When the London *Standard* newspaper's top
investigate team began to look into the School of
Economic Science, they met a wall of secrecy. What
they found is cause for public concern:

- Marriages are broken up, people brought close
  to breakdown.
- Schools educate children in a religious
  philosophy their parents know nothing about.
- Political parties and churches are infiltrated by
  people hostile to their fundamental tenets.

All this is in the name of what claims to be a
wholesome philosophy with Christian overtones. But
in reality this is a strange, eccentric, essentially
Eastern cult . . .

Peter Hounam is in charge of investigations on
The Standard, London's evening newspaper.
Andrew Hogg is a reporter on the *Sunday Times*
and was previously an investigative journalist on
The Standard.

SECRET CULT

PETER HOUNAM AND ANDREW HOGG

A LION PAPERBACK
Tring · Belleville · Sydney

Acknowledgements
The authors would like to thank the many, many
people who gave advice and assistance but who
requested anonymity. Their help was invaluable. This
book would not have been possible without the help,
too, of: Graham Dowell, vicar of Hampstead; Robin
Garton; Louis Kirby, editor of *The Standard*; Donna
Leigh; Bishop Michael Marshall; Canon Colin Slee,
Sub-Dean of St Albans Cathedral; Bill Temple-
Pediani; Joseph Vincent

Published by
Lion Publishing plc
Icknield Way, Tring, Herts, England
ISBN 0 85648 837 2
Albatross Books
PO Box 320, Sutherland, NSW 2232, Australia
ISBN 0 86760 605 3

First edition 1985

Printed and bound in Great Britain by
Cox & Wyman, Reading

CONTENTS

Introduction **The School**   7
Chapter 1   **Training the Perfect Woman**   12
Chapter 2   **From School to Cult**   29
Chapter 3   **Missionary Expansion**   57
Chapter 4   **The Ancient Knowledge**   83
Chapter 5   **Chronicles of Despair**   111
Chapter 6   **What is a Cult?**   141
Chapter 7   **A Private Education**   169
Chapter 8   **Illiberal Liberals**   218
Chapter 9   **The School and the Church**   232
Chapter 10   **Power − For What Purpose?**   254
Postscript   266
Appendix   **A letter to 'The Standard'**   280

The School

If religion were to be looked at as an industry, Britain's record in producing new products seems dismal in recent times. Imports have arrived here from overseas – the Moonies, Children of God, Scientology, Rajneesh – all profiting from a gap in the market provided by the young, the lonely and the spiritually disaffected.

But the trade has not all been one way. Secretly, but with formidable efficiency and success, a wealthy religious cult – British-born and -bred – has established a world-wide following. Its headquarters is in the heart of London's fashionable Kensington district, and its name is the impeccable-sounding 'School of Economic Science'.

For nearly forty years this establishment, in keeping with its academic image, has offered to the general public night-school courses in philosophy and economics. Many thousands of people from all walks of life have been through its doors, including barristers, housewives, policemen, students, journalists and labourers. Even a present British High Court judge was a student for many years.

But despite its apparent respectability, in recent years the SES has found itself under attack, not just in Great Britain but in a number of other countries where offshoot branches have been started. Former members have claimed that the 'School' practises subtle brainwashing techniques to ensure absolute obedience. Its disciples put in many hours of unpaid work each week looking after the movement's large property and holdings, and taking part in group activities. They are encouraged to isolate themselves from influences outside the movement, they are discouraged from discussing the School's activities with non-members, and if they leave the movement they become pariahs to those that remain. The demands placed on members are so strong, it is claimed, that marriages fail, families split up, and some students develop serious mental problems.

The first mention of the cult appeared in Britain's *Daily Mail* in 1968 when the paper investigated Maharishi Mahesh Yogi, the 'Beatles' guru', who at one time had close links with the SES. The story mentioned the cult's secrecy and the absolute obedience demanded from members — but surprisingly it took the matter no further. And there the matter rested until the mid 1970s after the movement had opened for business in Malta. Opposition to them grew steadily on the island until eventually the Roman Catholic Church there produced a pamphlet warning of the dangers of the School. They claimed that, instead of offering a straightforward introduction to philosophy or economics, the movement was a cult, simply out for new members. This was a remarkably accurate summary.

At about the same time, the *News of the World*, the raciest Sunday newspaper in Britain, found a story which was right up their side of Fleet Street. A man in the north of England was complaining bitterly that he had lost his wife to a philosophy group. Following her enrolment at a local SES branch, the marriage had gone seriously wrong. Presuming, probably quite rightly, that their readers were not so very interested in the finer points of philosophy, the *News of the World* concentrated their attention on the unhappy marriage. Little mention was made of just what the woman had been studying which had altered her feelings for the disconsolate husband, who by then was suing for divorce. Tucked away on an inside page, the story attracted scant interest.

In 1982 the SES were once more in the news, this time in New Zealand where the well-established Wellington branch had purchased for their activities a large mansion, something of a local landmark. Journalists who began to ask what the movement was all about soon stumbled on disgruntled former members. For the first time the word 'brainwashing' appeared in print to describe the cult's activities.

Coincidentally *The Standard* newspaper in London was

also in pursuit of this mysterious organization. As investigative reporters we began to take an interest after hearing of a marriage break-up where the wife blamed the matrimonial problems on her husband's involvement with the SES. The information we began to uncover was startling, so much so that it took more than a year of intensive research before the newspaper felt ready to publish.

We discovered a groundswell of very real concern about the SES. Several senior members of the Church of England were particularly forthright in their criticism, especially Michael Marshall, who at that time was Bishop of Woolwich. His concern stemmed from the early 1970s when, as vicar of a central London church, part of his counselling ministry had been devoted to a number of former SES members. From his experience he considered the movement 'evil' and 'corrupt', and at one time he even asked the Archbishop of Canterbury to issue a public warning about its dangers. His plea was met with silence.

Later we were to learn that as far back as 1977 the Society of Friends, better known as the Quakers, had banned the SES from using their large meeting-house in London's Euston Road. They had been concerned over reports of members leaving the organization with emotional or psychiatric disturbances, and had heard that the SES encouraged family rifts. When they met senior SES members to discuss these reports, they were further disenchanted with the secrecy surrounding the movement.

A number of organizations which investigate cults, such as Britain's FAIR (Family Action, Information and Rescue) and another Christian group Deo Gloria Outreach, also had grave misgivings. Their suspicions were reflected on the other side of the Atlantic with the Toronto-based Council on Mind Abuse also expressing anxiety.

We learned that in recent years the movement had been investigated by the Special Branch of the British police. Although they could find no evidence of illegality, we were told in a private conversation of continuing disquiet about the movement's activities.

9

As our research progressed we came to share all the fears and suspicions that had arisen. But the horror stories told by the many ex-members whom we contacted were not the full picture. We also grew to realize that SES members were playing key roles in several public organizations.

We discovered that the Chairman of the national Liberal Party, one of Britain's major political parties, was a senior SES member, along with several of the party's candidates at recent general elections. It also emerged that there were several vicars within the Church of England who had been members of the SES and appeared still to support the movement. And an official church organization, the European Christian Industrial Movement, which boasted the Archbishop of Canterbury's chief of staff as president, consisted mainly of SES members.

Particularly worrying were the four children's schools which the SES had set up in London. Ostensibly straightforward independent educational establishments, they introduced children to the rudiments of SES philosophy and encouraged senior pupils to join the movement. A sizeable number of parents knew nothing of the links between the SES and the schools, and some had noticed inexplicable character-changes in their children. A number of children were removed on the strength of *The Standard's* stories.

As we prepared to publish our findings, the Dublin paper the *Daily Independent* carried a lengthy investigation into the activities of the SES in the Irish Republic. Following that article and the stories which appeared in Britain, the Dutch and Belgian press also took up the debate, and there was renewed press interest in New Zealand.

The only material the SES has ever published about itself for public consumption has been pamphlets aimed at recruiting new members, and letters to newspapers objecting to criticism. Neither give the remotest clue about the organization's true nature.

In this book we examine the hidden side of the School of Economic Science: its philosophy, its idiosyncratic practices, its growth world-wide. We report the claims of its critics, and the counter-claims of some members. But regrettably we cannot present the views of the cult's mysterious leader, a former British barrister. He has consistently refused to be interviewed.

CHAPTER ONE

Training the Perfect Woman

Frith Oliver's frantic life of devotion to the School of Economic Science finally began to disintegrate one sunny summer's day in 1976.

In the garden of her home in Wimbledon she was screaming furiously at her two children who didn't want to come indoors. Frith had to get ready for one of the regular group meetings that, as a School of Economic Science member, she was obliged to attend. It was essential to arrive on time.

A neighbour over the fence yelled back at her to stop berating her children. Suddenly Frith was confronted with the increasingly erratic and irrational behaviour that was making family life unbearable. It bore in on her that she was close to breakdown, caused by her SES commitments — carrying out chores, attending group meetings or special classes and meditating for long periods morning and night. She was expected to follow the rules and teachings without question. And now that she was approaching the limit of her endurance, there was no one she could turn to for help. She knew literally no one outside the SES.

Fighting against everything the cult had drummed into her, Frith was forced to face the fact that her family life was more important than the organization that had ruled her from the age of ten. She began the process of disentangling herself from the grasp of the SES — a struggle that would last a traumatic three years.

In the cult she held a unique position. Frith Oliver was the School's first experiment in rearing a new breed of follower — the SES notion of the perfect woman. The experiment was a terrible failure and was to do untold damage to her and her children, and so she now feels compelled to tell her story.

The story begins in Wellington, New Zealand, in 1960. Frith was eight when she first began attending camps organized by the Society of Practical Philosophy — one of the names the SES goes by in that country. Both her parents were keen members, eager to instill the cult's philosophy into their young daughter.

She observed that all the grown-ups around her eagerly awaited these residential courses. They lasted a week and were an intensive programme of meditation, hard labour and lectures in the School's ideas. Occasionally there was the added excitement of a visit from London by the School's leader Leon (christened Leonardo da Vinci) MacLaren, who was then a practising barrister. In a movement already exerting a powerful hold on its members, the influence of MacLaren was staggering.

Said Frith:

I have clear memories of an overwhelmingly powerful personality — deep brown eyes of an extraordinarily compelling nature, a velvet voice with a depthless quality which could reassure and offer wisdom and love (how one longed for his approval!) or slash to the bone with alarming unpredictability. A trained lawyer's voice; he made very impressive use of it. I remember how everyone moved very quietly in his presence and leaped nervously to do his bidding at the slightest command.

At the age of ten Frith began attending group meetings every week to learn more about the beliefs and rules of the movement. Then, on a subsequent visit to New Zealand by MacLaren, she began to realize that he was singling her out as someone special.

His attention made a pleasant change to what was otherwise a difficult time for her. Life at home was very unsettled. Her parents were so involved in School activities that there was little time for normal family activities. And the cult's beliefs discourage overt affection between parents and their offspring. MacLaren's interest was flattering.

13

Leon MacLaren began to make the insidious suggestion, supremely intoxicating to a child, that I was somehow spiritually superior to most other people. (I think my sister was too, but that was something that had to be borne, alas.) It was suggested that I was somehow special, had some awareness that the poor grown-ups lacked. This wonderful quality I possessed would mean that my spiritual achievement would be far beyond the wildest dreams of other, less fortunate members of the School. As an added bonus, since such things smacked of worldly dross, I wouldn't have to bother too much about exams. This sounded like a good idea to me.

Looking back on this period of her childhood Frith can remember no suspicions about the way she was selected as something akin to a goddess in the School's eyes:

I wonder now what he was really looking for. An innocent mind more easily moulded than those of the more experienced adults? A mind empty of preconceived notions which could be satisfactorily guided in the path of his choice? (There, I need hardly add, he proved mistaken!) Whatever it was, I was delighted and felt extraordinarily privileged. What child would not be, when it was hinted that she was in fact superior to her parents whose authority appeared awesome to her — the hint coming from an authority which exceeded theirs? I felt a strong sense of gratification. Perfection in spirituality was desired by all, and I was a few steps up from the rest — a most satisfactory state of affairs. The division of the family widened.

Frith's parents, both successful professional public servants, accepted her new status with the School. But family life grew more and more difficult. Her parents consulted MacLaren about their daughter's outbursts of temper and wilful behaviour. Frith is in no doubt that it was MacLaren's idea that she should leave her family, fly to London and be brought up by the School.

She was just thirteen and the idea appalled her. But her parents fell in with the suggestion, believing it to be in her best interests. The School consistently taught that parents should not get emotionally involved with anyone, even their children. Emotion was a distraction, something to suppress at all times. Frith Oliver was put on a plane for London.

It is impossible to convey the depth of loneliness and misery experienced by a child of thirteen uprooted from all it knows and thrown unprepared into a strange country, strange company, huge, cold old streets of tall grey buildings and endless rain. The hopeless, helpless vulnerability . . .

And so the experiment began. Frith was sent to live with three women, all SES members, in a house used by the cult. It was not an atmosphere with much appeal to a youthful spirit.

These people had no notion of how to communicate with a child. They attempted, I suppose, to treat me as one of themselves as far as possible. They were all well into middle age, two of them with no experience of children whatsoever. The other should have known better: she was a teacher of many years' experience.

Academic life was equally unsatisfactory and unhappy. A place had been found for her in a well-respected Central London girls' school, but she found the curriculum unfamiliar and her classmates unfriendly. Her unhappiness broke out into rebellion, and at the age of fourteen she was removed.

Despite this set-back to his plans, MacLaren still viewed Frith as someone special. Closer guidance was obviously necessary to bring out the best, so she was now 'apprenticed' to a sculptor and woodcarver well established in the senior echelon of the SES. Frith did not demur. By that time she regarded the leader, known to some SES members as The Master, as a kind of 'ferocious father figure'. She alternately adored and feared him.

Her rebellion against the cramping effect of education at a traditional girls' school did not carry over into her SES activities. She was attending evening group meetings with the cult, as well as early morning sessions in music and the brand of mathematics favoured by the SES — a Hindu system known as Vedic mathematics which stresses the spiritual importance of numbers and of certain algebraic and geometric theorems.

By now she was also expected to follow the SES's strict routine, which they call Measure. This included making do on five hours' sleep a night, meditating at dawn and dusk, eating a special vegetarian diet, and wearing natural-fibre garments only. She also received regular private tuition from MacLaren in the beliefs of the cult.

I recall an evening during this period when I was staying at Stanhill Court, the SES retreat in Surrey. I was, as usual, in MacLaren's room, as I was privileged to be owing to my exalted position as his 'find'. I was allowed to serve him at table and listen to the after-dinner conversation. Sometimes he would talk to me alone. On this occasion he was expounding to me on the subject of women. 'All women always felt guilty,' he said. With much trepidation I ventured to argue. 'I don't understand,' I said. 'I don't feel guilty.' 'Oh yes you do,' he assured me. 'You just don't realize it yet because you're too young. All women feel guilty because of Eve's sin in taking the apple. And so they should. All women are guilty, and the only true aim of their lives must be to purge that guilt.'

Frith was even more unhappy because she found she didn't feel any guilt. She became more and more bewildered. The SES had told her that she must suppress emotions including sexual feelings, yet as a fifteen-year-old such feelings were running strongly inside her. She was taught that women were unequal to men and that she should always obey a man and suppress any feelings of doubt and resistance:

Feelings, I was told, were not true. If a person experienced, for example, grief, this was a negative emotion and untrue. It should be suppressed. A person who expressed such an emotion

16

was denying the Truth, and should be punished. The unbelievable cruelty of such notions was lost on me as a child; I simply believed what I was told. I have heard MacLaren state that anyone who was chronically ill or mentally handicapped was in that state because they wished to be so, in order to avoid making the effort to follow the Way of Truth. I believed him. So, astoundingly, did the adults around me. At least one must suppose they did; they stayed.

On top of this she was told not to form any views about anything:

In the very early groups I was told (along with the rest of the group) that the mind should be emptied of opinions. Opinions and beliefs were always 'false', as also were feelings. As I was too young to have formed many opinions, I tried in vain to abandon what I did not in fact possess. The result was a strange vacuum, wherein I believed that to profess knowledge on any subject constituted ignorance. This was compounded by such sayings from the Hindu teaching as 'He who says he knows, knows nothing'. Confusion, to say the least, resulted for many years! I stifled feelings and manufactured responses, but occasionally some underlying commonsense prevailed, the effort of dissimulation proved impossible, and I exploded.

These beliefs meant that within the SES's clearly defined pecking order there was little if any warmth and friendship. The senior members were cold and remote. They bullied the members beneath them and so on down through the hierarchy. People outside the SES were given no consideration whatsoever.

At fifteen Frith was deemed to have progressed far enough to join a senior group of the movement. She entered the Tuesday group, the second from the top, and although she was unable to understand much of what her exalted new colleagues were talking about, she felt ecstatic. In her new position she was close to the inner sanctums of the SES, with considerable power over people lower down.

But she had no friends outside the small circle that constituted the Tuesday group. Her work as an apprentice to an SES sculptor provided no more companionship. Everyone she knew well was much older. Frith hardly ever met anyone of her own age.

She now feels this was the cruellest wrong she suffered. Cut off from normal society she was still encouraged to think of herself as special, and at sixteen this was confirmed once again by another promotion – to the status of 'tutor'.

Within the SES a tutor is defined as standing in the place of the Absolute, the SES's idea of God. Every word spoken by a tutor must be regarded as springing from the Absolute. People under the control of tutors are expected to do exactly as they are told. More than that, the tutor must be consulted before a group member takes any major step in life, be it changing job, moving house, getting married, starting a family or seeking divorce. They become party to the most intimate details of the lives of their group members. Frith, despite her age, was no exception.

Puzzled mothers might ask me questions regarding the upbringing of their children, or young couples ask my permission to become engaged. Older couples brought their marital problems. I was far from adequately equipped to cope with such queries, and only too miserably aware of the fact. I spent the evenings in an agony of terror, desperately hoping that none of them would see through my pose as a 'tutor', and for some reason feeling that I was to blame for my lack of suitability for the job.

I turned, on occasion, for guidance from those above me, and was told it was my own fault I felt at a loss, because I was denying inner knowledge. (This was the kind I was supposed to possess in such abundance, the sort which obviated the necessity for proper schooling or exams.) I now felt guilt because of denying the knowledge. I was witholding it from 'my' students, a heinous crime. I also felt extremely guilty because of my manifest inadequacy as a 'tutor'; I knew damn well the will of the Absolute wasn't manifesting through me.

MacLaren's prophecy of women always feeling guilty was beginning to be fulfilled.

18

By the age of eighteen Frith was still living in the London house into which she had moved when first arriving in London. Despite the presence of the three hardline SES women members, she somehow contrived to become pregnant. Her deep-rooted unhappiness had led her to throw caution to the wind. The father was another SES member, a thirty-five-year-old bank employee lower down in the movement's hierarchy.

MacLaren was approached for permission for the pair to marry. After expressing his disgust at Frith's behaviour — the blame apparently rested entirely with her — permission was granted.

The union proved disastrous. The compatibility of the couple was not explored — they had little opportunity to get to know each other well. But the strain placed on any SES marriage is severe.

This is particularly so when one spouse is not an SES member. But even between members the pressure of SES duties and studies, the extraordinary code of behaviour expected of wives and above all the SES's attitude to sex all have an effect. (Frith attended 'ladies' groups' at which obscure biological evidence was produced to prove that women do not actually enjoy sex. It was taught that, unless you wanted to become pregnant, making love was a sin both for the husband and for the wife because it would stand in the way of spiritual progress. The School and its ideas had to be obeyed. Worse still, a member who strayed from the course of SES theology might be reincarnated as some inferior entity. So then as now many SES members remained celibate except when a child was planned.)

Marriages were equally threatened by the subordination of other important aspects of family life to the activities of the SES:

The husband in a family is told to 'put the School first'. Thus it is far more important for him to be about his SES duties (and these might be three nights a week, and one or even two days at the weekend — more as he becomes more senior) than to be at home with his family. Wives who complain of this neglect are dubbed 'wilful', 'destructive' and 'wicked'.

One example of the practice of this discipline is that when my daughter was being born my husband refused to be with me because he 'had to' attend a rehearsal of the SES orchestra.

Husbands are told that wives should be utterly subservient to them, and obey every word. They were not discouraged from physically abusing their wives if this 'obedience' was not forthcoming. (This occurred in my marriage.) Much was made of the wife's role in the home, with fanatical emphasis on cleanliness and perfection in everything. This led, of course, to much depression and misery at failing to achieve this perfection.

The School also taught that the way of carrying out tasks was all-important. Each task should be conducted with infinite care and concentration, without the mind wandering onto other things. This was the way to gain spiritual enlightenment:

There was also an insistence on Victorian methods of housekeeping, as being pure and virtuous. Hoovers and washing-machines were discouraged, for example, and old-fashioned boilers extolled. The use of detergents, plastics or any form of synthetic fibre was frowned on. (This, needless to say, involved financial strain as many natural substances are much more expensive than perfectly efficacious man-made counterparts.) Women were also expected to provide their families with a special vegetarian diet of uncooked food only.

The duties of a housewife had to be combined with an all-consuming commitment to SES practices. These began after five hours' sleep a night.
Said Frith:

One was supposed to rise at dawn, (or even earlier during the winter), meditate, then do an hour's study of the scriptures.

20

Another hour would follow on other SES practices such as calligraphy, or mathematics, and then an hour's Sanskrit practice was required. If one were in an activity group, such as the choir, a further three hours' singing practice also had to be fitted in during the day. Failure in any of the above was severely criticized.

The consequences of "disobedience" regarding "School duties" were very unpleasant. There would be haranguing interviews with an ascending series of tutors, and possibly even Leon MacLaren himself. I have frequently been humiliated to an unbelievable extent by these methods. One is left without any sense of self-worth and left ready to submit to any unreasonable demand just to try and regain approval.

A further problem was Frith's high position within the SES. People at a higher level considered themselves superior to anyone lower down, with greater spiritual powers. She says the cruelty this led to is difficult to convey:

You really did feel that God himself, or someone with his authority, was reprimanding your misdemeanours (this happened rather a lot to me — I wasn't a very obedient member!) and conversely, if you were correcting someone in a'lower' level, you felt that same power invested in you. You (I hesitate to say 'I', as I am now so bitterly ashamed of the belief) really believed that you were responsible for a person's soul if you were their tutor, and regarded them almost as a child. I have been told that when a tutor sits in front of his or her group the 'Voice of the Absolute' speaks through him, and all knowledge is available to him. Nothing he says can be wrong, and his word must be obeyed implicitly. This appealed in no small way to those with a power-hungry nature, and much heavy wielding of authority took place. Some very foolish instructions were conveyed and obeyed, and people suffered very greatly, both emotionally and in some cases physically.

In Frith's case it led to further strains on her marriage. Her husband was in the same level as her students and was thus accorded a much lower status. Inevitably it affected their relationship.

Damage was inflicted on the children too. Frith had two by the time she was twenty and as a loyal and senior SES member she was expected to put the SES's demands above their interests:

> I know now (and will suffer guilt for it all my life) that I neglected my children in the rush and scramble to be at my 'duties'. I left them too young and too often with assorted babysitters. I was more concerned with struggling to achieve all the standards set by the SES than with their happiness. I was, for instance, told that I must teach them to read, write and know their tables by the time they were four. When (not surprisingly) they didn't take to this I was wretched and desperate, and consequently bad-tempered. It was all unbelievably unhappy, and I am only now really realizing what the emotional damage to them must have been. The SES often condoned and even encouraged the removal of children from their parents, as in my case, and I have heard Leon MacLaren say that parents are the worst influence a child can have, and really *all* children should be taken from the sphere of parents' influence.

After six unhappy years the marriage finally fell apart. Frith got a divorce with custody of the children. But she was still totally committed to the SES, although always she had felt doubts about the teachings. Much was unintelligible and occasionally she realized that others found it so too. She put all this down to her own inadequacies and continued to feel guilty about it. As she had known no other type of life it never occurred to her to leave — until the incident in the garden where the confrontation with the neighbour brought home the way her life had become totally dominated by SES demands.

Perhaps what helped her to leave the SES was the contact she now had with people outside the organization. She was forced to find a way of earning a living. She had no educational qualifications, having left school long before she could have taken any exams. In 1977 Janet enrolled on

22

a secretarial course. She was still in the SES, but after the incident in the garden she had become more and more lax in her adherence to the SES code of behaviour.

She gave up limiting her sleep and abandoned early-morning study sessions. She gave up the meditation too, and gradually her view of the world changed. She began to realize that not everyone outside the movement was base, evil and ignorant. She was astonished to find that, contrary to what she had been led to believe, some were actually kind and pleasant.

By 1978 she had qualified and begun work as a secretary. Her confidence built up and at last she began to make friends outside the SES. But, though she was gradually separating herself from the organization that had ruled her life since childhood, her own children were now showing signs of harm. Ahead lay her biggest conflict yet with the SES and a legal battle that might have separated Frith from her children.

Both were now attending the private schools run in London by the SES. The curriculum, even for the very youngest pupils, included Sanskrit and SES philosophy. Discipline was severe, and her children were expected to spend much of their free time doing homework or attending SES functions.

Frith realized that her two children had become deeply unhappy, and tried to make up for it by making home life as pleasant as possible.

Whereas there was a rule that adults should have no more than five hours' sleep every night, children under twelve were supposed to have no more than eight hours. However, I let them sleep until they woke naturally; if they needed to relax I let them watch television, a pastime the SES did not approve of. And instead of restricting them to uncooked food only, I baked cakes and made shepherd's pie. I gave every reasonable support and help with their homework, but when I thought there was far too much I would sometimes write a note excusing the child from finishing it. I refused to force them to sit up until 10 p.m. or 10.30 to complete it, as I know many parents did.

23

For several years she did not consider removing the children from the schools — her SES conditioning was too strong for that. But gradually, as she began to sense freedom lying outside the cult, she found it more and more difficult to approach teachers and voice her worries. She was blamed for the children's unhappiness and lack of academic progress. One teacher said her daughter was the worst child she had ever had to teach. Why? Because Frith was not providing the right atmosphere at home.

Although I was growing anxious about my children's progress, I was still afraid to move them because I had no idea where they could go. I was wary of the state system. Leon MacLaren had frequently, in ranting speeches to SES groups, asserted that state schools were full of drug-pushers and violence. There was also a total lack of discipline, and a low educational standard. I was also quite aware that I could not afford the fees of any other private school.

I was caught in a bitter dilemma, because I dared not confess to my new-found friends outside the SES that my children were at an unorthodox school, and not doing well. I was being criticized by the SES, and was terrified of losing the good opinion of people who by now were the only friendly voices that I heard.

Besides, I knew that were I to move them I would face a tremendous struggle, possibly even a court case with their father. He would never have consented to such a course. I was very afraid of the psychological effect this might have on the children.

By 1980 Frith had been promoted and had a well-paid secretarial job at a college. She began to tell her friends at work about her life in the SES. But it was not until two years later — in the summer of 1982 — that the question of the children's schooling came to a head. Her son broke down and said he was being badly bullied. He also began to have headaches. The boy and his sister had both developed asthma. She felt the way the children were being handled at school was a strong factor in their physical and mental distress.

24

Around Easter 1983 Frith's son arrived home from school with a severe migraine attack. He was in pain and vomiting. It transpired that, despite letters to the school excusing the boy from games, he had been sent on a long-distance run with his classmates. It was the final straw. Frith decided that he and his sister would not return to their schools.

Arrangements were made to put them into a local private school, but there was the expected strong opposition from their father. He suggested instead that they went to live with him. Still an ardent SES member, he wanted them brought up in the cult's philosophy. And so did the SES. Rallying to his side, the cult helped him fight a legal battle for custody of the children.

The case was scheduled for the beginning of June 1983. She began collecting evidence to prove that the SES was a highly eccentric religious movement which passed on its ideas through the children's schools. Without such evidence, she feared the judge might well take the view that the movement, registered as a charity, was nothing more than an economic study group.

This is when we first met Frith. She learned that we were investigating the SES for a series of articles in *The Standard*. We could tell her of leading church figures and former members who had grave doubts about the movement. We knew by then of many people who would confirm the extraordinary hold it had on members, and the rigid code of behaviour they had to follow.

But the SES were able to provide ammunition from the other side. Frith's ex-husband received the most extraordinary support from the head of her son's school, and her daughter's headmistress was the teacher with whom Janet had been sent to live when she first arrived in London.

Both wrote letters supporting the children's return to their schools. The letters amounted to a direct attack on Frith's behaviour as a mother. It is just possible that other private schools might have been prepared to get involved in such a highly charged issue, but it is doubtful whether any other head teachers would have been quite so personal in their remarks.

In a written statement about Frith and her son the head of the boys' school wrote:

> Since his parents divorced he has lived mostly with his mother and has attended school here regularly. His home environment is plainly not helpful to him. His mother's behaviour is erratic and unreliable and has resulted in several outbursts against the school which seem to have little rational basis. The boy has not been well cared for at home: when he was younger he was frequently unwashed and poorly clad and we have had problems with homework and indeed with anything that required sustained effort. He has clearly benefitted from the school and from the companionship of the other boys and from the care of his Masters. We would certainly like to keep him in the school.

At the judicial hearing which took place at a county court in London the headmaster made even stronger comments about Frith Oliver and her family, even going so far as to say that the boy had criminal tendencies which could only be corrected by SES methods. But persistent cross-examination revealed his passionate devotion to SES ideas. His reference to the boy being 'poorly clad', for instance, referred to the fact that he turned up at school in clothes made of synthetic materials — not the pure wool and cotton laid down in SES doctrine.

The headmistress of the school that Frith's daughter had attended since the age of five wrote:

> At the moment her mother is not in contact with the school, and we find that the child achieves very little homework when she is at her mother's, but she does receive help when she stays with her father and then when she gets to school she enjoys the encouragement for work well done. We do not advise a change of school, because (the child) is being very well catered for here and because we feel that to continue in the same school, rather than change again at the age of thirteen, would ensure stability and continuity for her, when her home circumstances are not stable. She does enjoy the time that she spends with her father and she comes back happy and very well turned out.

Their evidence failed to make much of an impression on the judge, because many people were prepared to testify that Frith Oliver was a loving, conscientious and devoted mother. Nevertheless the matter was not resolved. The judge decided that Janet should not have removed her children so swiftly, and stipulated they must return to the schools for the rest of that term, pending the outcome of a hearing over the custody of the children.

A week later *The Standard's* articles on the cult appeared. And less than two months later Frith's husband abandoned the fight for custody, and failed to renew the injunction keeping the children at the schools. Her son is now happy and doing well in school. But her daughter is still facing grave problems in adjusting to normal relationships. Frith blames this on her child's contact with the SES through St James'.

Had Frith Oliver not rebelled, had she not failed to put the cult first in all things, her life would have been bizarre, even measured against the excesses of other members of the School of Economic Science. For by now she would have been the cult's epitome of perfect womanhood, existing in a serene, unemotional, zombie-like state. That was her destined role. As it is, her experiences are not unique, for similar stories have been told to us by many people who regret their involvement with the SES.

Some years ago Frith's parents left the SES. Her mother in particular regrets the way that Frith was sent from home at such a young age. She too wishes to remain anonymous, but she told us much of her experiences of the SES in New Zealand:

After about two years, when one has been initiated into the SES, one has begun to be enmeshed in the rules, which are very cleverly designed. (After all, Mr MacLaren is a lawyer.) The basic rule of never discussing the 'teaching' outside SES walls is one such. Another, never to communicate with anyone who leaves the organization, is a cunning protection. The highly organized network of meditation tutors throughout the School, requiring all students to report periodically concerning their

27

practice, is most extraordinary confidence trick. Most tutors admit among themselves that their experience of meditation means almost nothing to them.

Soon it is fear that holds the students. They are told they are 'special'; they are told that this unique experience of receiving the School's teaching will save them an infinity of lifetimes and that if they leave they are doomed to return to earthly embodiments until the end of time.

Anyone not practising the rules or questioning them will not be allowed to advance through the hierarchy. The 'personal growth' is said to involve all three levels of human development – physical, mental and spiritual. Here the failure of the church to provide sound spiritual guidance has meant that movements such as the SES must flourish, as there is no doubt of the hunger of Western man for spiritual knowledge and experience. The SES has a certain value for the short period in providing a limited sustenance until its inadequacy is realized.

However, any so-called spiritual organization that is held together by fear must certainly not be operating in the line of truth, which is founded in love. If there were love in the SES, people would be cared for, not discarded to one side when no longer useful.

CHAPTER TWO

From School to Cult

The fierce rules governing everyday life in the SES, which proved such anathema to Frith, are part of a process known in the cult as Measure. It is based on the belief that we all waste an inordinate amount of time and energy on thoughts and actions which are either simply futile or else positively harmful to our spiritual development. For our true purpose here on earth is to serve the Absolute.

The influence of the Absolute permeates the universe in a series of natural laws which we should endeavour to follow. Indeed it is our duty to do so, for if men cease to recognize these natural laws, the Absolute's influence becomes increasingly obscured, and evil and ignorance predominate. As an esoteric school which believes it has discovered what these natural laws are, the SES, in alerting people to them, are serving the Absolute. Thus work done for the cult is really work for God.

The 'natural' aspect of Measure accounts for the rules about clothing and diet, the traditional role of the sexes, and the condemnation of birth control and modern medicine. It also explains their horror of popular entertainment (which they consider a relatively recent phenomenon) and virtually all literature from Shakespeare's day to this. And it is the reason for their passionate support of tradition, which is held to embody natural laws that have been handed down from generation to generation.

Equally important is the effect Measure has on SES members. It is used by the cult as a way of destroying the personality. Brutal as that may sound, their philosophy clearly teaches that personality is false and must be eliminated. The SES believes that the further a person is from the Absolute, (as with new recruits or all non-members) the more rules they need to bring them closer to it. Rules based on natural laws will eventually lead a person to recognize that his or her inner Self is really one with the Absolute. The closer a person gets to that realization, the more the influence of the Absolute will work through him, exercising a benign effect on everything and everybody that person encounters. Personality — which the SES sees as a set of ego-dominated habitual responses — prevents that realization from taking place. It must therefore be harried until it dies, and the true inner Self emerges in its place.

By following Measure an SES member is also attempting to impose control and order on the way he or she lives. Thus the ideal day — usually only possible on their rigorous residential courses — involves rising at dawn and spending the morning in physical activity, which is usually a gruelling regime of manual work. The afternoon is a time for inactivity and stillness, which in SES terms translates into calligraphy, Sanskrit or mathematics classes. And the evening is a time for reflection, which in the SES means group meetings and possibly a musical recital. Bedtime, with the groups dividing into single-sex dormitories, does not follow until late — often around midnight. By prescribing such a formula for the day, they claim their members are following natural laws which will help them to develop spiritually.

All this should never become a matter of habit, for habit indicates lack of attention to the Absolute. The activities a member is called on to undertake will therefore vary greatly from day to day. And one day during a week-long course will be set aside for fasting. During that time the member is unlikely to be called on for particularly strenuous duties.

The approach to Measure is handled extremely skilfully by the SES. It has to be, for unless a convert has been properly primed by the cult, the regime is likely to frighten him or her off for good. If converts are led gently towards it, however, the result is usually a colossal tightening of the hold that the School has on their life. One former member, a professional woman in her late forties well-used to executive duties at work, claimed that the process built up a group dynamic so strong that it could stand alone as the explanation for the loyalty of the cult's members. In fact, as we shall explain later, there are a number of other factors which also engineer wholesale commitment to the SES.

The sheer mental and physical effort required by Measure occasionally proves too much for a follower. Former members claim that several suicides have taken place, but such claims must be treated with caution. (We have been unable to discover an inquest where blame has been attached to the cult.) Breakdowns, however, are not uncommon. And the treatment given can be really bizarre. A former member of fifteen years' standing told how one woman who snapped was forced to wash up all night in the hope it would calm her down. 'I know it's true,' he added quietly. 'I was the person ordered to supervise her. She washed up until dawn.'

Measure is naturally not mentioned to students when first they cross the threshold of the School of Economic Science. The SES in Britain attracts most new members from advertisements – on the London underground, in the national press and in local newspapers up and down the country. They advertise courses in 'practical philosophy' and may sometimes include the extra fillip of training in how to Know Yourself. Many curious members of the public pay a small fee, around fifteen pounds a term, fully expecting a Bertrand-Russell-type guide to the history of Western philosophy. Of course they receive no such thing. (In March 1981 one disgruntled ex-student went so far as to complain to the Advertising Standards Authority. They replied that 'philosophy' did not come within their terms of reference.)

Those with an individualistic turn of mind often do not last the initial course. They either leave of their own volition, or the SES tutor taking the course makes it apparent that their presence is not welcomed. For right from Day One the movement is carefully selecting those who seem likely meekly to obey the cult's rule. Some spirit is desired – it is easier to chip away at an abrasive surface than a totally smooth one. But tutors are looking for people who respond to questions in a way that shows they have taken on board

31

points put across earlier in the course. Personal remarks that students make, together with an assessment of their potential, are noted by SES members acting as observers in the groups. These details are later filed in a dossier held on each SES member. That dossier remains active for as long as they stay with the 'School'. What happens to them afterwards is not known.

If a student enjoys the course and stays, he or she will at the end of the first year be encouraged to sign up for a second. But whereas during the first year he will probably have been allowed to attend any evening of the week which suited him, he will now be asked to commit himself to one specific evening. Later in the second year he may also be asked to give up a second evening each week for 'duty'. This entails helping out at the hall where the courses take place, either cleaning the building or helping to organize refreshments. And at the end of that year comes the request on which his or her future in the SES depends. For one cannot progress beyond the second year without being initiated into Transcendental Meditation.

The course will already have laid the groundwork for this practice during the previous two years with intervals of 'pausing' in each session. Students are asked to still the mind and sit for several minutes at a time with back straight, knees together, head lowered and hands down turned on knees. (This is basically the same position as that in which the Egyptian Pharaohs are seen in many ancient statues − a credential apparently of some appeal to the SES.) Students are asked to continue the practice on the other days of the week, thinking of the group while they do so.

Those who agree to take up the meditation now face a ceremony purely Hindu in origin. They contribute a piece of white linen, to represent purity, flowers as an expression of beauty, and seeded fruit to symbolize their inner Self. A week's salary is also required − apparently people always attach greater value to something they have paid for. In return they receive a mantra − a single word of Sanskrit − which they must chant at dawn and dusk for up to half an hour. The word the SES always use is Ram, which is held to embody the Hindu doctrine of creation. We will explore the practice of Transcendental Meditation later. It is believed by some to have so many similarities with hypnosis that the two techniques can be seen as identical. But to the SES it is the process by which an individual can reach the inner Self and allow the Light of Consciousness, or the Absolute, to permeate his or her world.

With the technique firmly instilled, the SES member now embarks on a voyage of self-discovery where all maps and compass-points are supplied by the cult. Very soon after the initiation ceremony the recruit will be asked to attend a week-long SES course at one of the residential retreats. The regime is nearly all physical work, although some calligraphy and Sanskrit-sounding also take place. Meditation is done with the group, and dawn rising is introduced. But overall the atmosphere is far less intense than it later becomes. At this stage the diet is fairly traditional and can include meat.

This course is followed by a series of weekend retreats where the subject of Measure is first broached. Recruits are told what the idea means, and what relevance it has to their spiritual development. The SES wisely do not play down the rigours of what is involved, so that the idea of such a harshly regimented week assumes the form of a challenge. No one wants to be the first to back off, and instead of dread an atmosphere of excitement is created.

Once the week of Measure is underway there is no respite. Segregation of the sexes is introduced, and a vegetarian diet imposed. This goes far beyond the limits of vegetarianism, however, for the SES stipulate that only four foods can be eaten at any one meal. A typical lunch might therefore comprise a tomato, a piece of bread, a piece of cheese and an apple. Talking at the table is frowned on, and members have to be offered the food before they can take it. No one is allowed to help himself. Each mouthful has to be consumed slowly with the mind's full attention directed to this act alone. Curiously enough, wine is still supplied at the evening dinner, although it must be paid for. The result, after a day's intensive work and a limited diet, is often a speedy euphoria.

In summer members rise at dawn, but dark winter mornings are no excuse for a lie in. They will still be expected to rise between 3.30 and 4.00 a.m. and must fill in the wait for first light with extra lessons and scriptural study. Backbreaking manual work follows, with numerous group meetings and then the usual SES classes.

In the evening a large meeting of all SES members on retreat takes place, where observations are made about how the day's work was conducted, and reprimands delivered to those who have shirked or made mistakes. Dinner is followed by further group meetings, although this time the sexes are segregated. These meetings are used to underline the philosophy of the cult and usually last until members go to bed.

One former member summed up a week of Measure by saying:

> One of the strongest things I noticed was that you never had any time for yourself. There just simply isn't the opportunity to do anything which is not part of the routine. The effect is staggering. The group meditation sessions become very powerful – you can almost touch the atmosphere. When I arrived home after a week of this my friends became extremely worried. I seemed to be so far away from reality that they thought I had joined something like the Moonies!

Not everyone felt quite so reverential about the group meditation sessions; Frith Oliver for one. She told us:

> Life was not all so melancholy. Many glorious inanities took place in the School of Economic Science; when people abandon commonsense much hilarity prevails.
>
> I cherish fond memories of looking across a room of meditators on a warm summer's evening (illegal; you weren't supposed to open your eyes) and almost bursting with suppressed laughter as I saw rows of people swaying on their chairs as they fell asleep from tiredness or sheer boredom, then jerking abruptly upright, occasionally peeping round to see if anyone had noticed. (It was, of course, extremely infra dig to fall asleep in meditation.) This activity could achieve a certain regularity, so that the room took

on the appearance of a field of corn swaying in the wind. Sometimes tutors would stalk along the rows and pounce on unwary sleepers, who would shoot bolt upright, eyes still closed, and remain rigid.'

The week of Measure can be seen as the final step towards becoming a fully committed SES member. Refresher weeks are held every year, and members are also expected to attend several Measure weekends in between. Many of the practices are also meant to be carried over into the everyday world, with SES members attending early-morning sessions before doing a day's work. Further sessions are held several evenings a week, and most weekends. And many will be expected to perform regular duties, such as cleaning, at SES buildings.

All in all, the present-day practices of the SES seem a long way removed from the straightforward study of philosophy and economics. So how did this movement start, and how does it support itself? The answers to these questions are just as bizarre as some of the School's practices.

The story begins in Glasgow in 1883 with the birth of Andrew MacLaren to Irish Catholic parents. Life was hard, and at the age of ten he was put to work to supplement the family income. His contribution was the 3/6 (15p) he earned each week as a tailor's messenger.

From an early age the boy had displayed a strong artistic temperament, but despite his prowess with pencil and brush, economic necessity dictated that at the age of fourteen he became an apprentice in an engineering shop. Life soon became more tolerable when he was also accepted as a student at Glasgow School of Art – attending classes in the evening.

At the age of nineteen his apprenticeship was complete and he began work as an engineer. By this time, however, his job was merely the means of keeping body and soul together. His real passions lay elsewhere, in the field of the arts, politics, economics, philosophy and history. He began to develop a name as a penetrating amateur cartoonist. He took over the running of his father's church choir, and developed a love of Mozart which was to last all his life — referring to him later as 'my own musical god'. And he read extensively, absorbing influences ranging from Karl Marx to Cardinal Newman. At the age of twenty-five he read the book which was to change his life.

Progress and Poverty, by the American Henry George, taught that economic ills could be solved by one simple expedient — a taxation on land holdings rather than on income. This would automatically create a much fairer distribution of wealth. Young 'Mac' became a fervent believer, and held public meetings to preach the gospel.

Somehow he also found time to marry, and when he was in his late twenties his wife bore him a son. The happy couple obviously expected great things from their progeny, since they christened him Leonardo da Vinci MacLaren — though this was soon abbreviated to Leon.

At the age of thirty Andrew MacLaren decided to uproot his family and move to London where he would seek his fortune as an artist. He had become one of the most effective public speakers in Glasgow by then, and once in London he continued to champion the Henry George cause, his clarion cry quickly reaching the ears of the Land Reform Movement.

In 1914 MacLaren joined the Independent Labour Party, then later that year his strong streak of individualism was put to the test with the outbreak of the First World War. He quickly decided that the conflict stemmed purely from the 'bankruptcy of statesmanship' of all parties involved, coupled with their defence of vested interests. He became a conscientious objector.

Under the guiding hand of the Land Reform Movement he began to take a more active interest in politics with a view to securing a seat in the House of Commons. He gained some noteworthy support. 'If I were Prime Minister, I would make Mr Andrew MacLaren Minister of Land,' said George Bernard Shaw. MacLaren's parliamentary ambitions were not realized, however, until 1922 when he was elected for Burslem, a pottery town in Staffordshire. It was a shortlived victory: he was defeated the following year. But he went on to hold Burslem for another two terms, from 1924 to 1931 and from 1935 to 1945.

These days the late Andrew MacLaren is possibly the one man connected with the SES who is remembered with affection by disenchanted former members who remember him as a kindly, very spirited old man. His early days as Burslem's representative, however, seemed to win him few friends. After one particularly vitriolic speech the *Staffordshire Sentinel* thundered:

Mr MacLaren's address at Burslem last night is an insult to every class of the community in Burslem and Tunstall, the working classes most of all, and the Potteries generally . . .

The paper added that his references to other local figures of a different political hue 'carried their own condemnation with them by their vulgarity and their wantonly offensive personalities'.

His impact on the mother of all Parliaments was rather less potent. His obsession with land reform earned him the nickname 'the amiable fanatic', and before long his greatest claim to fame was the lightning sketches he drew of his parliamentary colleagues in the chamber. It is true that in 1931 Parliament came close to implementing a Finance Act which would have enforced a measure of land value taxation, but the act was repealed before it could take effect.

As a politician MacLaren was to hit the headlines just twice, both times for failing to toe the party line. The second of these, in 1943, led to his resignation from the Labour Party. Although he sat as an independent for two more years, he then lost his seat. His rejection of the Labour Party, he claimed, was the result of its transition from radicalism to a 'welfare-state mentality'.

His departure from the house had one advantage. It enabled him to devote more time to the unofficial group he had started in the mid 1930s called the School of Economic Science. As its name implied, the group studied economics or, to be more candid, how the institution of land value taxation could soonest be achieved.

But old age was creeping up on Andrew MacLaren and within a short time he relinquished control of the group to his son Leon, who by then was a practising barrister in London. MacLaren senior had obviously made a powerful impression on his son. Leon accepted the need for land value taxation wholesale and was eager to carry on the good work. But perhaps the impression was not quite as deep as one might suppose, for once Leon took the movement over it radically altered its identity.

Leon first entered the limelight when, after following his father into the Labour Party, he stood at Epping in 1939 against Winston Churchill. The elder statesman was able to see off his twenty-eight-year-old opponent in no uncertain fashion.

We next meet Leon a year later, at Conway Hall in Red Lion Square, Central London, where he was championing the cause of landladies who had refused to pay their rates because business was so bad. He was on hand to provide them with legal advice. Some bemusement was caused by the large sign he stuck up behind him. 'To thy own self be true' it read in large maroon letters.

Leon had been called to the Bar in 1938, but his career as a barrister was not the stuff from which court-room dramas are made, although he did raise eyebrows in 1950 when appearing for British Railways. They were opposing the licence of a coach company running a service from the Midlands to a seaside resort on the East Anglian coast. MacLaren's claim that there were already too many vehicles on the road and the public should be forced to go by train prompted the opposing lawyer to remark that such a suggestion would make 'some of us think that pre-war Hitler Germany must have enjoyed a lot of liberty'. But much of his career seems to have consisted of routine appearances for one London council or another in opposition to plans to raise the fares on public transport in London.

Politically he struggled on for a few years after his trouncing by Churchill. In 1945 he dutifully followed his

38

father out of the Labour Party, entering instead the ranks of the Liberals. He fought two elections for them, failing both times to get elected. His second Liberal attempt was at South Hendon, part of North London, in 1951. Curiously enough, the Liberal candidate in Hendon North at that time was fellow-barrister Kenneth Jupp, who had earlier tried to win the Canterbury seat. Jupp went on to become a senior figure in the SES for some years. He is now Sir Kenneth Jupp, sits in the High Court, and has not answered our letters asking him about the SES.

Leon's control of the SES became total in 1947 when the Fellowship of The School of Economic Science, its legal body, became a formally constituted trust. He became chairman, and trustees and an executive committee were also appointed. Apparently the arrangement was necessary because,

> A considerable number of Subscribers to the funds of the School have expressed their desire and intention of further supporting the School and maintaining and extending its work, and have therefore agreed to enter into Deeds of Covenant.

The rules of the Fellowship of the School of Economic Science state that its first object is 'To promote the study of natural laws governing the relations between men in society and all studies related thereto and to promote the study of the laws, customs and practices by which communities are governed, and all studies related thereto'. This suitably unspecific approach obviously covers a wider ambit than pure economics. And in pursuance of that object, the SES was to change from being an economic study group into a full-blown religious cult.

Throughout the 1950s the movement remained small and tightly knit, without the fierce regimentation which exists today. The change that was to come stemmed from Leon MacLaren's increasing conviction that the economic problems of the world could only be changed by transforming the nature of mankind. He believed that philosophy held the key to how that transformation could take place, and what course it should follow.

His studies led him to the teachings of two twentieth-century mystics. The beliefs of the Svengali-like Greek-Armenian George Gurdjieff (?1877–1949) and his errant disciple, the Russian intellectual Pyotr Ouspensky (1878–1947) are central to SES philosophy today.

They claimed to possess an ancient knowledge which had been handed down through the ages in a series of esoteric schools. That knowledge was nothing less than the formula by which men can leave behind the suffering of the world, and achieve immortality.

The process involves discarding personality in favour of the inner Self, which is part of the Absolute. If this is done, one's consciousness increases until eventually the world of matter is left behind and one progresses to higher levels of existence.

Ouspensky brought the Teaching, as it is called, to Britain in the early 1920s, and gradually built up a small group of followers. He had spent four years of instruction under Gurdjieff, but the two men had fallen out. Whereas Ouspensky, the gentler of the two, favoured an intellectual application of the system, Gurdjieff settled in France and established a centre where his followers underwent a regime of intensive hard work. Only in such a fashion, be believed, could the hold of their personalities be smashed.

Ouspensky began to harbour doubts about Gurdjieff the man, but for most of his life he had no doubts about the Teaching. Just a few months before he died, however, he radically altered his views and, assembling the faithful around him, he told them that they must seek new methods of attaining immortality. The organization broke up soon afterwards.

Out of the debris a number of smaller groups then began to emerge, all heading off in different directions in their search for spiritual salvation. One such group went by the name of the Society for the Study of Normal Psychology, which became known simply as the Study Society. Its principle was a Harley Street consultant called Dr Francis Roles, and throughout the 1950s they hunted for a new path to follow. It was a difficult business and they were later to refer to that period of their history as the Dark Age. For in the main they were a highly educated, intelligent group of people from the upper strata of British society who were not about to join up with the first guru they encountered. Much of their work therefore consisted in going over the already familiar ground of the Gurdjieff-Ouspensky system.

It was this group that Leon MacLaren joined, eventually absorbing enough of the Teaching to become a 'group-taker'. And what he learned from their society he began teaching to his own School of Economic Science. Today the SES regards itself as the latest in the long line of esoteric schools which have safeguarded the secret of immortality.

Throughout this period the man who was to prove the answer to the prayers of the Study Society was deep in meditation in the Himalayas. His name was the Maharishi Mahesh Yogi, who would go on to become world-famous in 1967 when the Beatles joined his disciples. Both the Study Society and the School of Economic Science were to play a direct role in introducing him to the British public.

The Maharishi (the word means 'Great Sage') taught a system called Transcendental Meditation which he believed could eradicate all disease and violence in the world, if only enough people would take it up. In 1959 a group of Americans who had heard of his claims paid for him to make a round-the-world trip to spread the message. He arrived in Britain in December that year and the first public meeting took place at Caxton Hall, London, on New Year's Day 1960.

At that time the arrival of a long-haired, bearded Indian guru was still a newsworthy event, and the Maharishi attracted national press coverage. The Study Society pricked up their ears. Could this be what they were looking for? A small group of members went along to find out. They were initiated into the technique, and although cautious to begin with, became firmly convinced that Transcendental Meditation was a valid method of focussing attention on the inner Self.

News of the technique spread quickly through the Study Society and more people went forward for initiation. MacLaren was not far behind, and he then instructed members of the SES to take it up. The SES was now poised to become the Hindu-based cult which it is today.

Events moved swiftly. In March 1961 MacLaren organized the Maharishi's first world assembly in London's prestigious Albert Hall. All SES members were instructed to attend and some 3,000 tickets were sold at prices ranging from £1 to 3/6.

The following month a group of senior Study Society members, led by Dr Roles, left England with the Maharishi to meditate further on the banks of the River Ganges. There they met the guru whose teachings the SES still follow, the Shankaracharya of the North, who belonged to the same Hindu school as the Maharishi. Where the globe-trotting Maharishi had devoted himself to meditation, the Shankaracharya had much else to say besides about the wider philosophies of the tradition. The belief grew among Dr Roles and his colleagues that they had found the original source of the Gurdjieff-Ouspensky Teaching. There were too many similarities for it to be otherwise. Ouspensky's indictment was quickly forgotten. This was The System and it came with an extra bonus – the meditation, which was a way of reaching the inner Self at will, something that had proved difficult to achieve by following the Teaching.

Returning to London Roles was ecstatic. Invited to address a meeting of the SES he told them: 'All your worries are over. I am just four days old. I was only born last Thursday.' MacLaren was keenly interested in this development, and decided to go and see the Shankaracharya for himself. He made the pilgrimage soon afterwards and was suitably impressed. The transformation of the SES was underway.

The conversion of both the Study Society and the School of Economic Science to Hinduism was not achieved without cost. Members left both organizations rather than go along with the new doctrine. And later, when both groups fell out with the Maharishi, more members left to follow the Indian mystic.

The reasons for the split with the Maharishi are difficult to pin down. None of the parties involved has any desire to talk about it. What is known is that in 1961 a School of Meditation was established by members of both the Study Society and the SES. Its purpose was to pass on the technique of Transcendental Meditation, with initiations being carried out by some of the group who had gone to India. The Maharishi was apparently not as fully involved in this venture as he would have liked, and some reports say he took exception to it. A remark in the *Daily Mail*'s 1968 investigation of the Maharishi's finances would seem to bear this out. The paper reported Dr Roles as claiming that the Maharishi 'was keen that we should give everything to him,' but was refused. A former trustee of the Meditation Society, the legal entity of the SOM, told us, however, that the Maharishi broke away when he realized that the TM technique was being linked with other philosophical ideas — the Gurdjieff and Ouspensky Teaching.

The School of Meditation still exists today, occupying two premises, one in Lower Belgrave Street, Central London, and the other in Holland Park Avenue, West London. That building was donated to them by an SES member who later left the cult. The house, however, remained the property of the SOM.

The School of Meditation are anxious to play down their links with the SES. Spokesman James Hudson, an advertising account director, told *The Standard*:

> The only connection is that we teach their students the technique of meditation. Only .05 per cent of people who come here are from the SES. There's no reason for people here to be members. Why should there be?

But Mr Hudson neglected to point out that the Chairman of the Meditation Society, which is registered under the Friendly Societies Act as a non-profit-making body, is Bill Whiting, a senior member of the SES who several members of the cult claim made several visits to the Shankaracharya on behalf of the cult. He neglected to mention that one of the three trustees of the society is Mr Timothy Glazier, a leading light in the SES. He refused to reveal the identity of the two English people who today conduct meditation-initiation ceremonies, and he at first denied that his organization taught meditation to youngsters attending SES schools.

In fact, Mr Hudson's rebuttal of his school's connection with the SES deserves to be treated with the utmost scepticism. One former member of the SOM, who had a close relation in the SES, told us:

I was spending a lot of time with someone who was heavily involved in the SES and I was interested in what she was doing. I did not agree with all the hours she was putting in, however, so she recommended I went to the School of Meditation instead.

I was initiated and had to go back several times over the next few months to have my meditation "checked". This meant meditating with a senior person and discussing what I had got out of it. Invariably it ended in discussions about my personal life. After a while it was suggested that all I was doing was taking from the school, and I should start to put something back. I volunteered for a duty which meant making coffee or cleaning the building, and I joined an SOM philosophy group.

After a time I realized that it was virtually the same as the SES. We were told of the danger of negative emotion and the importance of the inner Self. Dossiers were kept on all of us — I know because I saw mine. I stayed for about four years and by the end of it I was spending nearly all my time on SOM activities. I had a group meeting one night a week, duty another night and drawing (which included some calligraphy) on a third night. If my meditation needed checking, that would take up yet another evening. I had to be up at dawn every morning to meditate, and was also expected to practise Sanskrit-sounding and drawing for an hour before work. And on top of all that I was expected every now and again to spend the weekend decorating for them.

I left after the husband of my tutor made a pass at me. I had

44

had told her during the course of one of my meditation checks that I was having sexual problems in my marriage and had found I was frigid. I wanted to know if that was a result of the meditation — or something unconnected with the school. The next thing I knew, the husband of this woman had put his arm around me in the kitchen and said, 'If you're having problems, I'm always available'. I was just a kid at the time, twenty-one or twenty-two. I was horrified.

The meditation sessions were also beginning to upset me. I felt frightened, as though there were bad vibes in the room, and I couldn't feel my body. I thought I was going to levitate.

Another former member had some knowledge of the Gurdjieff-Ouspensky Teaching before he attended the SOM. He said:

I knew nothing of the SES at the time. When I joined a philosophy group and started to receive the Teaching I couldn't believe my ears. I left after I saw a woman member who was obviously having emotional problems roundly chastised for some minor infringement. It was all too much like Gurdjieff to my taste.

The Study Society, based in Talgarth Road, West London, seems almost as anxious to play down its connections with the SES, even though those connections are now history. It is admitted that MacLaren was once a member but claimed that there has been no association with the SES 'for a number of years'. They therefore could not help our enquiries.

But at one time there was a close rapport, with the two groups holding joint meetings. The strong links are borne out by an agenda in our possession which was drawn up for a meeting of the Study Society's Management Committee on 21 October 1965. It includes recommendations from several members. Under a section entitled, 'Extending our Influence', one member, an accountant living in Surrey, advised:

There seem to be two main avenues:
A Direct influence on the general public through:

- Extending sphere of SES. What does this involve in the way of finance, staff and accommodation?
- Extending meditation, e.g. outside London.

B   Influencing leaders of thought today:

- Philosophy;
- Science.

The author of these recommendations told us that he could not remember submitting them, 'probably because none of the suggestions were carried out'. The relationship with the SES, he added, was 'comparatively short-lived and experimental'.

Following his trip to India MacLaren began to devote all his energies to the SES, giving up his work as a barrister. Whatever spontaneity there had been about the School now disappeared under a barrage of rules which demanded greater and greater commitment from the followers. The idea of Measure made its first appearance, and a country mansion, Stanhill Court in Surrey, was leased for residential courses.

This strengthened commitment brought the cult financial gains. Even today members are under no obligation to contribute anything, except the cost of their courses and residential retreats. The cult keeps these fees as low as possible. But donations, bequests, endowments and covenants also ensure that the coffers are never empty. And for special projects, such as the purchase of a new building, renewed appeals are made to members to give what they can. The result is that during the last twenty years more than two million pounds has been raised. Much of this has been invested in property. Wisely, in 1964, the Fellowship of the School of Economic Science sought and was granted tax relief as an educational charity – a privileged position it still holds.

In the early 1960s most London meetings of the cult took place either in a leasehold building in Suffolk Street, close to Trafalgar Square, or at a house in Chepstow Villas,

Notting Hill Gate. By the end of the decade their headquarters had moved to a building in Queen's Gate, Kensington, which SES members lovingly restored. One ex-member remembers using toothpicks to strip old paint from the ceiling cornice.

In the early 1970s the cult's property holdings extended to include a second country mansion, Waterperry in Oxfordshire, where MacLaren now lives. The purchase was made possible by a gift of £100,000 and two other gifts, one of £30,000 and one of £20,000. Another member gave a house in Harbledown Road, West London, for sale towards the cost of Waterperry. It realized £35,000.

At about the same time Sarum Chase, a mansion on top of Telegraph Hill, in West Heath Road, Hampstead, was bought from the British Council of Churches for £85,000. The house, built by the portrait painter Frank Salisbury in 1933, is on the edge of Hampstead Heath, on one of the most pleasant sites in North London. Today it is worth many times its 1971 purchase price.

The next big purchase took place in 1973 when Nos. 91 and 92 Queen's Gate were bought at a cost of £390,000. Together with No. 90, which they had already acquired, this site in fashionable Kensington, must be worth more than a million pounds at today's values. The same year a house in Sheffield was bought for the cult's Yorkshire operations. Students there were all asked to donate.

In similar fashion a substantial part of the cost of Preston Brinscall Hall, purchased in 1974 by the Manchester branch of the SES at a cost of £51,000, was met by students' donations.

And still the money rolled in, until in 1976 came one of the strangest gifts the cult has ever received — Necker Island, one of the most remote and beautiful atolls in the Caribbean. The island, part of the British Virgin Islands, was given to the cult by a British member. Its subsequent sale raised £124,214. By a strange irony for a movement which abhors present-day pop music, the man they sold it to is Richard Branson, the multi-millionaire head of Virgin Records. He is now transforming it into a no-expense-spared hide-away for jaded rock stars!

In 1976 the SES was also given a flat in Bournemouth,

a genteel holiday resort on the south coast of England. Its sale raised £30,000. And the following year they began to receive regular gifts of silver. The first such contribution amounted to £1,135, but each year since they have received £1,111. (The figure one is the numerical equivalent of the Absolute.) In 1978 a woman member died leaving the cult two properties. One was sold for £15,400. The other, in West Byfleet, Surrey, is held by the SES subject to a controlled tenancy. The following year another member, Mr Frank Thomas, died and left cash and property. The cash alone was expected to amount to around £50,000.

Accounts with the Charity Commissioners in London reveal that between March 1970 and March 1982 — the latest year for which figures are available — the cult received a total of £1,053,090 in fees and £670,479 in endowments. Total income over the period was £2,197,657, while total expenditure was said to amount to £2,207,832.

Despite this apparent shortfall, fixed assets held by the cult had risen from £204,747 to £1,081,825 during the same period. Net assets had risen from £144,140 to £924,618. These figures, however, do not tell the full story of the cult's wealth. For Sarum Chase was said, in the accounts for March 1982, to be worth just £4,000 more than it was ten years earlier, while the Queen's Gate premises were said to have increased just £1,463 in value from March 1975. The true appreciation is of course much more.

The expenditure of the SES since March 1970 has included a total of £144,866 spent on 'Research and Special Studies', and £219,131 spent on advertising. Since March 1974 a total of £68,032 has been spent on Motor and Travelling. And remarkably, given the insistence of senior members that they have no connection with overseas branches of the cult, the accounts for 1971 show that £2,770 was spent on payments 'relating to the work of the School abroad'. In 1972 a further £4,109 went on similar activities. In 1980 the SES apparently spent £12,201 on overseas visitors, and in the year ending March 1982 they spent a further £3,477. Former members claim, in fact, that staff running overseas branches visit Britain periodically for pep talks from MacLaren.

Another curiosity in the accounts is the Debtors section in the current assets. For ever since 1972 this section has included several thousand pounds deposited 'with the Bank of Baroda towards the eventual provision of accommodation in India from which linguistic researches can be carried on in Varanasi'. Varanasi is the ancient city of Benares — one of the most holy places in India. From 1972 to 1974 the amount was £10,000, from 1975 to 1979 it climbed to £14,000 and from 1980 it went back down to £10,000. Whatever accommodation was envisaged has taken a very long time to materialize. The lack of it did not stop MacLaren and other SES members making regular trips to the sub-continent to consult with the Shankaracharya.

As the fortunes of the SES prospered, the cult's control over its members grew ever stricter. The suggestion to members in the early sixties that they might find it advisable to discuss changes in their personal lives with their tutors hardened into an edict that permission had to be obtained before any major decision could be taken. And the tutor's word had to be taken as law.

New disciplines were introduced. The study of Sanskrit was started as a direct result of the Hindu belief that the universe is born of sound. Sanskrit is apparently the nearest language to that original sound. Calligraphy was introduced as an exercise in overcoming outside distractions and focussing the mind, guided by the inner Self, on the difficult business of drawing perfect circles and flawlessly straight lines. As such it is a good yardstick for assessing how successful a member has been in following the philosophy of the cult. Less than perfect drawings indicate a wavering concentration.

One former member found that the greater his disillusionment grew with the SES, the more impossible it became to practice this art. Vedic mathematics was also introduced, former members claim, as a means of loosening the hold of strict logic on Western minds.

By the early 1970s long skirts had become compulsory for

49

women on SES courses. It was the prelude to the start of the women's and men's groups where the traditional roles of the sexes were taught. The vegetarian diet was also introduced, taken from an obscure 'gospel' — purportedly the secret teachings of Jesus. (The book is strongly suspected to be a twentieth-century forgery.) Senior members of the cult had already been experimenting with these practices for some time.

The attitudes instilled in the men's and women's groups were too much for some members and a number left the cult rather than conform. Those who stayed found they were to strive for a completely new way of life. Janet Parker explained:

After the advent of the 'Diet', in the early 70s, cooked food was not allowed. Lengthy discussions took place in the ladies' groups about the various merits of different methods of baking bread (it was even mooted once, I remember, that it was impure to bake it at all — perhaps it should be dried in the sun? more natural?), the difficulties of obtaining English fruit (only fruit of the native country bearing its own seed was permitted, no vegetables or salad — a severe strain in winter!), and the benefits of cheese, honey and yoghurt were learnedly discussed. People developed large hips under their long skirts. At one time we were told that babies should be fed on fresh breadcrumbs soaked in water or unpasteurized milk. The babies, very sensibly, had a great deal to say about it, and the practice was not followed very much.

The 'material' discussed in the ladies' groups was a most curious mixture. Whilst the general concept that women were inferior to men and owed them total obedience was reinforced, the women were also assured that in a mysterious and subtle way they were superior. (The concept of superiority and inferiority runs very strongly throughout all SES teaching, though students are assured right from the very start that everyone is the same!) Women, we were told, provided the subtle substance without which men could not function at all, so we were terribly important. This was satisfactory. We had the power, we were told, to provide good or bad 'substance'.

('Substance', I gathered, was a sort of subtle and unspecified influence pervading the atmosphere around the woman, upon which her family depended.) Providing good substance, a woman was a good and benevolent influence for her family and for society. This meant never voicing a negative emotion, never complaining in the slightest degree however outrageous the behaviour of husbands. This was 'putting the Truth first'. A woman who provided bad substance, however, was beneath the contempt of the lowest. No punishment was too cruel for her (and I heard of some in my time). A woman who dared to argue with a man was beyond redemption. Providing bad substance, I gathered, was if you complained or lost your temper or needed some comfort or cried. Requiring any emotional comfort from your husband was unnecessary and might put a barrier between him and his attainment of enlightenment. You, of course, should provide comfort and security for him.

The man stood to the woman as the Absolute (the word God was not particularly encouraged), and her only hope of discovering Truth was in total obedience to him. The Absolute, apparently, could be trusted to look after the family as long as the man continued to 'put the Truth first'. The Absolute, unhappily, maintained his unmanifest condition; he did not put up shelves, repair decaying paintwork or provide company in the evenings.

No one ever questioned, as far as I recall, the basic idiocy of these ideas. The outcome, of course, was that many families in the SES developed a most strained and unnatural relationship.

All these developments were, of course, extremely puzzling to the fiery old Scot Andrew MacLaren, and apparently fell far short of his approval. He would occasionally be invited to lecture to members of the School on economics, but privately he would voice exasperation with the Eastern influences which began to appear.

One former member claimed that this exasperation boiled over once into anger. Hearing of an SES meeting taking place at Church House, the headquarters of the Church of England at Westminster, he attempted to gain entry, loudly proclaiming that the movement had become a travesty of

51

the organization he had started. His way was barred by a group of SES members at the door of the room.

He died in 1975 aged ninety-one. His obituary in *The Times* made intriguing reading, for no mention of the School of Economic Science appeared. Nonetheless, after referring to his 1945 election defeat the obituary read:

> From that time he devoted his energies to passing on to young minds his love of Art, Economics and Natural Law; a work in which he found more real hope for the future than in his solitary stand in public life. Among those who have imbibed of his wisdom and experience are many two or three generations his junior. He would wish no other memorial to his life than their determination to carry on his unfinished work.

The eulogizing tone of this valediction raises suspicion that it was penned by an SES member — possibly from within *The Times* itself. For the paper is the only one which is recommended reading in the SES, and a number of members have been employed there in the past.

In 1977, to mark Queen Elizabeth's Silver Jubilee, the SES went public in a hitherto unheard-of manner. They organized a festival at their Waterperry estate called Art in Action, which has since become an annual event. Traditional arts and crafts are displayed, and the festival is open to members of the public. But even in the organization of this innocuous event, the influence of SES philosophy is felt everywhere.

Artists who are SES members have to keep a tight rein on their work. It must be purely representational. No emotional, political or experimental input of any kind is allowed.

One sculptor invited to show his work at the festival told us:

> The work there was very bland. It was about the standard of a provincial art society, though far more professionally done.

There wasn't any work there with a message to convey. The emphasis is really on craftsmanship. The business of the individual artist doesn't appeal to them at all. It's rather a sort of tourist-type art that they're concerned with.

Apparently some one had recommended me to them, so I was invited to exhibit before they'd seen my work. But what I'd produced was far from the serene kind of work they wanted. It was fairly expressionist, violent and left-of-centre. It became quite clear that I wasn't the sort of artist they wanted at all.

It was more than just the standard of the work at Waterperry which puzzled the sculptor. He went on:

In all the time I was around there was no hitch of any kind. They make an absolute fetish out of organization. If you were someone who thought that was what life is all about you couldn't have helped but be impressed. They were always getting in touch with each other on walkie-talkies; the whole business of communications was far more than was needed. It seemed like a training exercise; there were more men than were actually necessary.

And the event did provide training for many things. You had the young people there being trained in obedience, peeling potatoes, washing up and so on. There was the preparation of food for large numbers of people, and they were getting training in organizing large numbers of 'dopey' civilians.

I said to one chap, 'You're looking tired'. And he said, 'We were up at half past three . . .,' then he stopped himself. The young people seemed to be treated like slaves. One youth came up looking very depressed and said, 'Would you like another cup of tea?' I asked if he would like one too and he said, 'Oh no. I can't'. I asked him just what the set-up was and he said, 'Actually, I'm not supposed to talk'. I told him I was sorry and that I didn't want to get him in trouble, but I was intrigued. He looked to me like a chap having a nervous breakdown, yet he couldn't say why he was doing it. He just said, 'Oh well, if you believe in it then it's worthwhile'.

That night we were invited to dinner up at the house and I

was told we could leave our children with some teenage SES girls. The young people there had a camp, sort of ex-army tents lined up just like in the services. It was absolutely quiet, there was no larking around.

So we left our children with these girls and went off. We came back to find everyone, even the older girls, playing like children. Obviously it was quite a release for them. But as soon as they saw older people they immediately went into their defensive attitude, and this somehow horrified me more than anything else. They were so over-disciplined.

Another London-based artist who exhibited at Art in Action told us of the discipline, and the feeling that Big Brother was watching. He said:

The men all wore dark suits, collars and ties and seemed to spend most of the time lurking behind bushes with two-way radios . . . I found the whole affair oppressive: it reminded me of the TV series 'The Prisoner'. There was a wind ensemble making music and I almost expected to see giant balloons emerge from the lake.

For the SES the event is now quite a moneyspinner. In 1977 it raised £769, but a year later the figure was £12,235. In 1979 it had dropped again to £6,502, but by 1981 it was back up to £12,093.

The organization of Art in Action is indicative of the awesome efficiency with which the cult as a whole is run. There are now more than twenty SES branches around Britain concentrated in the main on major cities, including London, Birmingham, Manchester, Leeds, Sheffield and Southampton. The names they go by vary – in Colchester, for instance, the branch is known as The East Anglian School of Philosophy; in Birmingham it is known as The School of Practical Philosophy. Similar names are used elsewhere.

Membership figures are hard to determine. Peter Green,

principal of the SES, told *The Standard* that the Fellowship of the School amounted to about 120 people. He would not supply a list of names. He added that there were probably about 2,500 general SES members in London, and the same number again elsewhere in the country. The SES claim that some 50,000 people have been through its doors since it was started.

An SES Communications List for 1983, indicating the duties of many senior members of the cult, shows a structure more reminiscent of a large corporation than a philosophic school.

The SES is divided into a series of levels, the S level being the most senior. It is followed, in descending order, by the R level, O level, Middle School, New and General Groups. Young people between the ages of sixteen and twenty-five are catered for by special youth groups. The S level (we have never satisfactorily discovered just what the initials stand for) is divided into two, a Tuesday group and a Friday group. These are generally people who have been in the movement for years. Of the two, the Friday group is the senior, and is tutored by MacLaren.

His teachings are then passed down the line by members of the Friday group who tutor the Tuesday group. It is then passed on by tutors from the Tuesday group who take the R group and so on.

No mention is made in the Communications List, however, of a mysterious section of the SES called the Preparatory groups, which stand outside the main hierarchy. Two groups, about a hundred strong in total, have taken part in rigorous self-examination sessions called 'humouring'; their devotion to the SES is total. 'Humouring' is the process where SES members, on a one-to-one basis, explore the most intimate aspects of their personality with a senior member. It is not a technique the SES are happy to discuss, and is usually confined to the senior echelons only.

The prep groups are all young men and women who grew up in the youth groups. They follow the rules of the SES to the letter, and it is within these groups that arranged

55

marriages are alleged to have taken place.

Quite what their purpose is remains a mystery. Indeed, many SES members know nothing of their existence.

Missionary Expansion

Leon MacLaren has exported the SES to other parts of the world with great success. In only thirty years the cult has become an international movement as strong as many of the better-known new religions such as the Moonies and the Scientologists.

From the 1950s onwards senior SES members from London have left like missionaries to set up offshoots overseas. In some instances well-established study groups founded in the Gurdjieff/Ouspensky era were persuaded to adopt the SES ideology and pledge allegiance to MacLaren.

The SES's London headquarters in Kensington became the central clearing-house for start-up funds, lecture material and advertising copy. Care was taken to make sure that SES followers, in whatever foreign branch, received the same systematic programme of indoctrination, beginning with the introductory course of twelve weeks.

MacLaren began to spend many weeks every year flying from country to country masterminding the expansion programme. He stamped his authority on each new branch and devoted many hours to lecturing — some would say hectoring — the senior officials delegated to nurture SES ideas in their own regions.

While other cults were attracting great notoriety, the SES managed to multiply almost unnoticed. Only in a few centres was there any public comment, let alone opposition.

That the SES succeeded in expanding so quickly is a tribute to the dedication of MacLaren and other SES leaders, the beguiling attractions of the introductory course material and the resources pumped into each new project. There was another factor which may have helped to recruit new members in commonwealth countries — the SES's devotion to British traditions and old-fashioned values. Here was a movement dedicated to Victorian-style morality and dress — rekindling the spirit of the old Empire. For some at least it must have been a comforting mantle to adopt — despite its more alien Hindu ideology.

Today the SES is active in Australia, New Zealand, the United States, Canada, Greece, Cyprus, Malta, Belgium, Holland, Spain, Ireland, South Africa, Trinidad and even Fiji. The network may be even bigger, for this is not an exhaustive list. The secrecy of the cult extends as much to its overseas operations as to its activities in the United Kingdom.

One factor that makes the SES difficult to spot is that it does not have an internationally standard name. In some countries it is called the School of Philosophy, in others the School of Economics and Philosophy, in others the School or Society of Practical Philosophy. This has led some senior SES figures to claim that these overseas organizations have no connection with the SES at home. The evidence is strongly to the contrary. The entire world-wide network is still centred in Queen's Gate, Kensington. SES leaders gather from overseas regularly in England for conventions dominated by The Master, Leon MacLaren. These apparently happen every other Christmas.

If further proof were needed there are the stories of people who have joined SES branches overseas and become besotted with its ideology. They closely mirror the experiences of SES members in Britain — the familiar catalogue of family break-ups, nervous breakdowns, subjugation to the SES's strict code of discipline, special dietary and dress rules, lack of sleep and the meditation.

Wherever foreign branches have shown a tendency to depart from the SES's rigid dogma, the evidence is that leaders have been encouraged to leave or fall in line — and not allow the branch to evolve in its own direction. Thus an SES recruit from New Zealand would feel at home transferring to a group in New York, Sheffield or Dublin.

A few years ago senior members of the branch in Wellington, New Zealand, fell out with MacLaren and the cult of personality which they felt was developing. There was no question of their remaining within the cult. They left and set up their own, less demanding organization.

What follows is a digest of how the SES has expanded outside these shores. We begin with the School's most successful foreign operation − Holland. Here the cult is nearly as active as in Britain.

The branch in Holland is called the 'School voor Filosofie' (School of Philosophy). It has acquired a portfolio of properties that rivals the SES holdings in Britain. The cult has seven buildings in Amsterdam alone and other centres in The Hague, Deventer and Driebergen. An imposing million-pound estate and mansion is rented at de Breul, not far from Utrecht: here most of the residential courses are held.

The SVF was started in 1962 by Franciscus van Oyen and his wife Toos, a wealthy banking family. They had been converts to MacLaren's ideas in London. Today Toos van Oyen is the head of the Dutch school and her son Paul is the administrative driving force. He too has spent time in London and at Waterperry learning from The Master. His sister, Doreen, has spent many years aiding MacLaren in Britain.

No doubt Holland has always been a fertile breeding-ground for new religious movements, but the SVF's growth has not been among the hippy colonies. Its appeal has been among the well-educated and well-groomed professional and executive class. Over the last twenty-two years it has enrolled over 22,000 members. It was growing quickly, unhindered until one of its more devoted followers defected.

When Joseph Vincent left the SVF he went through the familiar withdrawal problems and verged on total mental breakdown, but he recovered to head a flourishing opposition movement to the SVF that has brought the cult into the public eye and made recruitment of new members much more difficult.

We visited Vincent in Holland and were surprised at just how well-entrenched the SES branch there has become.

There is no evidence of members dabbling directly in politics, but the Dutch secret service has been taking a keen interest in the cult.

Certainly the SES is remarkably interested in the Dutch royal family and has published transcripts of royal speeches that in some instances seem to follow an SES line.

Vincent's story is almost as remarkable as Frith Oliver's. He joined the cult at seventeen years of age in London, quickly moved to its branch in Malta, ran away to England again and ended up in the higher echelons of the SVF in Amsterdam and The Hague. Each time he joined a new branch it was with the hope that he would find a solution to a question that had been tormenting him. If the cult had really discovered 'The Truth', why were its leaders so lacking in humanity, so flawed? By the time he arrived in Amsterdam he was tortured by the knowledge that the School was not satisfying his emotional and spiritual needs. But he could not give it up. It nearly wrecked his marriage, and his mental stability.

It appears that Vincent, like Oliver, was something of an experiment in MacLaren's eyes. Only a few months after he joined the organization, Vincent was 'converted' and enrolled in the meditation. He was invited to become a caretaker-cum-administrator at the School's house in Malta and given a twenty-four-hour regime of work duties.

I had a timetable for the whole week from 5 a.m. to 12 p.m. and told exactly what to do. Soon my whole critical faculty was blocked out. I was effectively spending my entire existence working for the School. I worked as a salesman to pay for my board, my groups, materials and books.

I was taught that sexual energy was energy in the wrong place. Any kind of sexual growth was repressed. After two years I completely snapped. The pressure was too great. They always wanted more from me. I was going into a complete fantasy world. By meditating and eating very little, the lack of proper nutrition and the lack of sleep, you lose all sense of reality. I was a complete zombie, going into trances and finding it difficult to come out.

Vincent upped and came to England to see if somehow the School had lost its way. He joined the youth groups at Waterperry and remembers vividly being encouraged to become politically aware by joining the Young Liberals. Once again the pressures forced Vincent to escape. He started working on an oil rig, taking his vacations in Holland.

The SES still preyed on his mind and one day he saw an advertisement for the introductory philosophy lectures in a Dutch newspaper. He was hooked again, started at the bottom of the SES pyramid, and worked his way into a senior position.

> I'd tried to stop when I arrived in Amsterdam but it was still so much in my subconscious. You only need a trigger word to put you back in the same, zombie-like state of mind.

Vincent got his Dutch wife to join the groups and she attended for six months. She left and this began the process of conflict that led to Vincent leaving. The marriage was on the rocks because he was so committed to attending SVF meetings and doing his work duties. He was now a meditation-checker with an awesome power over his charges. Yet he was obliged to keep everything secret at home. He became increasingly domineering – in line with the SES view of the male's role in marriage. When he went to his tutor with his problems a stark choice was presented:

> I was told I must choose between my wife and 'The Truth', that is The School. When I said I would have to choose against The Truth I was immediately shown the door. I became a complete mess. I'd lost something I'd invested twelve years of my life in.

The cult warned Vincent that it would create mental problems if he left:

They said that if you try to go back to sleep again having gained the knowledge, you can never sleep. They also said that if you try to exploit the knowledge and talk about it to outsiders then you will go crazy and end up in an asylum.

Vincent says he had a complete identity crisis.

You can't relax or resocialize. I thought of committing suicide but stopped because the SES had taught me that I'd only come back again and repeat the whole chain of events.

Now working in the oil industry and happily married with a daughter, Vincent can look back on this episode and talk about it without any sign of upset. But he says it took him at least a year to get over the worst traumas and begin to think for himself again:

To me 'Don't Think' sums up the SES's entire philosophy. Undoubtedly I was brainwashed. I only began to recover from it when I began to meet people outside the cult and test their view of reality against mine.

Vincent introduced us to other ex-SVF members who had similar stories to tell. Arij van der Stelt, an architect and planner, described the SES indoctrination process as a form of brainwashing. Like Joseph he has put a lot of energy into attacking the SES and courageously being interviewed by numerous newspapers because he is against the cult's recruitment methods and secrecy.

The Dutch press have taken a close interest in the attacks made by Vincent and van der Stelt and Paul van Oyen's attempts to portray the SVF as a harmless academic institution. A weekly news magazine *De Tijd* devoted five pages to the controversy under the heading *The cast iron grip of the School of Philosophy,* and in another issue carried no less than twenty-seven letters from readers. The article, in January 1984, caused a stir among SVF members in Holland and has led to an internal questioning of the direction the cult is following — a reaction similar to that caused by *The Standard* articles in Britain. It is evident that the SVF has now been forced to explain itself publicly in a way that was never necessary before.

Also in January a radio feature on the SVF, broadcast by the national VARA network, included an interview with Paul van Oyen. A translation of his remarks shows how easily the interviewer could have been talking to any of the SES leaders in London. Here is an extract:

> *Question* What does the SVF actually propagate?
> *van Oyen* . . . human development, especially in the sense of spiritual development . . .
> *Question* Is the SVF a religion or a religious movement?
> *van Oyen* No certainly not, or er, we study a philosophical system, that we have developed ourselves which originates as much from the Socratic as from the early Christian as from the Advaita Vedanta philosophy from India.

Perhaps Paul van Oyen stumbled over this answer because the question was a tricky one for the SVF. In Holland it has special tax-exempt status because it is a religion. The tax authorities no doubt found van Oyen's answer rather revealing.

In the radio programme, van Oyen went on to make predictable remarks about the SVF's secrecy:

> . . . we have concluded the only real way to know what we do is to allow people to join us and to let them listen to what we have to say. . .

Van Oyen said it was very difficult to make public clear statements about what the SVF wants:

> We have come to the conclusion that as little publicity as possible is the very best for us to enable people to investigate for themselves what we have to do. . .

The interviewer bluntly accused Paul van Oyen of 'covering himself in darkness'. Van Oyen replied:

63

May I say not in darkness but in the radiant light of conscious silence.

Asked if the SVF was brainwashing people and exploiting them financially, the cult's Dutch spokesman denied it:

I don't know their meaning as I've never experienced them myself let alone applied them . . .

In another revealing question van Oyen was asked why SVF students were not allowed to discuss the organization's ideas openly. Van Oyen said students were allowed to discuss what they are doing but he added:

The only restriction we have is that we have trust that they only speak about matters which they have real knowledge about and that they really understand, and for that reason in the beginning period we lay emphasis on people being careful how much they speak about what they hear in the school simply because they can't control the consequences of these matters, and we want to draw their attention to the fact that they might end up in a difficult conversation which they can't get out of.

The Dutch banker was given a difficult time and the programme highlighted some of the problems faced by a covert group prodded into the public eye. It is impossible for the SVF to lie outright because it is ostensibly devoted to 'The Truth'. Many members' faith would be shattered by any such device. Instead van Oyen was faced with resorting to double-speak of which the cult has a rich vocabulary: for religion say 'philosophical system', for secrecy and evasion say 'radiant light of conscious silence'.

Joseph Vincent has a clear recollection of how such terms could be used to confuse or mollify any curious outsider. Perhaps the best example of SVF or SES double-speak is the term 'The Truth' itself. It can be accurately translated as 'our religious beliefs'.

The SVF is now regularly in the public eye in Holland and gets coverage whenever some new idiosyncrasy or tragedy occurs. It is the mental strain of being in the cult that receives the most attention. In Gouda the papers were full of the misfortune of a cult member found wandering suicidally down the middle of a motorway after walking out of an SVF work weekend. When we left Holland ex-SVF members were talking of a cult member who had committed suicide. They recalled how she had previously 'flipped' on one of the SVF residential courses, though of course this may have had nothing to do with her death. In 1983–84 the Dutch anti-cult group 'SOS' dealt with more than sixty people with SVF problems.

Undaunted, the SVF continues to develop. It has now established its own children's school – the Plato School – which only takes cult members' children. The children have a bleak academic and spiritual existence. We have a copy of what they were expected to do at Sunday school before the day school was set up. Children aged from ten to sixteen were brought from long distances to an SVF town-house in van Eeghenlaan, an expensive street in central Amsterdam. They arrived at 7.45 a.m. for half an hour's meditation. Sanskrit began prompt at 8.15 followed by philosophy at 9.15. After a tea-break there was compulsory boxing for boys up until the thirty-minute lunch-break, followed by fencing. Girls were taught philosophy and arithmetic, Hindu-style. Later in the afternoon came studies in rhetoric for the boys while girls were taking 'ladies' studies'. At 4.45 p.m. after eight hours of intensive tuition and character building, the children left for home. Sunday schools for SES children are run on similar lines in most other countries.

In Holland the SVF bureaucracy is nearly as top heavy as in London. A list of functionaries includes several hundred names.

SES operations are more tightly knit a few hundred kilometres south in Belgium. There are School of Philosophy centres in Brussels, Antwerp and Bruges. Some local interest had been aroused in Belgium and in Holland by the fact that the Belgian SES branch is headed by a well-known TV interviewer – Henri Schoup. An anti-cult group – The

Association for the Defence of the Individual and the Family — has been gathering information about the cult's activities following complaints from people attending courses that the true objects of the organization were being kept secret. The Association estimates there are 1,000 people enrolled on courses, with a hard core of 250 long-serving followers.

More complaints followed a recent exposé of the cult's activities by the popular Flemish weekly *Humo*. It accused the cult of keeping hidden the Hindu background of the teachings. It drew attention to the way Sanskrit was being taught and the spiritual influence of the Shankaracharya. Members, especially from the Bruges area, were bitter that they had not been told about these aspects of the organization. A number left their groups.

Oddly, as Joseph Vincent's story illustrates, Malta is the Mediterranean country where the SES has been most active. The cult set up shop there in the late sixties and has struggled ever since to fend off robust opposition.

The attack launched by Father Gallea, described in chapter nine, followed much controversy in the local newspapers, notably a daily called *The Bulletin*. In 1973 a correspondent writing under the pseudonym 'Cicacas' scythed into the cult, which in Malta is known as 'The Study Group':

> We have heard and read warnings made by learned members of the clergy, we have had protests by parents, and we have had public condemnations by His Grace the Archbishop. This is indeed gratifying but on the other hand it is distressing to note that certain people in authority remain inactive and insensitive and they have not yet stopped this dangerous nonsense.

The *Bulletin* article attacked the local SES branch for all the usual faults:

A few very unfortunate ones . . . remained attached to the group because, at least so it seems, they had become fascinated through application of suggestive methods reinforced by regular trance-like exercises and other auto-suggestive practices.

They remain captive within a circle of select clubmanship bestowing upon themselves a sense of respectability and intellectuality. These poor misguided individuals, albeit adult, give one the impression that they are living in a state of delusion and that they are completely unaware of being taken for a ride, that they are being used . . .

Cicacas attacked the leader and founder of the Study Group, Mrs June Matthews, and questioned the motives of her organization:

Perhaps the London School of Economic Science has plans to create a new society, to promote a new culture. We do not know for sure because of the secrecy.

The following year the newspaper was still attacking the Study Group. It noted that the SES's name was often confused with that well-established academic institution the London School of Economics, and reported that former members of The Study Group were being shunned by the cult and that new recruits were 'supervised with staring eyes'.

The controversy was still bubbling on in 1982 when the correspondence columns of *The Times* discussed the Study Group. One anonymous writer, calling himself 'Once Bitten, Valetta', said the philosophy has a brainwashing effect:

Every student is left in the dark until the light which comes only from the Study Group penetrates the different levels of consciousness . . . countless students including myself experienced spiritual crisis . . . there have been conflicts between husbands and wives, parents and children and also engaged couples.

In trying to understand the direction taken by the SES

branch in Australia one must remember how the cult views criminals. MacLaren has taught that they are lost souls on the way out of existence altogether. Thus it is that SES members in this former penal colony are looked on rather differently — as one of the cult's former top members has revealed.

Anthony Ravesi, a pharmacist, joined the SES, known in Sydney and Melbourne as the School of Philosophy, when it first began in 1967. It had been started by two Australian-born Greeks, Michael Mavro and his wife Nina, who had spent eight or nine years in London at MacLaren's knee before returning to Sydney.

Ravesi came to London in the late sixties and returned to Sydney in 1970, remaining at the top of the cult until the end of 1980. He describes himself then as a 'conformist'. He was a trustee of the SOP's million-dollar building in Kent Street, in the heart of Sydney. When Ravesi left, the SOP had 700 to 800 members there. Two others from the top group left at the same time — no longer able to accept the extraordinarily strict regime. On some residential courses women were made to swing ten- or twelve-pound sledgehammers until they were exhausted. Ravesi explains:

> We three are classified by the Leader, Mr Mavro, as disciples of the devil and the fallen of Lucifer's band. To describe the character of Mr Mavro could be best done by drawing your attention to the characters of John Calvin, Hitler and the notorious Captain Bligh of Australian history. It is quite a statement to make, but it is the easiest way to do it. The Sydney school itself is run like a penal colony, with all the severities of one, because according to Mr MacLaren and Mr Mavro we in Australia are the scum and dregs of Europe. These are the actual words used; they are not mine. As such we are 'unintelligent', we are 'not able to use our minds', we have 'a low level of consciousness', we are 'not able to think for ourselves'.
>
> You must remember that every remark made in the school by its hierachy, Mr MacLaren, Mr Green, Mr Pincham and

here — Mr Mavro, is part of the conditioning process. So, Mr MacLaren's remark that he still hears the ball and chains rattling in the streets of Sydney refers to Australia's heritage as being originally a penal colony, and as far as he is concerned we still are a penal colony with the mentality of one, so the members of the school in Australia represent or comprise the stigma which subtly sounds in the Australian culture. It is the work of school here to change that and become the aristocrats of Australia, but first we have to be educated so as not to be the scum and dregs of the School.

Ravesi describes the main bulk of SOP members as middle-class working people:

Compared to the SES school in London, the Sydney school would be the butchers, bakers and candlestickmakers of the system.

He says there are very few professional people but the SOP's youth group could be changing this.

When Anthony Ravesi left the SOP in 1980 his wife and three children also left. They had to cope with the physical, mental and emotional problems of living a normal life.

Ravesi has this comment to make about the argument, put by the SES, that thousands have been through the teaching programmes with no ill effect:

Thousands have passed through the doors of the Sydney school without any 'side effects' also, but this is in the first 2 – 3 years (6 – 9 terms) of their involvement with the school, which is the major part of the screening processes of the school system. The mental conditioning begins with the first lecture without the students being aware of it and continues throughout school life. However, students are sifted out during the first two to three years, the more promising ones, those receptive to the teachings and showing a willingness to co-operate, pass through six terms before being allowed to receive the meditation and thus enter the 'inner workings' or inner sanctum of the school.

It is from this point that you are expected to conform, obey and commit yourself to the work of the school without question. 'Your will must now be given over to a higher will'. These are the ones who suffer from leaving the school, although the screening continues even after this point. Nonconformists are placed in what is called 'side streams' as distinct from the 'main stream'. A student can find himself or herself in the side stream for years, for the rest of life if necessary. There are side streams right through the hierarchy of the school; it is an inbuilt safety mechanism to protect the school from the outside and thus it has been able to avoid scrutiny for so long.

Another senior member of the school who had also been a member for more than ten years was equally critical of the SOP:

Through personal experience I have found it to be insidious, destructive to family life, psychologically damaging and an 'emotional black hole'.

Not much has appeared in the Australian press about the SOP despite attempts by Ravesi and others to alert it. In New Zealand, however, the cult has been receiving much unwanted publicity. *The Standard* articles helped to fuel interest but even before these appeared an article in the *Wellington Post* questioned the activities of the local Society of Practical Philosophy.

Reporter Brian Woodley described the SOPP as a quiet little group which shuns publicity. It had recently paid $460,000 for a huge former Salvation Army hostel in the Aro Valley district of Wellington, and thus come into the public eye.

The article said the SOPP discouraged members from speaking about the Society to non-members. However some former members had contacted the *Post* alleging that members were subjected to brainwashing and that some suffered major domestic upheavals including broken marriages.

Head of the Society was named as John Walter, a local

landscape gardener. The *Post* said there were 200 members in Wellington with another section of the organization in Auckland. Among the case histories related by the newspaper was the following:

> One woman told the 'Post' that after five years as a member she had become so involved that, although she did not recognize it at the time, she was losing her grip and heading for a nervous breakdown.
>
> Subjected to menial tasks on special camps organized by the society, put on a special diet of bread, yoghurt and fruit that saw her shrink to six stone ten pounds (42.7 kilograms), instructed to lead a monastic life that included celibacy and no contact at all with people outside the society, and having to take part in meditation sessions that allowed little time for sleep over a long period, she now claims she was a victim of brainwashing.
>
> She said the idea was to achieve betterment of oneself by a strict soul-searching process. Her gripe with the society was that the process caused immense social upheavals, and that broken marriages and nervous breakdowns were not uncommon.
>
> 'The women did everything for the men. The men were the ones who were served. . . I'm sure it was brainwashing. We were so immersed in it that we couldn't see it. You couldn't see what was happening to yourself,' she said.

In reply the SOPP executive committee chairman Mr Bruce Luxford said there was nothing specific that the organization had to answer for. The *Post* article published the following response from Luxford to the allegations:

> 'We don't seek publicity, and neither do individuals within the organization.'
>
> However, 'the secret society bit just doesn't stand up,' he said. Other groups, like the public service, also had rules about not speaking publicly on matters.
>
> If society members found the pressures too much it was best for them to leave. There were no constraints on people leaving, he said.

'They're only asked please not to speak of the people they've met — not to go around criticizing and don't speak of what you've heard in the society'.

Mr Luxford said he could recall no marriage breakups that could be attributed to the society's activities.

A week later there was a shoal of anonymous replies to the article, a number praising the SOPP and defending its activities. One member calling himself 'Trees' had left after five years but had found it an 'immensely enriching experience'. Another said some marriages had been saved by the counselling provided by the society. A lengthy letter said the organization had begun in Wellington as long ago as 1956. The letter added:

Little by little, McLaren's methods became more and more bizarre. It was an extreme right-wing society. Right from the first term people are asked not to speak of what they hear, outside the group.

People after attending the 'school' for three years are invited to take the meditation. On the surface of it it is voluntary, but if they don't take it they can't go through with the group they started with.

The society leader's word was law, and eventually things reached the stage where members could not marry, become engaged or change their job without his permission. Members could still drop out of the society if they wished, 'but they reach a point that they believe that without the school's help and group work there is no possibility for them'.

Six months later the *Post* printed more criticisms of the SOPP, this time from a member who had left the Society because of the financial commitment he had been asked to make. A week's wages had been requested to pay for the mortgage on the Aro Valley building. The member had told the newspaper, 'People were becoming emotionally hung up on the school'.

The *Auckland Times* followed up *The Standard* articles

in London. Correspondent Dianne Haworth reported the allegations of brainwashing and the comment from churchmen in England that the SES was 'evil'. She then talked to the Wellington Society of Practical Philosophy and the Auckland School of Philosophy, both SES affiliates. There was a blanket denial of the allegations but the *Times* also discovered that there were plenty of people to back up the criticisms:

In the past few days the churchmen's claims have been supported by former members who have spoken out about the regime of fear that keeps members locked in the grip of the cult.

They spoke of practices that put huge strains on marriages, alienate children from parents, prevent members from openly acknowledging each other at outside gatherings, order members on how to dress, eat and do their hair, and demand absolute loyalty to the exclusion of all else.

'When members are on the residential weekend or week-long course, outside commitments, such as business or family, must be subordinate to the school's demands,' said one.

'One adult I knew couldn't get leave to attend a family funeral. Another man was not permitted to be with his wife while she had her baby. The school comes first.'

'I know I've been brainwashed, and I'm still afraid of them,' said one young New Zealand man. 'It's hard to know whether others feel the same, because there is a strict rule that those still in the school are permitted no communication whatsoever with those who leave. It leaves a huge void when you make the decision to get out.

'Many of the rules they abide by are good, if governed by love, but when governed by fear become diabolical.'

The *Times* described three buildings used by the cult in Auckland as 'luxurious residences'. A Sunday school provided a day-long programme of lessons at which children were taught they were special and the outside world ignorant. The article asked what attracted so many intelligent people to the organization:

One ex-member of the Auckland School of Philosophy said that it had, at first, seemed excellent. 'There was no hard sell; no pressure. Much of what they teach is good, and I looked forward to going. But by about the third term the message started to come through, and a bit of pressure was applied. We were invited to become involved in what they call second-line work.'

Second-line work includes gardening, maintenance, cooking and housework at one of the organization's houses — even ironing the shirts and polishing the shoes of the local head of the group are part of the duties.

Doubts crept in for the ex-member as those who began to question the school's philosophy at this more advanced level were publicly humiliated and put down for their beliefs.

'Quite a number fell by the wayside at this stage. They may have been uneasy at the way things were shaping up, but we were told, and believed, that they had left because they couldn't take the discipline.'

At that time people in the class were saying to the lecturer that their friends had noticed they seemed to have changed and were becoming different. They were told by a smiling lecturer, 'You are on the way. Be tolerant of the others, they don't know any better.'

'The school becomes more authoritarian, more hierarchical and tithing is introduced as you climb higher in the movement. What finished me off was a meditation course which was "sold" after two years. We had to give one week's earnings or pension, and go through some rites at the Upland Road house to be initiated.

'It was very cleverly operated, with fear as a control factor, I think, now. But really, if today's churches provided any real spiritual values, many of us would not have been attracted to this society in the first place.'

SES offshoots have taken root in New York, Boston, San Francisco and Toronto. The Toronto group has been struggling to survive against active opposition from the locally based Council on Mind Abuse (COMA).

COMA estimates there are only a hundred or so active members of the cult. Some Toronto buildings are in the

SES's name but introductory lessons are advertised in the name of the School of Philosophy. Recruitment is through newspaper advertisements and subway posters but COMA has been handing out copies of *The Standard* articles and the SOP has lost a number of members with COMA's help.

A number left in 1981 including three members with several years' membership. COMA says that it commonly took these people at least six months to get over the 'withdrawal symptoms'. COMA workers have a policy of offering assistance with deprogramming, having satisfied themselves that the SOP bears all the hallmarks of the typical cult. The first COMA knew of the SOP was in 1979 when a woman member came to their office complaining she was being harrassed by other members because she wanted to leave.

The SES has attracted little public attention in the United States. The New York branch — known as the Practical Philosophy Foundation or sometimes the School of Practical Philosophy — has over 700 members, but it is believed there are at least 2,000 SES activists throughout the country.

Head of the PPF in New York is Joy Dillingham, a former Ouspensky teacher from London who was an early convert to Leon MacLaren's new ideas. A one-time actress, Dillingham now commands great respect within the cult and not just in New York. She went there at MacLaren's behest in the early sixties, put an advertisement in the paper and got three followers. From this the organization has grown to one of the SES's biggest overseas branches with twelve levels of teaching beginning with the standard introductory course.

The PPF owns or leases several expensive buildings including a six-storey brown-stone, bow-fronted mansion in East 79th Street near Park Avenue.

This is now the cult's American headquarters. It is a former finishing school near Central Park in one of the most expensive parts of Manhattan. The premises are beautifully kept by converts — polished-wood panelling and paintwork have been lovingly restored.

The school runs courses on practical philosophy,

economics and a nursery and kindergarten for children between three and six called 'The Ark'. On Sundays it holds a Sunday school for children from five to ten which 'offers a variety of activities concerned with harmonious physical, mental and spiritual development'.

To casual enquirers, the PPF is presented as an academic institution. A woman at headquarters premises said:

> We are studying how the principles of many great philosophers can be put into action. We might study something by Plato or in the Bible and see how we can apply that today.

She said that the courses were taken

> by students who have been in the school for many years. If a student is interested enough after taking an introductory course they can go on to take Part II and so on.

One of the school pamphlets explains,

> Working together under the guidance of a tutor students are gradually led to stillness of mind and precision of attention, as they verify for themselves the essential truth of the teaching and at the same time gain a fuller sense of their direction and function in life . . .
> . . . Great importance is laid upon the need for proper work habits: whatever the work is, care, attention and generosity are the guiding principles.

A number of members were busy cleaning the building, sweeping down the steps to the house and wiping down the paintwork in silence.

The PPF is run as a tax-exempt educational foundation provisionally chartered by the Regents of the University of the State of New York. Children of members of the cult are expected to attend a Saturday youth club and a Sunday school run on similar lines to other countries. The Ark is a recent development. The fees are $2,000 a year. The

PPF says these are low compared with other New York nurseries – largely because The Ark pays no rent. It is run by Beverley Taylor and her sister – the only paid staff.

A remarkable insight into the SES and its New York operations was provided by one of the few people ever to penetrate the SES's inner circle without having to work their way laboriously up through the teaching levels. David Sklar is vice president of the huge Trump Organization which runs the Trump Centre in New York – a luxuriously appointed 'vertical shopping arcade' built inside a skyscraper.

Sklar taught at the Henry George School in the city for twenty years and is a devoted believer in George's economic ideas (see chapter 2) which the SES also embraces. He found out about the PPF through his wife who attended some of the introductory classes in the early 70s.

She noticed that the economic ideas were drawn from Henry George's theories and Sklar decided to attend a lecture out of curiosity. The PPF tutor appeared to be in difficulty putting over the economic theories. Sklar was soon recognized as an expert and two PPF observers were sent to Sklar's own lectures. The reports back to Joy Dillingham must have been favourable because he was soon invited to address forty or fifty members of her advanced class. Sklar says he was asked why Henry George's ideas had never caught on. He replied that the economics of the world could be transformed if 20,000 people could be educated in the ideas. Sklar says:

After the talk Joy Dillingham clasped me with an unusual display of emotion. She was usually calm and collected. She said, 'We'll get you those 20,000 people'.

There followed more invitations to speak to the senior hierarchy in New York and an invitation to London to meet Leon MacLaren. Sklar says he first met Andrew MacLaren on this visit and the pair immediately hit it off. Andrew MacLaren asked Sklar what he thought of the philosophy. When Sklar replied he could not see how it fitted with the economic ideas, MacLaren agreed. 'It's mere fluffery,' he said.

Sklar stayed in London for a while and lectured with Andrew MacLaren on economics to SES members. The advanced philosophy students seemed to have an imperfect understanding of the economics, though they were fully steeped in the SES's spiritual theories.

Shortly after arriving in London, Sklar was granted the audience with their revered leader Leon MacLaren:

> He literally held court at his home in Hammersmith. He had a waiting-room, a sort of ante-chamber, where all his visitors had to wait. When I went there Joy Dillingham was unusually nervous. We waited with representatives from the Holland School including the daughter of the leader there, and leaders of the South African School. It was like waiting for an audience with the pope. Eventually I was ushered into Leon MacLaren's study. Sitting at his feet was Joy Dillingham. He chainsmoked his way through the interview. When a new cigarette was needed Joy Dillingham jumped up to light it.

Sklar's interview was short but bizarre. MacLaren asked him to explain the nature of Truth. Sklar vaguely said it was like a wheel in which all the spokes lead to the same hub. MacLaren abruptly said, 'I recognize you,' in tones that made clear it was of some considerable significance. The audience was over, but it had a profound effect on his standing within the cult. Dillingham was overjoyed. 'He recognized you,' she said in astonishment and awe. Sklar assumed it meant he had been seen by the cult leader as some important figure from the past or future that he himself had never realized he was. When he returned to New York it was with greatly enhanced prestige. 'I never did find out who I was supposed to be,' he says, 'but it made me into a celebrity within the PPF.'

Sklar became a senior PPF economics lecturer, but not without the occasional difficulty. One of the people he supplanted could not accept Sklar's straight economic theory devoid of philosophical allusions. There was a row and Joy

Dillingham scolded her subordinate for breaking the basic rule of obedience.

Sklar began to dislike this aspect of the cult — its demands for total obedience, the lack of opportunity it gave members to exert their own imaginations, their own will. He describes Joy Dillingham as a model student at his classes, but when she entered a special chair was brought for her. One cult member said she could see an aura around Dillingham. Her word was law. Sklar recalls:

> If you had a wedding to attend but were expected to do something for the PPF there was no question which you would choose. The cult always came first, with the result that eventually all family ties are secondary. You are too busy to have any other interests.

His departure from the cult was even more bizarre and more abrupt than his entry. Sklar had been introducing new lectures into the PPF curriculum, on sociology. One day Leon MacLaren arrived in New York and asked to see him. MacLaren wanted to know about the sociology class. Sklar explained that he started with primitive man and the lectures developed from there. MacLaren was evidently upset. He said there was no such thing as 'primitive man'. Man had been more advanced in the past. 'Primitive man' was a terrible, erroneous expression. The audience was over and later Sklar was told by a distraught Joy Dillingham that MacLaren's message was it was time he started his own school:

> It was a charming way to tell me I was excommunicated.

Sklar took MacLaren's advice a little too literally for the PPF's liking. He rented space next door to the cult's premises and invited all the cult members to attend. For six lessons he had a hundred per cent attendance. The members had not heard of his excommunication and were simply following the basic rule of obedience. Sklar began to debunk the cult by drawing attention to the disparate sources from which the philosophy is drawn. After the first six lessons, no one from the PPF turned up. Clearly his subversive approach had been discovered.

Sklar is loath even today to condemn the cult outright. He believes the PPF is more an organized religion than a typical cult:

> I believe the economic theories which they teach are some of the most important ideas to get over. It is worth all the mumbo-jumbo that these theories have been surrounded with.

The SES still provides lectures in economics, but these could now be described as 'mere fluffery' compared with the main thrust of the SES's aims — spiritual enlightenment.

The SES established itself in Dublin in 1962. A small Ouspensky group linked itself with the SES in London. An article in the *Irish Independent* in May 1983 described how there was a split in the Ouspensky group as the SES began to exert more and more influence. The split resulted in the SES setting up its own local branch under the name School of Philosophy.

The cult now has 500 members in the Dublin area and its headquarters is a large four-storey Georgian House in Baggot Street, a wealthy central district. It has tax-exempt status as an educational institution.

The SOP has recently been holding its residential courses at Townley Hall Study Centre outside Drogheda. A former stately home, Townley Hall is privately owned, but the cult is now the largest user.

The *Irish Independent* article named the leader in Dublin as Edgar Deschant, an Irish citizen but of German origin. The principal is Alan Campbell, a Dublin auctioneer. The

Independent correspondent, Paul Blanchfield, talked to a woman who had finished the first course of philosophy lectures. She told the newspaper:

> I wanted to do something at night so I just went along. It was supposed to be some kind of a practical philosophy course. I'm not sure what it really turned out to be but I found the environment strange. No one wanted to tell anyone anything. They seemed to be very secretive people generally. There was a lot of mystery attached to the place; they didn't encourage people to write down anything and they didn't encourage you to ask many questions.

The woman said she was told it was better not to ask too many questions.

The article described the meditation, the study of Sanskrit and aspects of Measure. It concluded:

> The motivation behind the School remains puzzling. If it's based simply on the love of wisdom why are those involved unwilling to discuss their philosophy openly?

There have been several radio programmes discussing the expansion of the cult and some ripples of disquiet within the Catholic Church. One theological student began looking into the SES after a friend's girl-friend was found to be contributing £10 of her £85-a-week wages to the School. Someone else he met – an SES tutor – appeared to have changed in personality since joining the cult. The tutor and his wife 'now talked very slowly in an affected manner, ate health foods and refused ever to answer any questions'.

The student decided to attend a public SES lecture given by its principal, Alan Campbell. There were 250 present, all very well dressed. Campbell was never introduced and spoke extremely slowly for an hour. Everyone in the audience sat deadly still. The theme of the talk was, 'I am not my body. I go from unreality to reality, from darkness into light'. It is clear that the majority of people at the talk were SES members. At the tea-break they were delighted with Campbell's address.

In Dublin some SES members have formed their own choir which is rather antiseptically called 'Octave Management'. Performances are sometimes held in churches, including on one occasion St Anne's in Dawson Street which is Protestant. Predictably the choir sang mainly Mozart.

CHAPTER FOUR

The Ancient Knowledge

In many ways the SES is its own worst enemy, for without the secrecy that surrounds the cult, there would be no need for an exposé such as this. No one can question a movement's right to believe and to teach a particular philosophy — not even to practise it, however damaging some of the results — provided it is clear to recruits from the outset what that philosophy is and where it is drawn from. Secrecy, however, permeates every aspect of the SES operation, with the code of silence impressed on members from the very first term of their involvement. So this chapter is intended to open up the School's philosophy and show its antecedents.

We have already mentioned that Leon MacLaren took on board the teachings of Gurdjieff and Ouspensky. The reluctance of the SES to reveal anything of its background or methods is a direct result of their influence. Gurdjieff and Ouspensky held that a prerequisite of anyone studying their system must be secrecy. No novice could possibly explain it correctly, it had to be experienced to be understood, and descriptions simply led to distortion. This is a stricture that the SES have been happy to obey, although they have added a number of refinements to the Teaching espoused by these two latter-day seers. For while their obsession with secrecy may protect the SES philosophy from outside influences, it also acts as a very effective smokescreen against criticism and independent analysis.

And perhaps there is a further reason for this secrecy? They cannot be unaware that today controversy surrounds the name of Gurdjieff as naturally as fog surrounds a swamp. Present-day exponents of the system see Gurdjieff as the herald of a new dawn in human development. But his many critics paint a darker picture. Descriptions such as charlatan and trickster are common. He was an occultist, they allege, using his followers for his own unspecified purposes while remaining impervious to their sufferings. The case of Katherine Mansfield — the New Zealand-born writer who joined his group while in the last throes of TB — is regularly wheeled out against him. She was ordered to spend much of her time in a cow byre to combat the disease. Also spicing the case for the prosecution are the claims that for many years he was a Tsarist spy, and had links with Nazi Germany which included suggesting the Swastika as Hitler's emblem.

That his followers suffered — some of them grievously — there is no doubt, and his callousness is well-documented. Katherine Mansfield's involvement in the institute he set up in Fountainebleau near Paris was certainly bizarre and tragic, but perhaps more indicative of her free spirit than his mesmeric influence. His Tsarist connections seem to have been proved, but his involvement with Hitler remains far more speculative. As to the occult — yes, he admitted so himself, though his techniques seem far removed from the traditional concept of witchcraft. Beyond doubt, however, is the impact that his system of belief had on Western intellectuals during the fad-ridden 1920s and afterwards. The SES is living proof that the shock waves can still be felt.

Brought up in the central Asian town of Kars — now in Turkey, but then under Russian occupation — the young Gurdjieff distinguished himself with his academic prowess and his taste for the supernatural. He witnessed several events for which he could find no rational explanation, and while in his teens resolved that the wider world could provide the answers.

His search for wisdom was to take him on a twenty-year odyssey from the Pyramids of Egypt to the desert wastes of Mongolia, from Tibetan mystics to the Holy Land and on to Crete. On the way he assumed many roles — hypnotist, curio dealer, restaurateur, typewriter mechanic . . . And also, it would appear, Tsarist spy.

It was 1913 before Gurdjieff the Teacher, a role he was to play for the rest of his life, emerged in Moscow to pass on some of the wisdom he had acquired. By then he had gathered around him some twenty followers – a group going under the romantic title – Seekers of Truth. (It has been alleged that this group included one Karl Haushofer, who was to become one of the most important ideologists of the Third Reich. Documentary evidence of this is lacking.)

Two years later there poked into this throng of mystic marauders the suspicious head of mathematician and journalist Pyotr Demianovitch Ouspensky (1878–1947), then thirty-seven-years old and something of a celebrity in his own right. He found he had much in common with the mysterious Mr Gurdjieff.

The son of an upper-class Russian family, Ouspensky too had been intellectually headstrong from an early age. And he had experienced the supernatural – in his case an overwhelming sense that he had 'been here before', which at times gave him almost clairvoyant insight. His quest for an explanation of this phenomenon had led him to wide vistas of esoteric theory and techniques. He too had travelled widely, in Egypt, Ceylon, India, America and throughout Russia, and once back home supported himself through journalism. But his heart still lay in unravelling the mysteries of the universe. In 1912 his book, *Tertium Organum: a key to the enigmas of the world*, won him critical acclaim.

His credentials to join the Seekers of Truth could not have been better presented, and when he met Gurdjieff he quickly became convinced of the validity of his teaching. Soon afterwards both men fled the Russian revolution, and the system arrived in Western Europe.

Gurdjieff's philosophy was that mankind exists for just two purposes: to produce the vibrations necessary to transmit the higher forces of the universe to the earth below us, and to feed those higher forces by becoming enlightened enough to join them. Those forces, like us, emanate from an Absolute which created all, but they are closer to the Absolute than we are. Thus their influence is benign.

The only way each individual can fulfil these two functions is by the use of what Gurdjieff calls 'consciousness', or 'essence' (others may call it 'soul', or 'inner self'). Most of us ignore this still, small voice within us as we become caught up in the hurly-burly of everyday living. Because of this we fail to live up to our full potential. In this state our actions can be said to be mechanical, merely habitual responses which we seldom question. We are, to all intents and purposes, asleep.

There is no God of Mercy who will forgive us this dereliction of duty. That, according to Gurdjieff, is a sentimental idea clutched at by people eager to excuse their behaviour in the knowledge that they will be forgiven. If we fail to take our chance, we contribute through our ignorance to the ills of the world — and chaos and warfare reign. Men and women become ruled by their egos and desires. In this state we consign ourselves to the Circle of the Confusion of Tongues, in which we are subject to the law of chance and accident.

Something is needed, therefore, to awaken us to our plight, to re-engage our consciousness. Gurdjieff claims that people are made up of three centres: the physical, the emotional and the intellectual. In most people they are out of balance, and one of the centres predominates. Traditionally, he maintained, people have tried to achieve full consciousness by focussing on just one centre. The person with a preponderance of his physical centre has followed the way of the fakir, which has involved asceticism; emotional types have followed the way of the monk, which concentrates on religious feeling; and intellectuals have chosen the way of the Yogi, the way of reason. But Gurdjieff puts forward a Fourth Way, which is achieved by balancing all three centres in the individual. Once balanced, they work in harmony, and full consciousness follows. The advantage of this method, he claimed, was that it did not take years of discipline. Transformation could be achieved very swiftly.

How is this balance acquired? The first step, according to Gurdjieff, is that an individual must question his existence:

He must realize that he can lose nothing because he has nothing to lose; he must realize his 'nothingness' in the full sense of the term.

Here Gurdjieff was attacking 'personality', the public image we each present to the world and tend to believe in privately too. It is, he claims, a false state, comprising many different 'I's, some of them contradictory. In each individual it must be replaced by the essence, the unshakeable 'I' at the core of each person. For the only way of developing is to 'know yourself' — the glib phrase frequently trotted out by the SES to deflect questions about what they teach.

Gurdjieff seemed to take a real delight in reducing the personalities around him. Literary lions, Harley Street specialists and other eminently respectable dabblers in mysticism who flocked to his French chateau found themselves working until they dropped, on the most menial of tasks. The more unsuitable the job, the more likely they were to be selected to carry it out. And so the trend continues in the SES. Every residential course has a full quota of manual work to be done. And for the more difficult jobs, those members with the necessary skills have found themselves ignored in favour of those who lack the most rudimentary knowledge of what to do.

Once the personality has been subdued, then the work on rebuilding the individual can begin in earnest. This is accomplished by relentless concentration on the self, called self-remembering. Said Gurdjieff:

Self-study is the work or the way which leads to self-knowledge. But in order to study oneself, one must first learn how to study: where to begin, what methods to use. A man must learn how to study himself, and he must study the methods of self-study.

The chief method of self-study is self-observation. Without properly applied self-observation a man will never understand the connection and the correlation between the various functions of his machine, will never understand how and why on each separate occasion everything in him 'happens'.

Through this self-observation an individual becomes aware of the two laws which run throughout creation, the law of three and the law of seven (the octave). By observing them, he can reach a truer understanding of how the universe works.

The law of three is made up of two dissimilar elements, together with the balance, or understanding, which arises from their interaction. These include, at a basic level, man and woman producing child, and winter and summer producing spring. The Christian Holy Trinity is held by some esoteric groups, including the SES, to be a symbol of this triparite law.

This principle has a further application in the SES. Whenever members undertake a manual task, they are instructed to focus their attention fully on the 'point of work'. This is where the saw blade bites into the log, or the pen touches the paper. From the interaction of the two elements involved — saw-log, pen-paper — understanding should come of the best way of achieving the task in hand. (It also very usefully prevents the member using the activity as a chance to reflect on what he is doing there in the first place.)

The law of seven, or the octave, is said to govern the order in which any creation occurs. Gurdjieff asserted that the universe consists of vibrations which, at the point furthest from the source, become so dense they materialize into matter. The higher they are, through the seven stages which lead to the Absolute, the more rarified they become. The different levels in an octave, however, did not occupy Gurdjieff's attentions as much as the spaces between them. For Gurdjieff pointed to the fact that the spaces are not all equal. Two are less pronounced than the others. In other words, the octave appears to falter. This is borne out in the musical octave where only a semitone separates notes B and C, and E and F, whereas a full tone separates other notes. Gurdjieff compared the octave to a straight line running smoothly enough for the first three notes, but then at the first weakened interval dipping down at an angle. It runs along a new downward course for a further four notes.

Along comes the second weakened interval and it dips down again to a new course which it holds for the start of the new octave and so on and so on. Draw that straight line as it looks after plotting the course of six octaves and you have drawn a crude ellipse — we are going round and round, getting nowhere.

Gurdjieff taught that, unless special 'shocks' were introduced into the octave which would carry it in a straight line across the intervals, humanity cannot progress.

We see this theory of shocks borne out in his Golden Ladder, the seven levels of man's development. They are:

One   Instinctive motor man. Most people fall into this category. They are tossed about through life at the whim of their animal instincts and desires.

Two   Emotional man. He is aware of his animal desires and can at least manipulate them.

Three Intellectual man. Gurdjieff particularly despised this category — those who think they know everything.

Four   Transitional man. He is conscious that he wants to change. He has fallen under the influence of an esoteric school which teaches him self-remembering. This serves as the shock necessary to carry him across the interval.

Five   Integrated man. For the first time man acquires some real identity.

Six   Conscious man. He begins to acquire superhuman mental and physical powers. His knowledge is 'the complete knowledge possible to man'.

Seven The complete man in the final stage; he has acquired everything and is immortal. We know nothing of the shock required to carry immortal man to the eighth level, the Absolute.

The application of the law of seven permeates the entire structure of the SES. As we shall see, it is the basis of their view of the levels of mankind. And it even influences the length of time they spend away on residential courses. At various times shocks have been administered to the system when it was felt to be losing impetus. The introduction of the rigorous diet was one such event. Latterly some SES members have even seen newspaper stories criticizing the cult as the 'shock' necessary for their future development.

One aspect of Gurdjieff's teaching which the SES have taken firmly to heart is his advice on how to accumulate the energy necessary to help one's transformation, and how to avoid squandering it. In this we see the reason for the SES warnings against what they term 'negative emotion' and against fantasy and imagination.

Gurdjieff wrote:

> Energy is spent chiefly on unnecessary and unpleasant emotions, on the expectation of unpleasant things, possible and impossible, on bad moods, on unnecessary haste, nervousness, irritability, imagination, daydreaming and so on. Energy is wasted on the wrong work of centres; on unnecessary tension of the muscles out of all proportion to the work produced; on perpetual chatter which absorbs an enormous amount of energy; on the 'interest' continually taken in things happening around us or in other people and in fact having no interest whatever; on the constant waste of the force of 'attention' and so on and so on.

He advised that the way to acquire energy is to learn how to separate the fine from the coarse. For the human organism does not just rely on air and food for sustenance; it relies on the impressions that it receives. These impressions must obviously be sifted to ensure they are going to be beneficial. The way to achieve this is through self-remembering.

Today this emphasis on discrimination has become yet another smokescreen thrown up by the SES. By telling their members just what is fine and what is coarse, they are able to impose their totally arbitrary views about the world at large on their members. By accepting these views — MacLaren's loathing of Beethoven, television or the more popular newspapers, to name just a few — members allow the cult to control most of the outside stimuli they are likely to encounter. Such stimuli even include family and friends outside the cult, for SES members are encouraged to seek the company only of people engaged in a similar spiritual search — in other words fellow SES members.

Gurdjieff goes on to tell us that 'conscious men' who have passed on before us have left influences to act as our signposts:

Influences of this kind are usually embodied in the form of religious systems and teachings, philosophical doctrines, works of art and so on.

But these are not enough, for they are open to individual interpretation.

When a man, through his own volition, begins himself to start discriminating good from bad, then the good influences within him form a magnetic centre which attracts more influences of the same sort. These influences should lead him to an esoteric source to further his development. Such assistance, according to Gurdjieff, is crucial:

No one can escape from prison without the help of those that have escaped before. Only they can say in what way escape is possible, or can send tools, files, or whatever may be necessary.

The help must take the form of an esoteric school, and that school must fulfil certain criteria to be effective:
— It must be founded on the principles of the law of three and the law of seven.
— It must have a teacher, and the demands on its members must be rigorous. They must be bound to secrecy about the work they are doing. They must tell the truth at all times, and they must obey the rules. These rules, says Gurdjieff:

Can never be either easy, pleasant or comfortable. On the contrary, they ought to be difficult, unpleasant and uncomfortable; otherwise they would not answer their purpose. Rules are the alarm clocks which wake the sleeping man.

We do not know what caused Ouspensky to grow disillusioned with Gurdjieff, but it could well have been the pedagogic attitude those remarks illustrate. All Ouspensky would say was

> In the summer of 1918 I began to feel that I had ceased to understand him, or his views had changed; and I found it necessary to separate G. and the System, of which I had no doubts.

When they fled Russia, Ouspensky settled in London, but the British authorities refused to extend a similar facility to his one-time mentor. Tsarist activities, particularly in Tibet, had been a thorn in the flesh of the British Empire for decades, and they were not in a forgiving mood. Gurdjieff was forced to settle instead for France.

The two men seldom crossed paths again, and in 1924 Ouspensky formally broke all links. But he continued the Teaching for many years, building up several small groups of followers. Whatever the dispute with Gurdjieff, Ouspensky's followers were convinced they had unlocked the mysteries of the Universe, and were well on their way to salvation. That conviction lasted until 1947 when calamity struck. With only a few months to live, Ouspensky summoned 300 followers to his side. They were to begin again from scratch, he said, seeking new tools and new paths to enlightenment. Did this mean, came the faltering question, that he had abandoned the System? The reply was crushing: 'There is no System.'

MacLaren today seems to draw much of his inspiration from Gurdjieff and his teaching; self-remembering is taught from Day One in the SES. But the Hindu philosophy they learned from the Maharishi and the Shankaracharya was also crucial to the development of the SES into its present form.

In fact, as we explained earlier, MacLaren and others believed they had discovered in this philosophy the source of what Gurdjieff taught.

That religious doctrine is the Hindu school of non-dualism (mankind and the Absolute are one) known as the Advaita Vedanta. It was the philosophy of the Indian mystic the Shankara, who lived from 788 to 820 AD. He established four seats of learning in India to pass on his teaching in oral form. A recent Shankaracharya of the North was the incumbent of this tradition, who provided the SES with much spiritual guidance. He is Swami Brahmananda. Saraswati Jagadguru Bhagwan Shankaracharya.

Two notes of caution must be held firmly in mind. Firstly, criticism of the SES is not intended as a criticism of Hindu philosophy. It is the way that philosophy is applied which prompts our concern about the British-based cult. The emphasis on compassion that Hindu seers brought to the doctrine would appear to have been totally discarded by the SES.

Secondly, the relationship between the Shankaracharya, referred to by the SES as His Holiness, and the cult seems to have been fairly indirect. Anthony Ravesi, a former senior SES official in Australia, told us in 1983:

The interviews or audiences that Mr MacLaren has with the Shankaracharya can be likened to an audience with the Pope in Rome or the Archbishop of Canterbury to receive instruction and explanation on the theology and philosophy of Christianity.

His Holiness does not speak English and thus an interpreter is required to translate into English, and of course he is a member of the SES. The material which the students are given is the instruction received from the Shankaracharya changed to fit in with the ideals of the School. Simple things such as '. . . tell your people . . .' will appear in the material as '. . . tell the members of your School . . .';'. . . a guru or teacher teaches his students . . .' will appear in the material as '. . . a guru or teacher or a School such as this teaches its members . . .'. These are very simple examples to illustrate the way the teachings of the Shankaracharya are used to give members of the SES the impression that His Holiness has chosen the School and is giving it special knowledge to save mankind.

The answer which the SES believe they have found, through the original teaching of the Shankara, is that the universe and everything within it are a manifestation of the Absolute. This entity cannot be described, even by the word 'entity'; it is beyond definition or comprehension. As such, any definition or manifestation of it must be a distortion. (Think how woefully any love song or love letter fails to convey the truth of the underlying emotion.) Since the Absolute is ultimate reality, any distortion of it must be a lesser truth, or even illusion. Since it is absolute purity, any distortion must be impure. But still the truth must exist, within the distortion, for the distortion to take place. The problem is, how to recognize this ultimate reality, absolute purity.

It cannot be revealed to us why the manifestation of the universe has taken place. But we are told what prompts the manifestation. Co-existing with the Absolute are the three qualities of nature, or matter. To give them their Hindu names, they are Tamas, Rajas and Sattva. Tamas is the quality of inertia, Rajas that of activity, and Sattva the harmony or balance between the other two. (Recognize the Gurdjieff law of three?)

When they are in complete equilibrium, they exist in an unmanifest state. But, at the will of the Absolute, that equilibrium is disturbed and they spark one another off — first one the stronger, then another. They become the components of constant change. Birth — Life — Death; Winter — Spring — Summer; these are perhaps the most obvious examples. This continuous change accounts for the finite nature of everything within our perception. Hence man, a material being and therefore part of the distortion, can never be truly happy. For he knows, even while experiencing happiness, that it is impermanent.

This impermanence affects every aspect of our existence, with one exception. Our bodies change, our minds change, our perceptions change, our senses change. The one part of us that never changes is our inner self, or consciousness. That consciousness is the Absolute within us, at one with the unmanifest Absolute, at one with the true reality that lies behind the distortion or illusion of manifest nature, and at one with the truth inside every human being. The SES call this part of the personality 'the Atman'.

The vast majority of us have a problem. For the consciousness within each individual is trapped inside a material body, capable of exerting an extremely powerful hold. How do we know, for instance, the difference between the inner self and the pull of the mind, body or senses, which are all part of the illusion? Quite simply we cannot, unless we have joined the SES, who will give us the necessary instruction.

Those of us who fail to seek out and nurture the truth within us condemn that truth to living under the thrall of material distortion; we fail to recognize it for what it is. The material side of life forces consciousness down to the lower level, a process involving much pain. Instead of striving towards objective truth the individual becomes one with the subjective, the ego, and identifies with the distortion which is taken to be truth. Hence men and women become identified with their families, their jobs, their homes, friends, fashions, feelings and so on. All of this, of course, is a distortion of the Truth, which lies beyond these definitions. The only reality that should be sought is union with the Absolute. How, then, can a man or a woman see a marriage partner who is not engaged on a similar search as anything but a positive danger to his or her own spiritual development?

Neglect of our true nature will have the direst consequences. We will remain for ever trapped in the world of matter, the continuous chain of cause and effect. When we die, we will be doomed to be reborn throughout eternity, or for however long it takes for the inner self to break free from the shackles of material form. To the SES this is the equivalent of eternal damnation, for a law of nature is that everything runs from fine to coarse. Thus suffering, through ignorance of the Absolute and through the decay of matter, will be ever-present. Only returning to the Absolute can we transcend this unhappy state of affairs.

But to approach such a state while still in earthly form brings reward in plenty. For to approach the Absolute is to fall under its harmonizing influence, which will permeate every aspect of your life. Hence the implicit SES belief that virtue breeds success — although by that time you will have realized that material success is a mere illusion anyway.

The whole theory of the unchanging nature of our consciousness could be thought to founder on the fact that consciousness apparently deserts us in sleep. But this, we are told, is not so. In deepest sleep the material world is transcended and our consciousness comes closest to its true nature. So deep sleep is beneficial and necessary, though even here our ignorance of our inner self prevents us joining the Absolute.

In lighter sleep, when we dream, we are simply victims once again of the material world and all its impressions. We should therefore avoid this state; it is wasting valuable time when we could be awake and concentrating on our spiritual development. This is the basis of the SES belief that sleep should be limited to between four and five hours a night, and you should get up when you wake up. Fitful dozing is merely indulging the body.

The SES also found echoes of Hindu philosophy in Gurdjieff's theory that the universe was born of vibrations. For in Hindu philosophy it is traditionally held that the manifestation of the universe is precipitated by the greater manifestation of space, and the unique sensory characteristic of space is said to be sound. (Did you ever wonder why in the film *Close Encounters of the Third Kind* it took a certain combination of musical notes to enable the alien spacecraft to materialize?)

Hence the SES reverence towards Sanskrit. They believe that this, the most ancient of Indo-European languages known to us, is in fact the original language, containing the manifestation of the cosmic sound which created us all. As such its sound, together with the concepts contained in early Sanskrit religious works, reveal the ancient knowledge about God, or the Absolute. By simply chanting Sanskrit, the cosmic sound is created, allowing the influence of the Absolute to flow.

At the heart of the Indian religion are four ancient

testaments called the Vedas. (Two of the SES schools for children were called St Vedast!) These testaments were handed down orally in Sanskrit; many Hindus hold them to be eternal, and not ascribable to human authorship. Western scholars date them somewhere between 1,500 and 900 BC. The knowledge they contain is said to be supreme truth, which is periodically revealed in the world to those enlightened enough to receive it. This is not dependent on the enlightened ones being Hindus; they can be of any faith or nationality.

As with all religious works, the Vedas are open to interpretation, and within present-day Hinduism there are at least six separate schools of thought with widely differing beliefs on even the most fundamental issues. Three of them in fact are atheist.

The school which the SES follows is the Vedanta, the most important of the Hindu schools with a theological stance. This school grew out of two later additions to the Vedas, works called the Aranyakas (600 BC) and the Upanishads (600–300 BC). The Vedanta was thought by Indians of that time to be a necessary addition, for when the last of the Vedas appeared, it seemed the religion was stagnating into dogma and ritual. As is common throughout the history of religion, a spiritual rebirth became necessary.

The Vedanta sought to penetrate the symbolism of the rituals and probe once again the nature of God, and our relationship with our creator. For the first time, the concept of an Absolute was introduced, together with the belief in reincarnation. There was a corresponding reawakening of interest in inner mystical experiences. It was within this Vedantic tradition that the Shankara later set out his philosophy of the Absolute and mankind being one, with mankind existing in ignorance until realizing his unity with the Absolute.

It would seem that it is to the Vedantic tradition, with extra ideas culled from Gurdjieff, that the SES turns in instructing its members on how to achieve self-realization. The Vedantic method they adopt is a hard road to follow, known to the Hindus as the Way of Knowledge. Few choose it, preferring another Vedantic tradition, the Way of Devotion, which holds that we can more easily rejoin the Absolute through sincere devotion and passive surrender.

The Way of Knowledge requires nothing less than that men and women should be utterly transformed before they realize their unity with the Absolute. In the Hindu tradition, this transformation can only be achieved through the oral instruction of spiritual knowledge from a guru — or teacher — to a pupil. The guru need not be fully realized, but he can point the way. (This accounts for the SES's far-from-perfect tutors.)

We need to read the scriptures to underline what is taught, but the scriptures cannot in themselves provide all the inspiration which is necessary. This is why no notes are provided to first- and second-year students at SES philosophy courses. They have to hear the message first, and then read it. The huge attraction of this method, of course, is that when students do eventually read from the various sources, they will interpret what they read in the light of what they have heard.

It is also plain to see why many new students remain confused about which part of the teachings they hear comes from established sources such as the Bible, Plato or the Vedas, and which parts come from the SES. In SES terms the scriptures are not just the Vedas, but all works which they see as representing eternal truth. And while references are sometimes given, they are too general to allow the student to go away and check them out for himself. The last thing the SES wants is an individual assessment of the accuracy of their interpretation. It also accounts, of course, for the intolerance shown by tutors at these courses to those of an argumentative or sceptical disposition. For the students are not taking part in some philosophical free-for-all. Although no one has yet told them, they are receiving instruction in the Truth.

Both at the introductory classes and further on in the School, notes are made during group meetings of what each student says. These enable the cult to keep an eye on those exhibiting the most signs of compliance — and those likely to cause trouble. Particularly pertinent comments may be trotted out by the tutor at later sessions, giving their originators a warm glow of appreciation. Good and bad attitudes alike, however, are duly noted on each student's dossier.

Within the Vedantic tradition it is stressed that the greatest influence a guru can bring to bear on his students, to hasten their transformation, is compassion. This is more likely to make a real impression than anything he says. In the SES that particular virtue, perhaps through the influence of Gurdjieff, appears completely absent.

How then, according to the Way of Knowledge, is a person transformed? First he must acquire four basic disciplines. The first is discrimination between the unreal and the real. (What this means in SES terms, of course, is complete acceptance of their arbitrary approach to truth and falsehood, as illustrated by their attitude towards Mozart, Plato and so on.)

The second discipline is renunciation, by which you disregard all earthly pleasures because of their finite nature. Ultimately even the hope of eternal bliss must be disregarded before it can be achieved. (In SES terms it also involves spending as little time as possible on anything not connected with the Absolute.)

The third discipline is called the Six Treasures. These 'treasures' prepare the individual for self-knowledge, acting as foundation stones. The first is calmness − our minds dwelling on the Absolute and dismissing everything our senses perceive as illusory. The second is self-control, which means restraining the inner self from identifying too closely with our actions or perceptions. It should remain detached, in communion with the Absolute. If this is practised, our actions and perceptions will eventually be governed by the Absolute. 'We are not out to create anything,' SES members meeting at Queen's Gate were told in 1973, 'for that is the business of the Absolute.'

After self-control comes the third 'treasure' − realizing the utter self-sufficiency of our Inner Being. The fourth is forbearance — the ability to endure all feelings and problems perceived by the senses without identifying with them, expressing anything about them, or, with physical suffering, even seeking relief. This obviously goes hand in hand with the SES strictures against falling prey to 'negative emotions' such as anger or grief; it also explains their attitude that sickness is the result of sin.

The fifth treasure is complete concentration upon the Absolute through the teachings of a guru and the scriptures. And the sixth is faith, the complete acceptance of everything the guru says as true — not an unquestioning belief, but a positive attitude towards what is taught.

'Neither accept nor reject anything,' the SES tell their members, echoing the creed of Gurdjieff's French groups. But by their very presence in the room the students are in a state of acceptance. They adopt a positive attitude by being there in the first place.

The six treasures make the third discipline. The fourth discipline is the longing for liberation from the shackles of the mind and body so that reunion with the Absolute may be realized. This longing must be fierce enough to penetrate all earthly illusions. It is shown by an utter devotion to ultimate Truth.

With these four disciplines we can then embark on the three steps which lead towards the realization of our unity with the Absolute: hearing-receiving instruction from the guru, reflecting-thinking constantly of the Absolute, and meditating on the ideal of union with the Absolute.

The SES do not slavishly follow this formula for salvation to the letter, nor do they tell students where it comes from. While they say that they are following the Way of Knowledge, a number of ex-SES followers expressed surprise that the Way was so well signposted. Terms like the Six Treasures, for instance, are never used. And while some of these disciplines are stated practices within the cult, others arise naturally out of the behavioral rules. An SES member will not, for instance, be told to renounce all earthly pleasures because they are finite. But the timetable members have to follow, plus rules about dress, diet, sexual relations, popular entertainment and so on, all have the effect of renunciation. The group dynamic too plays a major part in keeping members to a reverential attitude towards their inner consciousness.

The Vedantic tradition borrowed various disciplines from the Yoga school of Hindu philosophy, and these too have been assimilated by the SES. They include cleanliness, of both mind and body. In the SES this means that women members should clean their homes everyday, the children clean their schools, and even introductory members may find themselves expected to act as part-time caretakers. One elderly woman novice who objected to paying her fee for the privilege of cleaning the branch building was told in a letter from her tutor:

> I feel that it would not be right for us to arrange cleaning of the building by outside contractors because, quite frankly, there is very little possibility that it would be cleaned in the right way.
>
> The tradition of the School to take care of its own buildings is long established and, I believe, founded on the right principle. It is a question of learning, in practice, how to care for the Creation and how to nourish it both in its animate and inanimate aspects, through work with the fullness of attention and intelligence. In this way the flow of force of consciousness is maintained for the benefit of all creatures. The very fabric of a building requires this nourishment, and it obviously helps to create an atmosphere conducive to the study of philosophy in the group meetings.

Another Yoga practice borrowed by the Vedantic tradition is posture, holding the body erect with legs together and hands on knees. This position, claimed as an aid to relaxation and inner tranquillity, is adopted by the SES when meditating. One former member, a woman who left the cult more than ten years ago, hardly altered from this position once in an hour-long interview, during which she decried much of the cult's teachings.

The meditation technique used by the SES is, of course, transcendental meditation, which also sprang from the same

Vedantic tradition. To the cult the practice is of paramount importance.

In short, TM is said to bring into prominence the quality of nature known as Sattva, the principle of balance. This enables self-observation to be practised more easily. And through self-observation the light of consciousness reveals the Will of the Absolute. TM therefore enables the practitioner to realize his union with the Absolute. Naturally at first this realization is elusive, but that is the eventual aim. However much of the Absolute is glimpsed while meditating, it cannot be sustained in everyday life, so a half-hour's meditation at dawn and dusk is prescribed. This way the influence of the Absolute will permeate an individual all through the day.

Meditation can also be done at other spare moments, and is a useful practice for coping with moments of stress and other 'negative emotions'. One woman suing her SES husband for divorce looked on in amazement as he went into a trance in her solicitor's office when the negotiations became particularly stormy.

As we explain elsewhere, the practice of TM is regarded in some quarters as a long way from the universal cure-all which its devotees constantly claim. There are real suspicions that it may be simply an elaborate process of self-hypnosis.

But Hinduism and Gurdjieff's philosophy are not the only exponents of self-realization, as the SES sees it. Others too have been party to the hidden secret of salvation.

They believe that Plato (427–347 BC) received the knowledge, partly from his mentor Socrates and partly from foreign travel, and then passed it on through the Academy which he established in Athens.

We need not enter the debate which has raged over Plato's philosophy in recent times, with brickbats such as 'totalitarian' and 'racialist' being flung at him by perfectly respectable academics. People have been stirred to outrage by Plato's claim that rulers may at times be justified in withholding the truth from their subjects.

Much of this censure has been aimed at his best-known work, *The Republic*. Here Plato depicts democracy as one step removed from tyranny. He advocates instead a fiercely authoritarian society, divided into three classes. The lowest is to be the class of farmers, production workers and merchants who, if they want to exist in that society, must show total obedience to their superiors. The only guarantee of their life within the community is absolute service.

Their immediate superiors are the Guardians, an elite of men and women highly trained in body and mind to defend the 'Republic'. Their strength and ruthlessness are combined, however, with a sheepdog-like restraint, so they do not attack their charges, provided of course that they present no threat to the community.

Above the Guardians are a small elite of philosopher-rulers who rise through the Guardian ranks to take on the job of leading the community.

In both of the upper classes, both private property and families are abolished. Plato felt that possessions could lead to greed, and corrupt both Guardians and rulers. And he also felt that families would prove a distraction from their duties. His second criticism of families was that women should play a fully equal role with men in the community, and so should not be hampered by their offspring. Children should be brought up in state institutions, where of course their education is firmly controlled.

This vision does not represent Plato's only word on the ordering of society. In his work *The Laws* he holds out rather more hope of a freer society bound together by a comprehensive set of laws.

There are definite parallels between Plato's vision of a perfect world and SES beliefs and practices. The absolute obedience of the lower class, for instance, accords with that required of rank-and-file SES members. And the emphasis on the duties of the upper two classes to the community reflects the demands of the cult. The more one serves the SES, sacrificing career or even family, the higher one rises − at least in theory. Plato's sympathy with equal rights for women, however, can only be anathema to the cult.

In the training of young Guardians, Plato puts an accent on physical training. This can be seen reflected in SES schools, where for the boys strong emphasis is placed on boxing and circuit training and, for senior pupils, membership of the army cadet force. He also wanted to censor the popular poets of his day; he felt they would lead young Guardians astray. Is this perhaps echoed in the SES vehemence against pop music and television, not to mention virtually every poet and many major composers over the last few centuries.

Even the structure of Plato's perfect society would seem to have a strong parallel with the SES's perception of the natural order of mankind. For the SES believe that mankind is made up of seven levels, with the Absolute forming the eighth. In other words, it fully accords with the Law of Octaves:

7) MANKIND: The work of men such as Krishna and Christ in leading us towards salvation.

6) MASTER TEACHERS AND LAW-GIVERS: Their job is to help civilization grow. Examples include Abraham, Moses, Socrates and Plato.

5) NATURAL LAW: This shapes culture through education, the arts and the sciences. Exponents include Shakespeare, Mozart and Newton.

4) TRADITION AND CUSTOM: Only to be adhered to if still showing vitality (in other words, if the SES feel they are still relevant). They may include manners, dress role of sexes, and so on. They are embodied in nations, governments, universities and churches. Into this class too the SES put men who upheld tradition, ranging from Alfred the Great to Churchill, and including Blackstone, the nineteenth-century legalist.

3) MERCHANTS AND BANKERS: Their job is commerce. Their place is the city.

2) MEN OF SKILL AND INVENTION: They combine trade with the element of production, in towns.

1) VILLAGE AND LABOURING COMMUNITIES: Their job is production, in villages.

Common sense tells us that in some ways this looks like the blueprint for a traditional society. But it carries with it a dangerous assumption — that those with power are closer to the Absolute than those without. The subordination of the lower classes, according to Plato, could only be guaranteed through rigorous control from above, an imposed discipline. But he never once suggested that his Republic was the natural order for the world. The SES appear to believe that their octave is. To judge by the way those within the movement, apparently well on their way to union with the Absolute, exercise their power, the rest of us are in for a hard time.

The SES believe that those furthest removed from the Truth need the most rules to guide them towards it. So does natural law according to the SES perhaps require as much control of subordinate classes as does Plato's vision? Elsewhere in his philosophy Plato taught that once man recognized true goodness he would want to follow nothing else. The rigorous control would become unnecessary. Is the same logic at work in SES recruitment drives and expansion?

This concept of society is also outlined in the caste system of Hindu tradition. At the top are the Brahmans or wisemen. Next were the warrior caste (from whose ranks Buddha and Krishna arose), whose job was to serve the wisemen. They in turn were served by the merchants, and at the bottom of the heap were the producers, whose task was to serve everyone above them. The iniquities of such a system, still a social reality in today's India although legally outlawed, have been well documented elsewhere.

There is much else in Plato to occupy the attentions of the SES. In another part of *The Republic*, and also in another work, *Phaedrus*, the SES find confirmation of their belief in reincarnation — although Plato only puts it forward as a possibility. And in *Phaedrus* we see Plato, through the voice of Socrates, putting the spoken word above the written word. A speaker can explain as he goes along; writing is open to individual interpretation.

The SES also echo Plato in the major role they assign to tradition in a well-principled society. He sees it as invaluable, for nurturing virtue in the young and sustaining it in the old. The SES, however, use tradition to confirm their own ideas and attitudes, discarding any which do not suit them.

And Plato, like the SES after him, saw proof of the existence of God and the immortality of the soul in the fundamental laws of mathematics. The reasoning is complex. Distilled to its bare essentials the claim is that, because by adding the figure one to any other number you can make odd numbers and even numbers equal, the figure one must be the Absolute, bringing unity to the disparate.

This brings us to possibly the most fundamental aspect of Plato's philosophy in which the SES can recognize a kindred soul. For Plato argued that if knowledge and truth exist they must be permanent, otherwise they would lose their true state. And if they are permanent, then there must be a realm of permanence, although it cannot be glimpsed with the senses. Our thoughts are not permanent. They change constantly. And so they cannot be the basis for any real knowledge. But somewhere in our intellect we do possess a permanence against which thoughts and sensory perceptions can be measured. And, so the reasoning goes, this intellect relates back to a unity in which all the fragments of truth can be seen in relation to one another.

This leads us straight to the crux of SES beliefs — that there is an Absolute of perfect truth, ultimate reality. To Plato, the way we achieve knowledge is through recollecting this unity — as Gurdjieff would have put it, by self-remembering.

According to the SES, Jesus too was party to the secret knowledge of Plato and the Hindus. In a movement as anxious for respectability as the SES, the desire to appear perfectly compatible with Christianity is natural. But the cult's image of Jesus Christ differs radically from that of the Roman Catholic or mainstream Protestant churches. It seems a clearcut example of turning to the Bible to verify already existing beliefs.

They claim that Jesus was a grand master of the Essene cult, a breakaway group of Jewish ascetics who they believe kept alive the secret knowledge of the universe in Gospel times. The 'Jesus was an Essene' theory has been an enduring belief among esoteric cults through the ages. The SES interprets the sayings of Jesus in a manner which bears out this belief, claiming that more traditional interpretations of his message are distortions of the truth. When Jesus said, 'I am the way, the truth and the life', for instance, he was really referring to the essential 'I', that part of the Absolute which is present in everyone. 'The kingdom of God is within you', said Jesus, but this is another reference to the essential 'I'. Other biblical passages are also used to bear out their theory.

Thus the opening words of John's Gospel — 'In the beginning was the Word' — are seen as proof of the cosmic sound which created the universe. It is as though the SES interpreted these words 'In the beginning was Sound', whereas Christians believe they say something quite different: 'In the beginning was Meaning.' A similar meaning is read into Psalm 19, where the first three verses read:

> The heavens declare the glory of God; and the firmament sheweth his handywork. Day unto day uttereth speech, and night unto night sheweth knowledge. There is no speech nor language where their voice is not heard.

A major influence on the SES view of Christianity is an obscure text called *The Gospel of the Essenes*, which includes a smaller work entitled *The Gospel of Peace of Jesus Christ*. At best, if we accept the claim that the book is a translation of ancient Aramaic and Slavonic texts, it can be regarded as a Gnostic gospel. (Gnosticism, itself a 'secret cult', was declared a heresy in the early days of the church. Gnostics believed that the material world is an evil which man has to transcend to join the higher good. Jesus was a projection of this higher good — and not God incarnate.)

There is much doubt about the authenticity of this 'gospel', however, which even quite senior members of the SES admit to. At worst the *Gospel of the Essenes* can be regarded as a twentieth-century forgery. The *Gospel of Peace* includes the diet which the cult now follow. (It also recommends regular enemas — advice the SES have understandably ignored!)

All this is a million miles away from orthodox Christianity. Any claims the School makes to be Christian are fraudulent, and Christian ministers who belong to it can surely only do so through ignorance.

Having established an understanding of the 'sacred science' to which the SES adheres, we need to explain one further concept which reveals the true purpose behind its search for disciples.

For the SES would appear to accept traditional Hindu cosmology which predicts the end of the world. Hindus believe that the universe is finite; because it is matter, it runs from fine to coarse.

The full life-cycle of the universe is called a Kalpa, and lasts for a period of 4,320 million years. But within that cycle there are a thousand smaller cycles called Maha Yugas, or Great Aeons. Each of these smaller cycles is divided into four Yugas, or lesser aeons, which descend from a Golden Age to a Silver Age, Bronze Age, and eventually an Iron Age. At the end of the Iron Age, the universe is destroyed before being reborn.

The Golden Age was the time when mankind lived under the direct influence of the Absolute in an earthly paradise. There was a fall from grace, with man forgetting the devotion that he owed to the Absolute, and so we moved down through the aeons. We are now in the Iron Age, otherwise known as the Kali Yuga. Kali, of course, is the Hindu goddess of destruction.

Here the coarsening has set in with a vengeance; ignorance and evil have begun to assert their influence. We only entered this state in 3,102 BC and it has a span of some 432,000 years, so there is no cause for immediate alarm. But something must obviously be done about the ignorance and evil.

The only thing which can stem it is the influence of a school possessing the ancient secret of the universe. That school, say the SES, is at present themselves. In the past it was the esoteric traditions already mentioned. And, so the reasoning goes, whenever such a school begins to make its influence felt ignorance and evil are stemmed and a Renaissance takes place in the world.

That is what the SES truly believe they will bring about, with their School in the vanguard. It can be regarded as the one overriding aim of many of their activities, including the music groups, calligraphy classes, Sanskrit sessions, and art courses.

For proof they turn to the Renaissance which originated in Italy in the fifteenth century. Flying in the face of all the historic evidence which characterizes the Renaissance as the fruit of centuries of intense intellectual endeavour, the SES finds its source in one Marsilio Ficino, a scholar and philosopher who lived from 1433 to 1499. Was he not so struck with the ideas of Plato that he started a Platonic Academy in Florence in 1462? Did he not strive to show how compatible Christianity and Platonism are? And did he not translate Plato from the original Greek into Latin? (Ancient Greek is that much closer to the original cosmic sound!) The explanation is obvious. He too must have known the universal secret!

All in all, an in-depth analysis of the SES reveals a very different picture from the public image they like to present. A person who begins an SES course is not just learning about philosophy. All unawares, he or she is being prepared for initiation into an esoteric group, among whom is preserved a secret knowledge which will bring the world to enlightenment. In the service of this task, a great deal is acceptable which most of us would hold to be dangerous or wrong.

Peter Green, the Principal of the SES, wrote in a letter to *The Standard*:

> The School of Economic Science is not a cult or a religious sect. These are designedly provocative and sensational words. Founded more than forty years ago it is a school in the Socratic manner whose aim is to study and teach the natural laws governing relations between men in society.
>
> From the early consideration of these laws in the realm of economics, students began to ask deeper questions about the fundamentals of man's existence itself. This step into philosophy, which is the love of wisdom, was most natural.
>
> Over the years, around 50,000 people have attended our courses in economics and philosophy which have been so widely advertised on posters around London and in your newspaper. Many students have discovered in themselves a meaning and purpose to their lives; others have found hitherto undiscovered talents and abilities beginning to flower.
>
> Many stayed to enjoy the company and good conversation, while many more left happy and content that, for a brief period in their lives, their minds had touched on the deeper questions of human purpose . . .

In short, it was all terribly worthwhile and perfectly above board. But Mr Green conveniently missed out several facts. The studying which he refers to is not the mere analysis of the problems facing mankind and how they can best be solved. It is a study where *the* answer to man's problems is supplied.

And while many former members have left the movement 'happy and content', we shall in the next chapter hear the stories of just a few of those we interviewed who left bitter, frightened and spiritually distraught.

CHAPTER FIVE

Chronicles of Despair

In building up a profile of the SES, more than fifty former members were interviewed, as well as a number of relatives of existing members.

While a major proportion of the letters received by *The Standard* appeared to be in favour of the SES, the telephone lines were busy — continuously so, for nearly a week. The overwhelming number were from people thankful that the spotlight of attention had at last been focussed on the cult.

The wife of one deeply committed SES member broke down in tears as she said:

> This week it's my birthday. You have given me the best present that I could have hoped for.

In the lengthy interviews which subsequently took place, it was apparent that for many former members simply talking about their experiences performed a kind of exorcism. And the relatives of cult members spoke of their feelings of relief that they were not alone in their predicament. So little had been known about the cult that they had felt totally isolated in their concern.

The following case histories are short extracts from interviews which often lasted several hours. In most cases, strict anonymity had to be guaranteed before people were willing to talk.

Our informants feared the power of the SES, and were anxious to avoid further alienation from loved ones still in the movement. It was obvious, too, that some people found it difficult to come to terms with what they considered to be their earlier gullibility.

Jane Brown (not her real name) is a high-school teacher of English literature and language, and a recent mature student graduate from Cambridge University. She was introduced to the SES in the mid-1950s by a boy friend, whom she later married; she stayed for thirteen years. She blames her membership of the cult for the death of her baby daughter:

My particular tragedy occurred at a time when the SES were teaching its members that medical science was 'evil', that hospitals were centres of negative emotion (one of the SES terms for sin) and that no School of Economic Science member should go to an ordinary doctor.

I became pregnant and went to my tutor to explain that I have a tendency towards high blood pressure, and I felt that in the circumstances I should seek medical care during the pregnancy. My tutor replied, 'You give me perfect trust, and I will give you perfect care'.

I gave him the trust he required and in return I was seen by an SES doctor and midwife. This doctor, one day when I was advanced in pregnancy, actually said to me, 'Aren't you scared?' I didn't know what he meant. I'd no idea that I was dangerously ill. I learned afterwards that he had told the Master, Leon MacLaren, that unless I remained in bed at the School's large country house, resting, he would take no further responsibility for me.

Eventually I was rushed to the South London Hospital for Women as an emergency case. The consultant who saw me there asked, 'However did you get into this state?' There was no comment when I told her. Premature labour was induced, presumably to save my life. I was in labour for three days. My baby was born perfectly formed and very strong, considering the tiny placenta she'd had to sustain her, but she died after two days' fight, on her part and on the hospital's, to sustain her breathing.

I remained dangerously ill for three weeks and in hospital for another three. During this time members of the SES pushed their way into the hospital, calling at all hours, uninvited, and pestering me with lectures about my attitude to what had happened. All this at a time when I was prostrate with grief and too ill to think about anything. In the end, I told the hospital to admit nobody but my immediate family, and I wrote to my tutor resigning from the school.

From that moment onwards no friend from the SES (and that meant all my friends after thirteen years) came near me. I was left to recover from the tragedy and the illness in complete isolation. Without wishing to over-dramatize a sufficiently bad situation, I feel that my daughter was murdered and that I, in my fanaticism, took part in that murder.

At the time I joined the SES I was a Sussex county scholar reading English at Kings College, London University. My prospects were bright. But I became totally entangled in the organization, which contains much perverted goodness.

The SES made such demands on my time, such inroads on my confidence, and poured such scorn on my studies that I panicked, became ill, and didn't take my finals. I was turned into a brainwashed automaton with no feelings of family affection or responsibility, and a total contempt for every fellow human being who was not a member of the SES. I had an inner conviction that I was a member of the 'Inner Circle of Mankind' – closer to God than everybody else and in due time (after many lifetimes perhaps) destined to join the Divine Circle of Self Conscious or Realized Men, who were said to include, oddly, Mozart, Jesus Christ, Leonardo da Vinci and Buddha. . . .

Ordinarily, of course, you would never hear about this. All SES members take a vow of secrecy. They promise never to talk to anybody about 'The Teaching'. I have long since realized that the extraction of this promise is just one more of their many devices to protect their hotch-potch of doctrine from rational questioning and discussion, and I have therefore absolved myself from my promise.

A sixty-year-old mother of five, living in Brighton, attended SES lectures in nearby Hove for two years, but balked at the course when meditation was introduced.

At the beginning, and for some time afterwards, I believed I was too stupid to grasp all that was being indoctrinated — especially the constant diagrams put up on the blackboard to illustrate their theories. Their teachings, to my mind, seemed to be aimed at reducing one's human feelings as far as possible and at freeing one's mind from one's emotions. This was illustrated by our tutor's reference to his mother's grief and suffering at the death of his stepfather. It seemed, according to their beliefs, that she wasn't allowed that sorrow.

All in all, the jargon and the symbols put up on the blackboard were confusing, bewildering and above all so remote from the kind of philosophy that I had read and understood hitherto. And that is why I feel I have been conned by them.

Right from the start we were directed into doing exercises, which on the face of it seemed very beneficial; a way of relaxing can't be bad. But tremendous emphasis was put on these exercises, stressing their importance. We were expected to do them at certain times of the day, bearing in mind the Group in the process. And by the end of the last term of my second year, we were informed that meditation would hereon take the place of the exercises, and that someone was coming from London to tell us all about it. This was a big event.

When the man duly arrived I asked him the perfectly straightforward question, 'What are the benefits of meditation?' Whereupon he slowly lowered his head onto his chest and didn't emerge for some long minutes, much to the surprise and amusement, I felt, of the whole class.

When he did finally raise his head, it was to answer my question by way of the blackboard with diagrams of circles within circles, the innermost one holding the word SELF. All gobbledy-gook to me, especially the jargon that went with it. All that he could come up with as an answer was to say that it was power and energy that we would ultimately gain from it. But looking at him I was totally uninspired in that direction as a more sleepy, inert individual I couldn't imagine.

I personally feel from my time in the SES that it's all very clever and extremely subtle brainwashing, on the lines of most cults, and I firmly believe dangerous and little to do with Philosophy, but everything to do with an Indian cult.

Iain Mitchell is a chronic schizophrenic and has hardly spoken a word for years. After many attempts at trying to control his condition, his parents have been forced to commit him to mental hospital under Section 26 of the Mental Health Act.

The cause of his illness is not known for certain but Iain's parents are convinced that his membership of the SES was a strong contributory factor. At thirty years of age his life is in tatters, a tragic contrast to the promise he showed before he joined the SES in 1974.

Iain Mitchell was a musician of great potential. After living in an Islington squat with his girlfriend, he won a place to study music at Southampton University. His friends and relatives were confident that he would have a bright career.

It was his girlfriend who introduced him to the SES and together they started the introductory course. Iain's sister watched what happened:

Before joining the SES they were lively, cheerful, unconventional people with a healthy disrespect for authority. The girl was rather left-wing. But the SES soon led to an about-turn in their behaviour.

As they went on courses they seemed to be concentrating on their personal spiritual development and leaving behind their former expressions of concern about the rest of the world and its miseries. They began to believe in the soul and eschewed those who didn't as people who lived 'on their stomachs'.

They became vegetarians and started to practise meditation after meals and at other times. If you were with them you got no warning — quite suddenly they were not with you but staring into space, wrapped up in themselves. The habit of staring fixedly and not speaking to anyone seemed to stick with Iain and got worse as time went on, until it was not meditation but non-communication.

Iain's sister was so concerned about his condition that she argued with him and tried to persuade him to leave the SES. She was particularly worried about his studies.

They were unable to say who ran the SES. They said they'd been told not to discuss the SES with outsiders because they themselves were in too great a state of ignorance to communicate the ideas correctly. They became more puritanical and irritatingly moralistic. Intolerance of other people seemed to be one of the worst effects, and it led them to reject those closest to them.

Iain's university career stood no chance. He believed the SES to be far more important and came from Southampton to London twice a week to go to SES lectures. He was also going for weekends in Oxfordshire for which he had to pay. Often he didn't go back to university for two or three weeks and stayed with me.

He'd become highly critical of his music course, saying it didn't have the spiritual importance to him of the SES. The university and our parents did everything possible to stop him quitting university but he could not be persuaded.

Iain's sister went on to describe how the final breakdown came.

Iain's girlfriend went to live in a flat which I think was owned by the SES. Iain wasn't allowed to spend the night there. His girlfriend had now become more critical of him. She'd been taught that men and women should play their traditional roles. Men should be strong leaders of women, breadwinners, wise advisers and so forth. Nothing could have been further from what she'd thought previously.

Now that Iain had left university he was unemployed. With his girlfriend living in the flat apart from him, his deterioration became more rapid. He got a job as a porter and about this time stopped going to SES lectures. Soon afterwards came the breakdown, which led to his hospitalization under a confinement order.

A forty-two-year-old medical secretary told us that when she left the cult, she found great difficulty in facing the world without the support of her group. An SES member from 1967 to 1978, she forced herself to leave when she felt she had learnt all that she could. To her, the SES is a laudable, much misunderstood organization.

It has structured guidance at all levels of physical work (a proper way to work), intellectual development, and spiritual growth. I searched for this in the churches and never found it. In fact, I found little comprehension that such a thing existed or was needed. 'Keep the commandments and do your best' was the general advice from the church.

In the churches a lot of momentum comes from emotional surcharges − love for Jesus, for prayer groups, etc. But such a thing is only one small drop of all the factors at work in real development. The churches don't seem to appreciate this. In the church I rarely saw fundamental changes in people. In the school it was a continual experience to see new people, more real people, emerging out of what they had been. It was a kind of maturity, depth, sensitivity, and sensibleness. All the trivia of the person dropped away.

However, any organization is made up of human beings with human querks and failings. This is behind many of the criticisms of the School. Individuals do step above themselves or impose their own interpretation of what is afoot. But over the long term, it gets ironed out and people are subtly put back into place perhaps by being given a duty which places them at the receiving end of what they've been doing. People are not experienced at running such an organization and have to gain this − just as parents have to gain experience at parenthood, sometimes at the expense of the children feeling their mistakes − and likewise it takes time and experience to work in a School, and some do get hurt whilst this process is going on. But lessons are learnt by it.

There has been publicity in the past over brainwashing tactics by the Moonies/Unification Church and other such organizations. The School is probably looked at to see if such a thing exists there. The fact is that there is a very fine line between brainwashing and re-conditioning. Re-conditioning is certainly necessary (as in all religious institutions, military services, learning institutions, etc). But no right-minded organization, despite the fine line, would assent to brainwashing, and I never saw it at School.

However, this difficulty is an inherent risk for any organization, School or religious institution or other. The truth can often disquiet the mind – what if I don't, what if I refuse, what will the ultimate consequences be, etc. But this wasn't used as a pressure to burden people with. It was used to open the mind to true options. I never saw threats or anything like that used.

What marks the School as different from the Moonies, Bhagwan Shree Rajneesh etc? It is difficult to say definitively, but a difference there is. It is tasted in the living through it but is hard to pinpoint. The School is not sloppy, nor sentimental. It has no part in engendering crushes or hero worship, though its leaders are held in respect. The quality of its fundamental values is very reminiscent of the highest Christian tradition, but also of the other great religious traditions, for they all meet at this level. It is ordered and clear-minded through the asceticism practised in everyday living and the ordering of the mind on profound principles. All these things are the type of thing necessary to produce higher levels of existence in people. This is true of all traditions. No saint in any tradition ever made such lofty heights by 'doing your own thing', 'letting it all hang out' and sentimental relationships.

Although order and discipline are very important, so also, perhaps more so, was the virtue of discrimination. People were constantly led to points of discriminating for themselves. This gave a combination of individual strength but within an ordered group. 'Follow my leader' behaviour was seen from time to time, but I saw it break down many times when it became clear to everyone what was going on. We laughed at the 'Emperor's new clothes' syndrome, and sense prevailed. But it required the experience of it to learn it.

It might be said that the School doesn't have the right to impose these ideas and regimes of living on the children. But it is also questionable whether we have the right to withhold them. They have the right to the greatest we can pass on, and this is not conquering space and interstellar warfare as the world at large teaches, nor is it the conditioning of crushing your rivals and climbing to the top, as the world and some educational systems teach. The highest we have is different in *kind* and the School is an attempt to pass on the 'other', that which is of truth-value in relation to the Absolute.

They become different children, but it could not be otherwise. All children are subject to conditioning (be it from living in Northern Ireland, living among uncouth and violent people, or be it from the ego-dominant, sex-dominant, violence-eulogizing media). These children receive a wholly different conditioning. Their minds, and their living practices, are not filled with all the junk of society. They are filled with wholesome ways of living and true precepts.

That isn't to say that things can't go wrong. Experience is being learned as it goes along and mistakes will happen, wrong emphases be given. But trying to form a perfect institute of learning which embraces the whole person to the heights – who can do it? I never saw such children in a Church Prep School that I was once in.

Regarding the School and Christianity: from my own experience, what is learned in School opens within a person a real appreciation of religion, such as is extremely hard to come by today in the religions themselves. I have seen people brought to the church through going to School and gaining understanding of what the church was really about. I have seen people leaving churches because they couldn't find that kind of reality of religion that could be found at School.

However, this fine line is made all the more difficult because:

– At a certain stage the individual has to suspend his or her own judgement and go by another's in order to re-learn. Hence the religious rule of obedience, and 'unless ye become as little children . . .' But it is in the overall context of a free assent to be there.
– The ability to acquire free discrimination at a higher level is founded upon a wholly different criterion and way of living, and therefore cannot be rightly assessed with an ordinary

119

worldly pattern of enquiry and thinking and experience. The new order of thinking has to be lived and experienced to be appreciated at all. It cannot be passed on in words — they may describe it but are without substance and meaning until experienced.

Hence, to an outsider or to certain levels within, certain stages could be misunderstood as brainwashing, but they are only a part of a process of ultimate liberation, unlike true brainwashing which results in ultimate subjection.

People are free to leave the School at any time. They can just walk out and never go back. A polite enquiry may be made and an offer to talk, but no other pressure is put on anyone to return against his or her will.

However, it can still be very difficult to leave School, and I found it so. But I can see now, in retrospect, that this difficulty was within myself and no blame attached to the School:

— If one feels insecure about standing on one's own feet without the support of a School, then there is nothing for it but to go through that insecurity and find that independence. (Only to find that it was always there anyway only not known to be.)

— By the very nature of what is being studied, people who do enter this work tend to give their whole being and faith to it. The seriousness of it reaches their depths, therefore they cannot just walk away as though they'd been studying Maths or Literature. They've glimpsed the black and white of the human condition (as did all the great saints — dramatically) and cannot regard the everyday sins of the world, or turning away from the path they have been on, as of no consequence. They know its importance. But this is the difficulty of individuals and their own inner level, not of any School or religious institution. The individual could attach this kind of difficulty to anything that they saw as a support to them. Nevertheless, anyone who has tasted true blessedness will feel of themselves a great difficulty in making the break. It is not a difficulty imposed on them, but one of their own perception, and going through all that is necessary to live in the world

120

unsupported by a School etc. may be just another part of
the same journey or growth, painful though it may be at the
time.
– There may be certain particular times when pressure is
brought to bear on a person not to leave. These are specific
times (on an individual going voluntarily through this process)
when a person meets something which he or she does not want
to face and wishes to run away from. I've seen and known
this. Those who really want to go are ultimately left
to walk out without any pressure. But those who really wish
to face the crisis despite their desire to run away are urged
to stay and are very grateful afterwards that some strength
was there which forced them not to evade but face their
obstacle. Whole areas within them then become liberated
through doing so, and this is made plain in their actual
experience.

A twenty-seven-year-old language teacher from North
London was in the middle of his second term with the SES
when he read newspaper articles about their activities. He
said:

During the first term everybody was quite lively and asking loads
of questions. But now people just sit there and accept what the
tutor says as though it was ordained by God. It's frightening.

We're constantly given diagrams to memorize and instructions
on how to do our exercises properly. It's all part of a process
where you try to strengthen your mind, not to make you an
individual but to try and close your mind off from the rest of
the world so that no matter what happens you have this benign
smile and can cope with everything.

I think unconsciously everybody is being brainwashed, but
the people there don't think anything is happening to them. It's
a very gradual process.

I felt suspicious right from the start and asked the tutor
whether they were some kind of religious sect, but you don't
really get proper answers. After a while people ask less and less.

All the way through I've probably been the most questioning person in my class and there was a tendency to try and shut me up. Last night a woman − I think she was a plant − turned to me and said, 'You do say a lot don't you?' I agreed and said I would continue to do so, adding that if she didn't like it that was her problem.

But in the last few weeks I've noticed that even I have become a lot less questioning. You just roll along with it. Looking back, the whole process is chipping away at you week by week.

A thirty-three-year-old secretary became so alarmed by the SES course which she attended in Croydon, South London, that she contacted several newspapers in the hope of launching an investigation. Her attempt failed.

I went along in the late 1970s thinking it would be a general study of philosophy. Aristotle one week and someone else the next. Various red lights came on pretty quickly.

I remember in particular one lady in her early forties who at first was very bubbly, vivacious and full of questions. The lecturer started to treat her with a very subtle ridicule which of course people don't like if they're on their own in a group of strangers.

Gradually her whole questioning persona became introverted. Instead of the course being a development for her, it put her back into herself. It was dreadful to see.

The SES say that you have a 'watchman' in your mind that they make you become aware of, so instead of lucid and flowing thought, you have inhibited thought processes.

It's a little bit like the story of the millipede that's going along quite happily until someone points out its legs and it begins to trip up because it starts thinking about them.

In the end your mind reaches standstill and from there all the SES notions get in because your critical faculties are largely knocked down. It's a definite brainwashing technique.

I was worried by what was happening and felt paranoid because I was aware these people were gaining power over individuals and no one seemed to know who they were. I contacted a few newspapers in the hope that somebody would

122

take it up, but the average person doesn't believe that they personally could be influenced by such teachings. They always think they're very strong and people who do get influenced have something missing.

There was a hypnotic quality to the whole evening. I can't help thinking what on earth we need cruise missiles for if the whole population are zombies anyway.

I think the SES preys on lonely people in the city. If there's nobody you can turn to, nobody who is understanding enough, then you'll get sucked into it. With the general lack of philosophy in our society, this sort of quest is going to attract people.

Ann Smith (not her real name) today looks back on her ten-year membership of the SES with incredulity — and a good deal of dread and bitter self-reproach. She claims the cult wrecked her marriage, gave her children a lasting taste of emotional chaos, and came close to destroying her life altogether.

Ann, a fiery, highly articulate woman, is proud of the fight she put up to provide her children with a normal upbringing, and keep a roof over their heads. Home is a private house in a middle-class London suburb where the pictures, books and records show a discerning but wide-ranging taste. Her husband is nowhere to be seen. He walked out soon after she turned her back on the cult, and remains a committed member. His subsequent diffidence towards the family means that Ann now takes her independence entirely for granted. She recently realized a lifelong ambition and enrolled as a mature student at a London college to obtain a degree in Social Sciences.

Ann was one of the first SES members to kick against the fierce strictures imposed in the late 1960s. When she saw the effect that the cult was beginning to have on her family — emphasized by her husband's desire to bring up the children in an SES fashion, she left. Together with a small group of ex-SES members she then helped run an escape route for other members she had known, who were disenchanted but lacked the courage to make the break.

Don't forget, our tutors were telling us that if we left, we would be cast into the confusion of tongues, the circle of Outer Darkness. The world was a jungle but SES members were living under the Divine Will. Those outside were just so much fodder to be used by the SES. Their lives were governed by the Law of Accident.

A small group of us who'd got out and could see the SES for what it was agreed to man the telephone and talk to those still in the movement. I personally helped about three or four get out. It was a question of assuring them that in fact life was good, that dreadful things wouldn't happen to them, and that they had their own strength.

We held small reunions in the early years after we left, but in the end it became too painful to keep reviving old memories. We were trying very hard to put it all behind us, and so gradually we lost contact with one another.

Then over the years it became difficult to convince anyone who hadn't been to the School just what it was like. It was so bizarre that if you talked to anyone they thought you were exaggerating. Your friends, local people, and even your relatives tended not to believe you. Some of my memories could simply be interpreted as the ravings of a middle-aged woman going through the menopause.

Ann joined the movement in the late 1950s. She was in her early twenties then, living alone in London and, a former scholarship pupil, was thoroughly disenchanted with the series of mundane office jobs which she took to support herself. Her parents were radical socialists and from them she inherited an interest in politics, and in the wider realm of philosophy and religion. The SES advertisement which she saw on an underground station wall could have been tailor-made.

In those days, she remembers, the SES were a far more democratic organization. She and the other young men and women with whom she met thoroughly enjoyed the chance to talk about the fundamental questions they had been asking themselves — free from the uncertainty of whether anyone else was really interested. In such a spirit the request that they should begin to devote two evenings a week to the cult was met without rancour. Many of them had already formed a social life outside the SES based on other members of their group anyway. And when requests were made that they should start decorating the SES headquarters — then in Suffolk Street, close to Trafalgar Square — that too was met without reservation.

Ann continued:

None of us seemed to have a really strong family or religious tradition, so we were looking for an inner strength. We went along to the SES and found others of our own generation who were willing to talk about anything. It was a time of austerity and elsewhere young people seemed to be of no account; the consumer market hadn't been invented for them yet.

As we progressed through the courses the idea was very gradually given to us that we were somehow special. We were the only ones on the track of truth. It was very flattering to our egos.

At first we were simply asked to notify the school of our change of address and that seemed reasonable enough. Then very subtly pressure was brought to bear that we should notify the school when we changed jobs and if we were considering getting married. We'd been told that our tutors were our 'neighbours' in the scriptural sense of "Love thy neighbour". Being young, we inevitably underwent crises in our personal lives and, because we'd become so close to our tutors, we turned to them.

Most of us were floaters in London anyway, and in exchange for the helpfulness of our tutors we were drawn more and more into the school. We were advised on our tastes — Mozart, Leonardo da Vinci, and Shakespeare. Anything written since Shakespeare's time was not considered worth reading. Eventually we were told where to live, we had to ask permission to change our jobs, and we had to ask permission to get married. The encouragement to devote more and more time to the school became continuous, and it wasn't just the tutors pressurizing people to toe the line — there was strong group pressure too.

A crisis at home threw Ann deeper into the movement than most. She moved into an SES house and the cult found her a job as a secretary. Soon afterwards, she married a man whom she had met through the cult. Terrified that she would be denied permission to wed, she went down on one knee to MacLaren to plead her case and he, presumably suitably flattered, gently rested his hand on her head and gave her his blessing. It was the beginning of the end of her time with the cult.

Ann quickly became pregnant and soon discovered that her condition brought scant consideration from her tutors. On residential weekends at Stanhill Court she was still expected to rise at 5 a.m. and carry out her manual duties.

On one occasion, when I was seven and a half months pregnant — so vast I could hardly walk — I was asked to climb a stepladder to pick faded blossoms off a flowering bush. It was a hot day and the bush was in a greenhouse. I protested and said, 'Look, I'm shaking, can't I sit down,' but a senior tutor said I had to carry on.

When I got back to London I felt so awful that I went straight to hospital where it was discovered that I had toxemia. Arrangements were made to admit me to hospital the following week and in the meantime I was sent home to rest. But two people from my group then arrived to take me to a meeting. I said I couldn't go and explained why, but all they replied was, 'Don't worry, God will look after you'. I replied, 'Yes, and I'll look after the baby', and I refused to move.

Just four weeks after giving birth I was ordered down to Stanhill again — I was told it was for a rest. I gave the baby to another SES family to look after and off I went. That's how committed I was.

Ann's alienation from the cult grew steadily as she tried to build a home for her family. She resented the rules which forbade a television or radio, but her greatest misery of all was the fact that for four nights a week she was left alone while her husband was out on his SES duties. In the months following her pregnancy, she left the cult. Her husband told her that it was the end of their marriage, and refused to speak to her. Only the intervention of a senior tutor made him break his silence.

Refusing to give up hope, Ann tried one last desperate ploy. She became pregnant again in the hope that it would bring her husband closer to her. The subsequent birth did not have the desired effect, and in the years that followed her husband went on to reveal the full extent of his SES conditioning.

I could see the brainwashing start when he started teaching my daughter Sanskrit when she was five. It's a beautiful language, but the SES don't just teach the language, they teach all the ideas behind it. He started her on calligraphy as well and we had a tremendous row. The marriage came to an end, and I started a divorce.

He'd consistently refused to behave as a husband. He told me that women had only three titles, daughter, sister and mother, and that I should go down on one knee and call him lord and master. I just laughed and laughed. There was no way I wanted my children brought up in such an atmosphere.

Swiss born Gina Bon, a former actress, was coaxed into joining the SES in the early 1960s by the boyfriend whom she later married. Her curiosity kept her in the cult for more than ten years, during which time she experienced at first hand the authoritative regime which keeps SES members in order. Outraged eventually by the cult's attitude towards Christianity, she left. For fifteen years she worked as a personal assistant to an internationally renowned psychoanalyst, which gave her enough insight into psychology to help put some of her own experiences into perspective. Now fifty-seven years old, working as the administrative secretary of a children's clinic in North London, she is fiercely critical of the claims of the SES.

I was never fully committed to the SES. I'm too much of a natural rebel to accept things that easily, but I was very curious about where it was all going to end. I was looking for something inside myself and that too kept me there. When you first join it is such an incredibly broad-based and catholic offer that you feel you can only enlarge your horizon. You would never suspect it is the dogmatic and rigid system that it turns out to be.

On one occasion, I was forcibly prevented from leaving Stanhill Court. No one had told me that women were supposed to wear skirts − long dresses hadn't then come in − while working down there. So when I assembled with my work party wearing jeans a couple of tutors looked most suprised, and ten minutes later I was summoned to see a senior tutor.

Words were exchanged and I decided that I'd had enough. I went to my dormitory and packed my little bag, but it was such a rambling building that I couldn't find my way to the front door. As I dashed around lost I came face to face with a committee that had been sent to find me − one of MacLaren's women aides and two men.

They asked if I was aware of the gravity of what I was doing. They added that if I didn't understand by then what all the rules were about, I would go on repeating my mistakes in ignorance for ever. I'd had a very tough and eventful life and I said: 'Are you threatening me with hell fire? Because if you are, believe me I've been to hell and come back. Nothing you can say will frighten me.'

I was so upset and shaken that I simply took off down the corridor. I opened the door at the end and it was the front hall, where MacLaren was standing with two more men. I fixed my eyes on the front door and ran past them, but the two men grabbed me, one on either arm.

My case was taken out of my hands and I was frogmarched out of the front door and down into the gardens. I couldn't believe what was happening to me. They were acting like film Nazis! Then MacLaren shouted and they stopped and he came up and said, 'Let's be sensible about this.' We walked on together and had quite a conversation and I decided to stay. That was the kind of hold they had.

The Stanhill regime was very fierce. When they brought in the rule saying you had to get up when you wake up, it was absolutely horrific. It's a very old story breaking people down by keeping them awake. I used to jokingly say that it was an indoctrination-brainwashing centre. I'd survived a lot of things which others there hadn't. I looked around me at people who were like puddings disintegrating. You put a finger into the dough and the mark stayed.

I witnessed one full-scale psychotic breakdown and heard about others.

The conditions were such that they could bring on breakdowns with people already at risk. It wasn't just the regime and the hardwork, but the intensive self-examination which took place. I know it was supposed to produce peace, harmony and unity, but for some people it did the opposite. The pressure was in the air. It was like Big Brother. You were somehow under constant surveillance, if not by someone else then by yourself. There was no place to hide.

When they brought in the Gospel of Peace I thought it was an absolute fraud. I happen to be extremely well-read in the Bible and I went to the tutor after the session and said if he thought I was going to buy that blasphemous document he could think again. I said I wouldn't touch it with a barge pole. He said I didn't understand.

One former long-standing SES member who left the cult in the mid-1970s but whose husband is still a member, had this to say about the effect on her husband:

Although I love my husband dearly and we're still together, it is pretty hard living with someone who is swayed in this way.

The brainwashing is terribly insidious. It is very, very gradual. It reduces them to cabbages, it really does. In the SES some some years ago there was room for another life to be led. In those days you could answer back. I don't think now that is true.

The awful thing is that they don't know — they don't want to know — what happens to people when they leave the SES. I know if my husband left he would be a lost man. He would only leave if he saw that there was something wrong with the organization — but when its faults are pointed out he doesn't want to know.

They spend all their time with the School and don't really mix much in the world. When they do look at the world, they simply concentrate on its ills.

They very nearly sent me mad, but in a way, since I've left, I've found myself and I feel that I've matured . . . I feel like something that was kept in deep freeze.

A mother of three, in her fifties, also complained of the change in her partner:

I began fighting these people twelve years ago when my husband got involved. In 1972 I wrote to my MP who contacted Mrs Thatcher, who was then Secretary of State for Education and Science.

She wrote back to my MP saying: 'This is a private establishment conducting courses for persons over compulsory school age. It is therefore not open to inspection by HM Inspectors and is in no way subject to this department's control. There is, I am afraid, nothing my department can do to help.'

When my husband first went he told me he was going to the London School of Economics to do philosophy lectures and I thought, 'Fine, it will do him some good'.

It wasn't until two years later that I discovered it wasn't what I thought it was. He began doing odd things like bringing home dirty tea towels to wash and preparing food at home for the group, spending more and more of his time on SES activities.

In the end it drove me to such lengths of despair that I felt like committing suicide. Then the School told my husband that I was going mad, and was wicked and evil. They did their best to break us up and for a while they succeeded. He left me, but then he came back promising that he wouldn't go back to the School. That was virtually the only source of contention between us.

But now he's resumed going. It's like a drug — he can't keep away; and I'm going through sheer hell again. He's not the same man when he's there. It's dreadful to see him. I went to see a very eminent psychiatrist in Harley Street some years ago who told me, 'Your husband will never be the man you married. He's been brainwashed'.

A seventy-four-year-old retired engineering representative living in Leeds, a widower, was persuaded by younger friends to visit the SES in Leeds during the mid 1970s. He stayed with the group for a year and a half.

My experience wasn't a good one and I came to the conclusion that it certainly wasn't for me. The initial stages aren't of a character that would antagonize you. It's a gradual progression. After some time I found I wasn't able to accept it at all.

There was an imposition of ideas which you had to totally accept — and almost totally surrender your own ability to think or do anything else to the tutors. If people do that the only thing that will matter is what they've been taught — nothing else.

It became obvious that the School and its activities were the first thing to be considered. Everything else was subservient, whether it was a marital relationship or career commitment. The School was to be the be-all and end-all of your life. It seemed to me that people with a lesser strength of character were in danger of being much more easily influenced, and becoming totally absorbed by the SES.

Its influence seemed very far from being good. I would go as far as to say that it was evil. An insidious, unwholesome effect seemed to percolate throughout the whole philosophy.

I took exception on one occasion when we were asked to make a financial contribution to the School, and each person had to declare that their donation represented a certain percentage of their gross annual income. I said I regarded the request as an imposition, and had no intention of divulging such information to anybody.

But the first real alarm-bells rang when we were invited to a big house they owned in Sheffield. All sorts of quite trivial, unimportant domestic tasks were allotted to us there. I felt like a schoolboy. It had no place in any philosophic teaching at all, and I began to rebel against the idiocy of it all. There was a lot of emphasis on something they called the point of work — where your hammer hit the nail or whatever — which was a nonsense.

Finally I wrote to my tutor and resigned. I got a letter back saying that Mr Marshall, the head of the North-East section, wanted to see me. I then received what amounted to an instruction to meet him in Sheffield.

I went at the appointed time and he kept me waiting. Then he walked in, switched on a smile and said, 'You seem to have a problem'. I said, 'Mr Marshall, I have no problem. You asked to see me. What's your problem?' After five minutes I told him we were both wasting our time, and left.

A London businessman joined the SES in the late 1970s in a bid to save his marriage. His wife was a committed member. The attempt failed and they are now on the verge of splitting up.

We married about fifteen years ago and at first everything was fine. But a couple of years later my wife was befriended by a woman living nearby who introduced her to the SES.

She went along to one of the courses and was soon hooked. After a while I became less than happy about what was going on. I could see this thing coming between us. She was totally committed to the SES, as though she'd been brainwashed. She was impervious as to what effect it was having on her home life. But the children suffered in particular. She would frequently leave them with me at the weekend, and off she'd go on some course. I considered her first duty was to her home.

After expressing my misgivings I was asked to go along and see her tutor who was very fair. She said, 'Don't knock it until

132

you've tried it,' so I went along to see what it was all about.

The only way to find out was to actually attend one of the courses. When you first join it's a fun thing. There's no obligation put on you at all. You can do basically as you please, but after a while you were instructed to carry out certain duties.

Then they try to discourage you from associating with people outside the group and you find that the only people you know are other group members. One chap had a duty during the week, and another duty was given to him at the weekend. He told his tutor that it would break up his marriage. The reply was that he had to decide whether he wanted to come to full realization or go through the world as a zombie. He stayed with the SES.

The change in the group that I started with after the residential courses began was frightening. I was a bit of a rebel and insisted that during the day I went back to London as I had my job to attend to. There was a lot of aggression when I kept reappearing. I was alien to them.

I stayed with them five years in all. By the end of that time all my old friends had disappeared and when I left it was very traumatic. But I couldn't put up with what was going on.

It worried me that the people there were in a very strong position where they could dictate or control a person's life, and they simply weren't qualified to do so. They were just dabbling. At tutorials you would have various questions fired at you about your personal life. In my case there were obvious family problems, but the tutors didn't help in any way at all.

Mayfair art dealer Robin Garton joined the SES in 1964 and left nine years later.

I now have to admit that I was brainwashed. It was a period of my life when I was looking for the answers to a lot of questions and eventually I was drawn into the movement further and further.

The week-long course at Stanhill Court was part of the conditioning process. You don't have a second to yourself.

You're woken at 4 a.m. every morning, work all day and have very little to eat. You stop dreaming, and are conditioned to get out of bed as soon as you awake.

It has a devastating effect. You lose your critical faculties and become extremely easily influenced. But surprisingly, although you're physically very tired and sleeping only three or four hours a night, you begin to get used to it.

At the time, Mr Garton felt the SES were answering many of his questions.

I'd always been religious and I was impressed at the way that the SES seemed to be involved in serious study of the great teachings. First, you go along one night a week, then two and then three until you're spending your whole time involved with the SES.

For impressionable people it's bound to be very effective and the individual becomes fodder to the power ambitions of the organization. It began to rule my whole life and it was a struggle deciding to leave. When I eventually made that break, I slept fifteen hours a day for a year. They tried to get me to return but I refused. It was a ghastly experience.

I've nothing against people believing what they like, but people should be aware when joining just what it can do to them.

David and Mary Jones (not their real names) gave more than fifteen years of their lives to the SES. It was a labour of love at first, but by the time they left in 1974 their allegiance had turned into an irksome burden that weighed down every aspect of their lives.

David, a self-employed electrician with a sound knowledge of mechanics, was used as a Mr Fixit at all the SES buildings, willing to help out any time of night or day when things went wrong. He moulded his working life around his SES commitments and still found time to attend early morning Sanskrit sounding sessions and Vedic mathematics classes at Chepstow Villas. His wife was an assistant group tutor and a member of the music group which required many hours of practice every week.

Ten years after leaving the cult the material cost of the time and effort they gave can be measured by the small council house in which they live in South London. Spiritually, however, they are rejuvenated. The years of intense self-improvement according to SES discipline are behind them, and they have found a new faith — in the Greek Orthodox Church. There they claim to have seen people display the qualities to which the SES aspired, but which they seldom reached.

Their warmth and sense of humour help keep the past in check, but one senses there are moments of self-recrimination for the guilelessness with which they accepted the teachings of the cult for so long. David was the first to turn against the cult, but unwilling to jeopardize the marriage, he hung on for another three years until his wife, whom he met through the cult, was also ready to leave.

The memories they harbour are not all bad. Both claim that, while there was at times a good deal of pain and frustration during their time in the School, especially towards the end, there were lasting benefits as well. They claim that the practice of observing the mind at work and controlling the attention, and the many practical skills they learned, have been immensely useful in many ways.

Being stretched to your limits both mentally and physically alters your rather small picture of yourself, they claim, making you more aware of your real possibilities. And they add that the love of stillness and beauty, which was an everyday aspect of School discipline, remains even when the outer discipline is dropped.

But above all they look back with regret at all 'the close and loving friends' they have lost since leaving the SES. Those friends are people they still feel affection for, mixed with sadness for those who 'have changed almost out of recognition from the early days — lost their joy in life, their spontaneity and warmth'. David and Mary say they feel no bitterness about the School and what they gave to it, but 'consider every member should be free to move on when ready'.

Said David:

I saw the poster on an underground station wall and it was a God-send to me. I was a stranger in a foreign country, just out of the RAF, and I was seeking something that would give me friendship and fulfilment. At first it was very welcoming. MacLaren was approachable and he would joke and laugh with you, and even exchange ideas.

But as the School grew they needed more tutors and consequently had to have a tighter hold on them to make sure they did exactly what they were told. These tutors ended up obeying the rules so totally they told people to do things which went against common sense.

I gave fifteen years of my life to the SES and I gave in some respects a hell of a lot more than other people. Not as much financially perhaps, although we paid out and paid out, but in expertise and commitment.

I was convinced in myself that I was well on the way to achieving some kind of self-realization, above material wealth or anything like that. I didn't try to buy a house, I didn't try to get a great job. I was prepared to do any old thing as long as it kept me going from one day to the next. I was probably the only person in my group who lived it to the full.

We used to say that we'd found the fourth way, that we were monks and nuns in the world. And we were quite prepared to be martyrs. We knew that the truth would be persecuted – we only had to look in the Bible for the evidence. Any outside criticism simply reinforced that belief. We not only closed ranks, it confirmed the truth of what we believed.

But when I reached the O level I seemed to go no further. Many of my peers were moving on and I was staying where I was. If a friend moved into a senior group, that was the end of the friendship. They had to be careful speaking to you in case they told you something they shouldn't and you would be careful speaking to them as they were senior.

In the end it became apparent that I could go no further because I simply didn't have the background. I was a foreigner

136

and a blue-collar worker. I realized that all the ones going up were the people with money, public-school educations and influential positions. I wondered why one needed such a background and then I realized that virtue bred success. If you weren't successful on the outside, you weren't truly committed on the inside.

Then it dawned on me that the tutors and superiors didn't live what they were teaching. That came to a head at Waterperry during the fuel crisis of the early 1970s. I was directed to lead a team digging a hole for a new tank. I asked what the tank was for and one of MacLaren's aides told me that it was to store additional oil for the central heating. I said it wasn't on. We belonged in a society and if the society went out of oil we should all go out of oil. I added that they would never be able to buy it, and was simply told, 'That's what you think'. I smelt corruption and that was it.

Mrs Jones' break with the movement occurred in a more traumatic way. The SES had banned its members from using birth control and she discovered that she was pregnant. With three children already she secretly decided to opt for an abortion, which was also taboo, but word got out.

The next thing I knew was that we were summoned to see Sheila Rosenberg, who forbade the abortion, saying that we had to obey natural laws. So I went ahead and had the baby, and it was stillborn. What I went through in those few months was enough to shake my whole faith in the SES.

A lot of dissatisfaction had already been building up. The feeling that things weren't going right. One wasn't getting the joy and companionship and the feeling that you wanted to give a hundred per cent that had previously been there. I had a tutor years younger than me. He was so ignorant and yet so pious and supercilious.

I look back now at how committed I was with amazement. We went away to Stanhill Court one weekend, leaving my baby son with a fractured skull. I dropped him in my rush to get ready. It was total panic. My first duty was to be with the group regardless of anything else. I left him with my mother for the weekend and when I returned his head was dreadfully swollen.

Another thing making us uneasy when we left was the way that children were swept along in the movement. They'd take on board all the beliefs of the School and do exactly what their parents wanted them to do. They weren't allowed to have any other way of life. They were very sheltered and simply didn't meet any other children. Heaven knows what it was like when they reached university or wherever. They just wouldn't have known what real life is like.

The organization seems to have a blank about how to get on in the world and what society is really like. They seem to be stuck in a set of middle-class attitudes. They can't open out. They're not big enough to absorb things and that must be wrong.

The children's schools were just getting off the ground when we left and it was highly recommended that SES members sent their youngsters. There was a lot of mental pressure to do so.

Mrs Jones added that even ten years later she still had nightmares about the regime at Stanhill Court.

One woman wrote an impassioned letter to the Bishop of Woolwich condemning the SES. She said the regime at Stanhill Court gave her husband the appearance of a zombie. He'd return from residential courses completely unable to relate to his family. As his wife was struggling to bring up young children, this not unnaturally caused major marital disharmony.

The woman explained that when they'd first married her husband had already embarked on the SES introductory course, and was attending once a week. At first all was well, but as he became drawn further and further into the movement, he began to change.

He took up meditation, went onto the diet, and studied Sanskrit and the scriptures far into the night, getting up at dawn to resume the work. His sense of humour disappeared, and the couple began to drift apart, the husband firmly convinced that the SES were the harbingers of a new Renaissance.

Eventually the woman was asked to visit the SES to meet a senior tutor.

> I was then subjected to a cold, calculating lecture. He said it didn't matter what I thought of the School. My husband was needed, he was going to stay, and I'd better get used to it. I had to knuckle down and be a loyal wife or we'd no future together.
>
> I was terrified and confused and could see my whole life disintegrating. The power of this man over me was extraordinary. (These people really do have enormous psychological power over others.) I wanted to run but was rooted to the chair.

In desperation the woman resolved to join the SES in an effort to understand what was happening. But she found the cult oppressive. She came to the conclusion that in the SES families were unimportant, and women expected to play a subordinate role.

Unable to accept their teaching, she left. Matters with her husband didn't improve. When she became pregnant again and fell ill, his SES commitments meant he was seldom at her side. But eventually even he began to have doubts about the cult, and broke free from their grip.

The impact of the SES on their lives had been so strong, said the woman, that they would 'never be free of the shadow it cast'.

> It's always there deep in the background. It caused such damage that we'll never be able to completely heal the hurt it caused. We're now a happy, united family but it has taken much time and patience to rebuild our lives.

All this evidence casts a very strange and doubtful light on what Peter Green, Principal of the SES, told us:

> Anything which one person is keener on than another could

be divisive. A cricket club or a political career can be very divisive. I don't think it's more than that at all. We believe very strongly in the importance of the family.

CHAPTER SIX

What is a Cult?

In this book the SES has been labelled a cult. The word has emotional overtones, but has not been used lightly. We need here to establish the evidence on which we have based its use.

That SES members get up to many dotty exploits cannot be doubted. The stories of ex-SES members described in Chapters 1 and 5 illustrate that. But does it all add up to more than an eccentric study group? There is abundant evidence that it does.

We take as our yardstick the twelve marks of a cult which have been drawn up by the Citizens Freedom Foundation of the USA, and which have been endorsed by the British group FAIR.

By fulfilling each and every one of these criteria, the SES finds itself, doubtless most unwillingly, in the company of such rather better-known bedfellows as the Moonies, the Scientologists, the Hare Krishna Movement, along with a host of other eccentric faiths. The doctrine is naturally different, they all are, but the techniques are essentially the same.

We can also state categorically that the SES, either intentionally or accidentally, has established within its movement an environment which can have a brainwashing effect on the unwary.

That does not mean that every member of the SES is a mindless zombie, instantly recognizable as a member of a bizarre religion. Our task would have been a lot easier if that were so. The very respectability and apparent middle-class gentility of the organization protected it from criticism for many years, and still stands in its favour with those who are unfamiliar with its practices.

It is obvious too that not every member allows the cult

fully to permeate his or her life. We can remove from the picture straightaway the many thousands of people who attend introductory courses with the SES for a year or two and then leave, happy or otherwise with what they have learned. They receive very little information about the true nature of the SES – its background, hierarchy, organization or resources. Indeed, the introductory courses can be regarded as an elaborate vetting process. The SES does not want people who are not prepared to accept the doctrine and commit themselves fully to its application. Those who show the wrong attitude are quickly made aware that no progress is possible.

It is tempting to say that we can also remove from the picture members in the senior echelon of the movement who may be perfectly happily married, perhaps holding down a position of considerable influence in public life, and keeping only in a token fashion the swingeing rules on dress, diet, behaviour and attitudes. They are apparently quite happy in their membership and no one would be foolish enough to question their right to follow their beliefs. Former members are adamant, however, that such figures only occupy their roles in public life at the behest of the movement. Told to change jobs, move home, or adopt a stricter approach to the SES, and they would do so or have to leave. If this is so, we have to question why these figures are allowed such leeway? Could it be that in their public roles they are actively carrying out a different kind of duty for the movement? One thing is certain, this discrepancy between the gospel as preached by the SES and the lifestyle and attitudes of the senior echelon, most of whom have been with the cult since it first evolved into a religious body some twenty-five years ago, is one of the main reasons why some committed members further down the ladder become disenchanted and leave.

Our real concern lies with the 'lumpenproletariat' of the movement: those who arrived after the movement's burst into religious fervour in the early 1960s. They must seek approval for every major decision in their lives, they are encouraged to alienate themselves from the 'negative' influence of non-members, (be they family or friends) and they are encouraged to spend all their time carrying out cult practices.

It is here that the real problems arise, and these are exacerbated by their belief that they are members of the movement through their own intellectual and emotional choice, so if things go wrong it is them at fault. We would argue that in fact their free choice has been grotesquely narrowed, much in the way that people will buy goods from high-pressure salesmen, firmly taken in by the sales patter.

These members will not usually have been drawn to the SES out of any desire to join an all-embracing movement. SES advertisements at London underground stations and in various newspapers around the world simply offer courses in philosophy and economics — suitably general topics to cover a wide variety of approaches, but nevertheless implying academic disciplines rather than a gateway to salvation.

Having gained people's allegiance, the cult shows a callous negligence in the way they wield that power. People who suffer breakdowns are abandoned as quickly and as cleanly as possible. Others begin to entertain real doubts about the movement and perhaps leave it. They then face the nightmarish task of trying to build new lives, with no one to turn to, for by that time their only friends will be other SES members.

The intention of this book is not to pillory individual members of the SES. They would all claim that they belong to the movement for the best possible motives. They genuinely believe that they have found the path towards truth and ultimate goodness, which can only make them better human beings.

Yet that path entails membership of an organization which has caused and is still causing immense misery to a good number of people. Its precepts are aimed at stifling the natural thoughts and feelings of its members into a set of preconditioned, and therefore sterile, responses. The emphasis on obedience within the hierarchy allows group leaders, termed 'tutors', who may be natural bullies, insensitive or simply lacking in common sense, to hold complete sway over subordinate members, with the ability to interfere in almost every aspect of their lives.

And while the cult may be aiming at ultimate truth and goodness, their approach is wholly elitist. SES followers are taught that only they possess the key to the door of eternity.

This is characteristic of most of the new religious movements which have sprung up in the last twenty years. In America the success of these movements has been a much bigger challenge to the established churches than in Britain. It has also created a far bigger problem for psychologists and therapists trying to help those who get 'hooked'.

The American Citizens Freedom Foundation is one of the larger groups in the United States helping ex-cult members. It has drawn up a list of the features by which a typical cult can be identified. There is a remarkably high correlation between this list of twelve aspects, and the characteristics of the SES.

1) **A cult is usually characterized by a leader who claims divinity or a special mission delegated to him or her by God.**
2) **The leader or founders (usually living) demand absolute and unquestioning obedience and are the sole judges of the member's faith and commitment**.

The SES's term for God is The Absolute and the man closest to The Absolute is Leon MacLaren, the SES's seventy-three-year-old leader. MacLaren receives spiritual guidance from his guru, the Shankaracharya in India, but SES followers derive their guidance through tutors and on up through the pyramid structure to Leon MacLaren, The Master.

MacLaren's hold on his followers is quite extraordinary. If he decides to hold a meeting it would be inconceivable for any loyal SES member to play truant. Lawyers, teachers, civil servants, business executives are all willing to rearrange their lives for the honour of hearing their leader speak. As the following account of such a gathering shows, this is more than just personal enthusiasm on the part of the cult

144

followers. There is a reverence for The Master that smacks of the typical cultish desire for a charismatic mentor. Here is how one former SES member remembers a MacLaren meeting:

In my time with the SES, it used to be the practice for all senior students in London to be invited to the regular end-of-term lecture. I think I am right in saying that one had to have completed Part One, at least, to qualify for an invitation. These lectures were our mass rallies. They were characterized by rigid discipline and by the total silence of the participants; by mass, hypnotic passivity; an impressive phenomenon where hundreds of people are assembled in one building.

It should be understood that Mr MacLaren is an orator of extraordinary power. He has a beautiful voice with a vast range of pitch and expression. He uses this to good effect in a style of oration which is Ciceronian in its balance, measured construction and persuasiveness. To listen to Mr MacLaren speaking publicly on any subject whatever is a seductive enchantment. Physically he is ugly. His face is wolfish, his hair greasy and sparse. He dresses dismally in dark, crumpled, cigarette-ash-sprinkled, waistcoated suits which do not conceal his well-developed paunch. His gait is stooping; his posture droops like that of a vulture. Indeed, his whole demeanour is vulpine, threatening. How then to explain his charm? His magnetism? His personal power over people of all sorts?

Some of this can be attributed to his undoubted taste for and skill in bullying. Weak people congregate round a bully and bask in his approval whilst enjoying the discomfiture of his victims. Victims even enjoy their humiliation sometimes. At least it is a form of notice, of notoriety. There is, too, for braver spirits, the challenge of 'taking on' a bully. All these reactions could be observed in students' attitudes to Mr MacLaren.

At the end-of-term Lecture, Mr MacLaren reigned supreme. Students would arrive in their hundreds, class by class, and line up in total silence under the watchful eye of their 'tutor'. No matter how long we had to wait, there was never any disorder or noise of any kind. Once seated in our places, the hypnotic silence deepened until Mr MacLaren entered in a beaming good

145

humour, snuffing up the holy atmosphere of submission through his big, black nostrils; savouring the silent discipline embodied in the obedient mass of humanity before him, ready to listen and be played upon as he thought fit.

I suppose, put simply, it was a case of mass hero worship. We were encouraged to speak of Mr MacLaren as 'the Old Man' and to think of him as the father of us all. Here was somebody thoroughly 'awake'. He would lead us all to a heaven on earth, and then beyond. We were all 'below ground level', worms sunk in stupor in the earth, as he repeatedly told us. But he would show us the light of day, put us on our feet and make us into supermen and superwomen. The fact that he was a poor physical specimen himself, a chainsmoker and a heavy drinker, never seemed in the least incongruous to us. It is only now that I am astonished to remember that, because Mr MacLaren smoked continually, unlimited smoking was approved in that puritanical community; and because Mr MacLaren had a weakness for claret, so did we all!

MacLaren's ability to rouse people and win their minds has been mentioned to us over and over again. Even the most bitter ex-members will say that there is something uncanny about the way he is able to mesmerize people in his presence. Unfortunately we have not had the opportunity to find out at first hand. MacLaren has refused our requests for an interview.

As befits a leader of a cult, MacLaren is treated like a Maharaja. It is clear that financially and physically he is entirely supported by the SES. He lives in luxuriously appointed apartments at Waterperry, with other accommodation Stanhill Court and Sarum Chase, the SES's lavish mansions in the South of England, and at equally well-appointed residences when he travels to SES offshoots abroad. He is chauffeured in a black Rover, a gift from an SES member, and travels first-class when forced to go by plane. He is supplied with the finest of all available clarets, silk shirts, immaculate wool suits and lotions. He is attended by nubile young SES members specially selected for their loyalty and spiritual potential.

146

SES leaders have told us that they see this as something of a recompense for all that he has given to the world in spiritual inspiration. One has the notion that apart from his taste for claret and cigarettes MacLaren is wholly engaged in spiritual self-improvement and uninterested in worldly pleasures, in the belief that with enough loyal disciples he can achieve unity with The Absolute.

The unquestioning obedience asked of such followers has in recent years taken a new turn which SES members are reluctant to discuss. A number of SES couples who have brought their children up in the SES faith appear to have been invited to have their adolescent daughters formally enrolled in the cult in a manner which can result in an arranged marriage.

At sixteen the child will be brought before MacLaren in a virginal white gown and a ceremony performed in which she dedicates her life to The Absolute. The child is talked to by MacLaren so that he can apparently assess her needs and character. Later a husband will be approached — usually someone a great deal older — and a betrothal will take place. A seven-year age gap is considered optimum.

We know of several marriages that have been arranged in this manner. There is no evidence that they are anything but happy at this stage. However, to MacLaren's role as supreme spiritual authority within the SES can now be added that of matchmaker. A number of SES members have admitted they are worried by this development, but they are powerless to act. As we shall see later, any criticism has to be stifled.

3) **Established members are often guarded, vague, deceptive or secretive about beliefs, goals, demands and activities until the recruit is 'hooked'.**
4) **A cult often encourages exclusivity and isolation using the excuse that all outside the cult is totally evil or satanic.**

Within the SES it is widely argued that people outside the movement are 'asleep' and of lesser merit because they are not seeking true enlightenment through the School. A read of the SES's leaflets — all the branches produce similar material — would suggest the SES is simply an educational trust offering lectures in philosophy and economics. The purpose of this book is to show that there is more to the SES than that. But how has the movement been so successful in attracting so little public notoriety for so long? Here is what an ex-member has to say about the way the Teaching has to be kept whole by swearing a vow of secrecy:

This vow is one of the main reasons for the 'School's' magnificent cover over the years. Early in the Philosophy course, students have to promise *never* to discuss anything they do or learn inside the 'School' with outsiders. The solemnity of this promise cannot be exaggerated. The reason given for the necessity of the promise is subtle. It calculates upon the temperament of the average 'School' member.

The 'School' attracts excellent people; people who are honestly disillusioned with materialism, honestly alarmed at the danger of world war, honestly sickened by the vulgarity of the mass media, the mass ideal of life as projected, for instance by advertising — and who honestly long to improve the level of their own life and that of the community. To such temperaments it would not be convincing to argue directly that because they have discovered something valuable, they should never speak of it except to the privileged few. No. We were persuaded to say nothing for the sake of the whole of humanity. We were taught that an 'essence' or sleeping soul is infinitely precious and fragile. The 'Teaching', on the other hand, is powerful and dangerous if introduced outside 'School' surroundings. Expose a sleeping soul in ordinary life to the 'Teaching' before its proper time and it would react violently and become damaged so that, instead of one day blossoming, it would simply rot and decay and fall out of the chain of existence altogether. We were taught to believe that to speak of the 'Teaching' outside the 'School' put other people's souls in danger of perdition. We truly believed this and so we never, never spoke. Had I, for instance, had the sense to talk about what was going on in the early years to my family or friends, I am sure they would have laughed and reasoned me out of it. There is, after all, that recent case of the don at St John's College, Cambridge, whose wife had the sense to talk things over with *him*. He saw the evil and the flaws in the 'Teaching' at once. It is only now, when I am convinced of the real evil and possible insanity of Mr MacLaren and the 'Teaching' that I am willing to break that solemn promise made so long ago. I do not believe for a minute that anything I tell you or the world about the 'Teaching' can do anything but raise a laugh or two, horrify considerably and perhaps call up pity for anybody involved in such a mess.

However, this solemn promise of secrecy could help to explain the apparently obstinate silence of many ex-'School' members. Cynically, it has occurred to me too that they might be reluctant to admit that they were ever such presumptuous and blasphemous fools as to believe that they were singled out from the rest of mankind in the way the 'School' taught; that they thought they were approaching admittance to the Inner Circle of Mankind which was supposed to contain such company as Jesus Christ, Buddha, Muhammad, the Maharishi and, by implication, Leon MacLaren, Dr Roles and approved artists such as Mozart and Leonardo da Vinci.

Keeping the aims of the SES secret becomes a problem when the cult tries to recruit new members. Over the years a very sophisticated recruitment programme has been developed which attracts hundreds of new followers every year yet succeeds in blurring the aim of the movement.

In centres all over the world an introductory course of lectures is advertised. The lectures are so carefully formulated that they are almost exactly the same whichever lecturer is giving them in whatever country. If anyone enquires what the outcome of the courses will be, they are told that they must take the course to find out. One of us – Peter Hounam – enrolled in the course with that in mind. It was soon clear that the course had little to do with the academic study of philosophy:

It was held in a bare lecture room in Old Gloucester Street, Holborn. As I enter three men in neat suits, well-groomed, sit at desks enrolling the new intake. We pay £15 for twelve lessons.

An SES attendant compiles a seating plan for the lecturer. It is a poor turnout, only eight of us have come, but there are further meetings here every night of the week and others at the SES's HQ in South Kensington. Quietly, the empty chairs are cleared away leaving us sitting apart staring at an empty blackboard, a rose in a vase and the lectern.

Nothing happens for five minutes and then the lecturer walks in. He introduces himself as James Gibbons (a London barrister) and proceeds to explain that the SES is a registered charity, non-profit-making and dedicated to the study of great teachings.

What do we think wisdom is? What is knowledge? What were the characteristics of wise men? Gibbons waits for one of his students to give what he believes is the right answer and then moves on, referring all the time to a written list of points that hasn't changed materially in the last fifteen years. What are the great virtues? Wisdom, temperance, justice, courage . . .

Then follows one of the key teachings of SES theology — the different levels of consciousness. When I ask if these are accepted as a philosophical fact, I'm told that they are by all sensible people — and watched thereafter for being too inquisitive.

He tells us that as we become more and more serious students of the SES we will learn to climb up the pyramid to the highest levels of consciousness — at which point we will be able to know everything that is going on around us, and eventually everything that is going on in the world.

After two and a half hours of our so-called philosophy course Gibbons suddenly leaves the lectern, sits in a chair and tells us he is going to give us some homework in practical philosophy. We are asked to sit straight upright in our chairs, hands on knees 'and let all the busy thinking slip' away. The room falls silent and we are asked to hear all the tiny sounds in the room. After three minutes our lecturer gets up and tells us to practise the exercise three times a day until we come back again next Monday. He adds that if we don't turn up we shouldn't be surprised if someone rings up to find out why.

Without giving away anything about itself, the SES has got eight strangers to accept the notion of spiritual enlightenment through the SES's brand of theological study and the practice of meditation. It is a remarkable feat for one two-and-a-half-hour lesson.

My next two lessons were at 90 Queen's Gate, the SES international headquarters. There are more students but the teaching flows on in the same vein — higher levels of consciousness can be attained by accepting the great SES truths and practising the meditation 'exercise'. We are read snippets from great teachers of the past and asked to accept them. Above all, we are urged to keep trying out the exercise. One student is admonished for thinking it is possible to do it on a motorbike.

The final and possibly most important point that we are asked to accept flows from this question: How do we know when we have been asleep? People stab at the answer, looking for something deeper than is required. The answer, we are told, is blindingly simple — we know we have been asleep when we wake up.

Thus it follows that we only know that there are higher levels of spiritual enlightenment when we have reached those levels. In our present fuzzy state of 'waking sleep', we simply have to accept that those higher levels exist. And with that acceptance the class puts its faith in the lecturer and the SES, and is hooked.

If Peter Hounam had remained a loyal student and finished the introductory course, it would still not have been evident just what the SES is all about. Students have spent a year attending courses and still not realized that the teaching is a refined form of Hinduism laced with other forms of mysticism.

The unwillingness of even new SES converts to talk about their faith is thus partly the vow of secrecy and partly a profound ignorance of what is behind the beliefs. The relationship with their families and friends begins to deteriorate as questions are left unanswered and the convert withdraws into what many have described as a "zombie-like state".

According to the American Citizens Freedom Foundation here can be detected two more marks of the typical cult:
5) **Meaningful communication with family and former friends is sharply curtailed and the cult becomes the convert's new Family. In most cults every attempt is made to blur or eliminate the convert's conscious memories of his or her former way of life and personal history.**
6) **Cults systematically employ sophisticated techniques designed to effect ego-destruction, thought reform and dependence on the cult.**

Some critics of the SES would argue that the School's exclusivity, breaking the link with the past, with family and former friends, is a form of imprisonment. Certainly people who have left the SES have found themselves in a world suddenly new and unexplored; they feel insecure and have to struggle to readjust.

The alienation that begins as people get involved in more and more SES activities is described like this by an ex-member:

> Mr MacLaren's attack on what he called 'identification' was consistent and sustained. Roughly speaking, he labelled all natural and family affection as 'identification'. He said that such identification was evil and one of the main forces in life that kept people asleep and helpless. He taught that there was no place in the 'School' for a student who felt that his or her husband or wife, parents or children were more important than 'School' work. We were told that the newest member of Part One, whom we may never have met, was in reality closer to us than our own family, because he or she was at least a developing essence which had been attracted through the magic doors, whereas our own families were sleeping monsters, connected with us by accident rather than by choice, likely to make unreasonable demands upon us; likely, indeed, to resent the time and energy we spent at the 'School'.
>
> In the SES, family life was attacked overtly and covertly. Overtly, the attack came in the form of the drive against

'identification'. Covertly, it came in the form of the organization of the 'School' work and the students' daily life.

After Part One, students were subjected to repeated invitations to partake in voluntary activities to help the 'School' on other evenings of the week than that on which they attended their own class. Failure to volunteer meant all-out failure in the organization, and anybody who did not do extra work progressed no further in the organization. They would never qualify for admittance to the senior levels of the 'School' and they would certainly never meet Mr MacLaren.

Time and again we have been given examples of wives in hospital being abandoned by their husbands because they *had* to attend an SES course. The effect on family life was in many cases disastrous — quite often it was the catalyst for marital breakdown.

The purpose can only be to put the SES group before family or other commitments. It can be described as ego-destruction. The group does everything together, working as a team and suppressing any instinct to act spontaneously, imaginatively and as an individual. One member proudly explained how his group had stripped the cornices from a ceiling at the SES headquarters in London by arming themselves with toothpicks and painstakingly removing the old whitewash covering. It had taken weeks to complete. Continuing our ex-member's comments:

Married people were in no danger of indulging in identification with each other. They were never put in the same tutorial group, as a matter of policy. This ensured that they spent at least one evening of the week apart. They were separated, too, in their voluntary duty groups which increased in number with seniority and length of association with the School. (I call the duties 'voluntary' — this is a bit of a misnomer in that one did not choose the kind of extra duty one preferred. One could be told to join the sewer-diggers, the plasterers, the caterers, the film-makers or the cement-mixers — and that would be that. Discontent or disobedience were out of the question.)

Towards the end of our career in the 'School', my ex-husband and I each had separate duties at 'School' premises on every single night of the week and often at weekends as well. We both had full-time jobs until I became a mother. Either way, we seldom saw one another.

Why should people allow their lives to be manipulated in this way? For some it provides a cosy retreat from the difficulties of decision-making:

The benefit to the cult is that a habitual transference of interest from oneself to the group, faithfully practised over the years, really does weaken self-interest and, incidentally, healthy individual characteristics such as common sense and the instinct for self-preservation. Concentration on the group encourages unthinking obedience, mass reaction and response, and fosters distrust in individual initiative.

The benefit to individuals is obvious. They are relieved of all personal anxiety, all feelings of personal inadequacy or insecurity. The group will sweep them on to their first awakening, to 'self-consciousness', to godhead. They need never worry about right and wrong or about evil again. Personal responsiblity for themselves, and indeed for anything else, is at an end.

Thought reform begins early within each group gathering through the specific admonition neither to accept nor to reject what is taught:

This is an excellent brainwashing precept. It is introduced to students in the following way. They are told that they may always make up their own minds about the 'Teaching'. Nobody is forcing them to believe anything. They should, however, be prepared to keep a more open mind about the secret teachings of the Inner Circle of Mankind than would a sleeping

154

individual member of the human race. There must be no criticism, no instinctive rejection, no 'negative' argument about anything. There must be no strong feeling of any kind. The student who wishes to become enlightened must simply listen, look and take neutral note of everything presented. In time, what is true and acceptable will (with the help of group effort) become clear of itself.

This sounds reasonable. In fact, it induces a state of unthinking acceptance and quiescence which soon becomes habitual. The human mind is such that it either accepts or rejects. If it does not reject, whatever may be said in all piety about 'holding certain things neutrally in mind', it accepts. This may be why Christ said, 'Whoever is not with me is against me'. He was expressing a psychological truth which Mr MacLaren clearly appreciates. He has no need to force agreement. He simply uses this technique to stifle disagreement at birth.

Individual will is also destroyed by giving group members exhausting duties. While providing the SES with a ready supply of free labour, such duties would seem largely pointless to most outsiders. In the context of the increasingly scientific discipline of group dynamics, or of Gurdjieff's own theories, the object is seen to be precisely that they are *deliberately* pointless.

The duties could be exceptionally menial and humiliating. Joseph Vincent, the long-serving SES member who now campaigns against the SES in Holland, told us how he had been made to clean the lavatories six times, not because the first time he had not done them properly but because he had not done them in the right frame of mind — concentrating on the act of cleaning and on that alone.

7) **Indoctrinated members put goals of the cult ahead of individual concerns, interests, education plans, career, health and well-being.**
8) **The cult may maintain members in a state of heightened suggestibility through lack of sleep, engineered diet, intense**

spiritual exercises, constant indoctrination, controlled group experiences and manipulated 'spiritual' encounters.

9)   Converts may display symptoms of extreme tension and stress, fear, guilt, lack of humour, regression in communication skills/critical judgement/judgement-logic skills and reality-testing.

Why do so many members of the SES allow the organization to take over their lives? Why are they unnaturally suggestible? The meditation, the curious diet, the special dress for women, the lack of sleep and arduous residential courses must help to make them so. But without indoctrination such devices would be of little value. Among many pages of tutors' notes written for the SES's women's groups are many examples of the way this indoctrination is carried out. Here is part of a lecture on the place of women:

> At the centre of most homes is a lady. For good reason, we shall not call her woman or female, but lady. She is at the centre of the home; her dimensions determine the circumference of the home; and her substance permeates the home. Furthermore, that which she carries in her voice determines the nature of the vibrations in the home. Let us, therefore, carry in mind throughout this week, the question, 'What is the function of a lady's voice in the home?' Listen to your voice as you deal with tradesmen, correct the children, welcome your husband, think about the ironing, practise universal sounds and all the rest; and find out what the sound of the voice actually *does*. It is a severely practical question: 'What is the function of a lady's voice in the home?'

Through page after page the tutors are taught the SES line on women's place in society, how to keep the home clean and set aside a room where 'negative thinking' is banished; how to curtsy and how to bring up children. Even children must behave in an unemotional way:

> Tears spring up very easily in relation to a sudden shock,

156

however slight. They may also be a valid expression of confusion or uncertainty. Of course, they should not be condoned or encouraged; especially with small boys, it is important that they learn early that men do not cry. If fact, some men do — justifiably; these are the men in whom the higher emotional centre has been unlocked, and when they weep, it is for imprisoned humanity. Jesus wept; Buddha wept. We know nothing of such tears.

So, ordinary tears should be discouraged in children, but the cause of the tears should be noted.

Expanding this a woman ex-member explained the SES's concept of 'negative emotion':

Excitement or strong feeling of any kind is discouraged in the 'School'. It is called 'negative emotion' and, again, it equates with 'sin'. After a few years a practised SES member will have become, outwardly, an emotionless monster. Impossible to upset, to discompose, to disturb the *outward* equilibrium of such a person. I stress the word 'outward' because I know, from experience, that inwardly one could be a seething mass of passion whilst outwardly expressing no 'negative emotion'. The 'School' tolerates never a raised voice, nor a hurried, unconsidered movement. It cultivates physical rigidity. It is forbidden to sit with crossed legs. The hands must rest, each on one knee. It is forbidden to fidget, or to slump or lean against anything. It is forbidden to raise or lower the voice unduly. The mind and body are supposed to be quiet, ever-alert — ever-tensed and ready for the onslaught of new 'awareness'. (What really happens, of course, is that people become almost blind and deaf in the effort to take in impressions keenly and to 'observe' themselves.)

After a year or two of sincere effort, the outward control acquired by all this repression of natural emotional and bodily expression becomes formidable. Insult, berate, accost a 'School' member as much as you like — he or she will not react. You will receive, after a pause, a measured reply which baffles the best interviewer or reporter in ordinary life. None of the ordinary gambits or rules of life apply and, unless you

157

know better because you have been subjected to the same discipline, you might conclude that this person really has superhuman control, superhuman calm, superhuman power.

The American Citizens Freedom Foundation have three final hallmarks of the typical cult and all apply in some measure to the SES:

10) **Members are pre-occupied with fund-raising, recruiting and workshop activities.**

11) **The cult may be found to be exploiting its members' finances.**

12) **Some groups exploit members through unpaid employment and poor working conditions.**

Elsewhere in this book we have shown how members are involved in donating their spare time and cash to the SES. Some people say they were asked to give up to a fifth of their income to the cult. Others were simply requested to make gifts for specific projects. The SES also makes money from the courses it runs. The fees appear modest but the running costs are minimal. Nobody is paid a fee for taking a class or acting as an attendant.

At the SES's country houses nearly all the routine maintenance work to the buildings and grounds is carried out with obsessive dedication by the cult's followers. They live in simple dormitories, prepare their own food and pay their own travelling expenses.

A vivid illustration of how well-organized this aspect of the SES has become can be gleaned from the cult's communications list – an internal telephone directory which runs to six closely typed pages. The list is only of senior and middle-ranking SES members in charge of the cult's activities. There are nearly 300 entries and though some names are duplicated it shows just how carefully structured the operation has become.

People are appointed as accountants, librarians, public-event organizers and arts organizers. There is a long list of tutors in charge of the different levels of tuition. A section is devoted to Sanskrit studies, sound and calligraphy courses and mathematics. The buildings are looked after by an army of people with property managers, stores, survey and maintenance chief, electrical consultant, an architect, a provisioner, bookshop tutors, decor advisers and housekeepers. All are devoted SES followers giving their time free. Such is the dedication of the movement that people are even tutors in charge of cleaning, catering and house and garden work. There is someone in charge of 'ladies at home', 'renaissance', rhetoric and drama, economics research, textiles and needlework.

One of the biggest contributors of free labour is the 'youth group', headed by ex-sergeant major Michael Nash. When we first started looking into the SES we were invited to meet Nash at his home in Kent. He has his own advertising agency and is engaged every weekend putting sixteen- to twenty-five-year-olds through a rigorous course of physical and mental exertion.

Members are awakened at 5 a.m. every morning to begin a daily round of work, study and discussion. The food provided accords strictly to the prescribed diet.

From these courses they graduate onto week-long stays at Stanhill Court, near Guildford, where a similar programme also includes fasting for thirty-six hours.

Nash, who once stood unsuccessfully as a Liberal county council candidate, said:

I'm chief brainwasher of the youth movement. I put forward proposals based on the traditional values of human development. They are utterly basic and founded on three principles – live honestly, harm no man, and do unto others as you would have them do to you.

If that is brainwashing, if that is conditioning, then I stand guilty, guilty, guilty. It can be seen in that way, there's no doubt about it.

It all depends on the nature of the person; I've been through it and always kept an open mind and two feet on the ground.

'In my time, 25,000 people have been through the School of Economic Science. The number of breakdowns and difficulties we have had in that time is so minimal compared to 25,000 in any other group elsewhere in society that I really don't think it is a strong subject for criticism.

People are upset by the most extraordinary things which to them are totally important, quite rational.

I was a sergeant in the army and all I have really done is transfer that attitude to the youth group. I love my country, I love my Queen, and I love my fellow man. I stand for the traditional virtues. Ever since I was a boy I have been a defender of the weak. I believe wholly in the concept of the good soldier.

Nash said he warned people before going on the courses what to expect. Once a course was underway, he would 'roundly admonish' people who did not work hard enough.

He explained that the courses helped to focus a person's attention while refreshing them mentally.

Undoubtably something happens to one. You come to a greater realization perhaps of which direction your life is taking.

An entirely different point of view has been expressed by many former members of the cult who believe they were brainwashed by the methods so strongly advocated by Nash, the meditation and other disciplines.

Experts agree that it is highly unlikely that any absolutely foolproof way of brainwashing an individual has ever been devised. There will always be those individuals who, however deep in their psyche it is buried, nurse the flame of rebellion and individuality. Secondly, individual traits of an environment which can trap and brainwash people can be found in most forms of social conditioning, whether it is adherence to a religion, pursuit of a career, or the holding together of a family. It is when eight particularly powerful features are found in any one environment — be it a nation,

160

political group or cult — that the need for extreme caution arises.

We have taken as our reference one of the standard psychological textbooks on the subject; *Thought Reform and the Psychology of Totalism: A study of 'brainwashing' in China*, by Robert Jay Lifton MD (W. W. Norton and Company, New York).

Dr Lifton is an acknowledged expert on the subject. His findings are based on extensive interviews with people who fell foul of the Communist take-over of China in 1949, which was the first the Western world learned of the practice. (Brainwashing comes from the Chinese *hsi nao*, to wash brain.) His research then went on to include interviews with American servicemen captured during the Korean War, and with people imprisoned during the Chinese Cultural Revolution in the mid 1960s.

Dr Lifton defines the practice as 'thought reform'. It consists of two basic elements:

> Confession, the exposure and renunciation of past and present evil, and the re-education, the remaking of man . . . aimed at social control and individual change.

He then goes on to outline the eight psychological factors which would seem to be prerequisite to the setting up of a brainwashing environment.

1) **Environment control** Controllers of the environment (in this case the SES) try to exert power over everything an individual sees, hears, reads, writes, experiences and expresses. Just as importantly they also seek power over what the individual thinks — denying that individual a chance to stand back and decide personally whether he or she wants to be part of that environment. The regime at the SES's rigorous residential courses would seem to fit this description — as would the code of behaviour for SES members in the outside world. The most detailed practicalities of speech, thought and action are supposed to reflect SES teaching at all times.

2) **Personal manipulation** Controllers set up an environment in which specific patterns of behaviour and feelings are demanded. The behaviour and emotions then create an effect on the individual which appears to arise quite naturally. Because of the apparent spontaneity of this effect, it appears to be almost mystical. With the SES this would include the powerful feeling of kinship and unity which builds up at group-meditation sessions and on residential courses. Ex-members still speak of this feeling with awe years after they have left the cult. Such feelings have been specifically provoked by the cult's practices. This would also explain the feeling of 'self-control' which members enjoy. This 'self-control' seems to the outsider an unhealthy repression brought about by the cult's doctrine and methods. This mystique also infects the controllers. It confirms their sense of 'higher purpose', of 'having directly perceived' a new course of social development, and of 'being themselves the vanguard of this development'. Lifton adds:

> By thus becoming the instruments of their own mystique, they create a mystical aura around the manipulating institutions – the Party, the Government, the Organization. They are the agents chosen (by history, by God, or by some other supernatural force . . .)

3) **The demand for purity** This is the division by the controllers of everything into either the pure or the impure, the absolutely good or the absolutely evil. The good, needless to say, is that which is consistent with the brainwashers' ideology. Anything else is said to be bad or impure. Lifton points out that this attitude sees absolute purity as obtainable, 'that anything done in the name of this purity is ultimately moral'. Could this explain why the children's schools neglected to point out their links with the cult? Or why new members are not warned what lies ahead of them? The search for absolute purity is certainly the foundation stone of their beliefs. But, as Lifton points out, no one can reach a state of perfection, and the guilt and shame which

arise with constant failure make members even more vulnerable to their manipulators.

4) **Confession** is another factor which activates the guilt mechanism, extending the manipulators' hold on the followers. In the SES, confession takes place when the member is ostensibly having his meditation checked. He will be asked questions about his personal life to discover whether he is deviating from the SES path. For very senior members, the process known as 'humouring', when one member will probe the life of another with endless questions, would also seem to fulfil this function. A milder form of confession is encouraged at group meetings when members are asked to relate how what they have learned ties in with their behaviour since the last meeting. Lifton points out that confession becomes an act of symbolic self-surrender, an expression of the merging of the individual with his environment. It also brings with it the total exposure of the person confessing. The underlying assumption here is that the environment and its instigators have total ownership of each individual within it. Sharing confession also creates a strong sense of unity within the group.

5) **The sacred science** This is the aura which the brainwashing environment builds up around its basic dogma, 'holding it out as the ultimate moral vision for the the ordering of human existence'. There is little doubt that this is how the SES view their beliefs. Lifton claims that, however illogical the dogma, exaggerated claims are made for its airtight logic. 'In this way, the philosopher-kings of modern ideological totalism reinforce their authority by claiming to share in the rich and respected heritage of natural science.' SES members claim, of course, that they are following 'natural laws'.

6) **Loading of language** The ideological concepts are expressed in words which become shortcuts through the thought processes. Such words can take on a power of their own – conveying the ultimate in good or evil. In the SES,

terms such as 'truth' and 'negative emotion' would seem to fit this description. Says Lifton: 'Also involved is the underlying assumption that language, like all other human products, can be owned or operated by the Movement.' The jargon acts as a verbal straitjacket. By restricting the language used, capacities for thinking and feeling are similarly narrowed. (Remember how Joseph Vincent found that certain key words acted as triggers to bring him back into the SES way of seeing things.)

7) **Doctrine over person** Once a person enters the new, controlled environment, all his or her previous experiences are re-examined. They are interpreted in terms of the new set of beliefs, not according to the person's own true thoughts and feelings. Says Lifton:

> This doctrinal supremacy requires that character and identity be reshaped, not in the way they would normally develop — thinking and feeling for oneself — but in a manner which will shape the doctrinal mould.

The underlying assumption here is that the doctrine is ultimately more valid than any aspect of 'human character or human experience'. From their very first SES meeting, members are firmly encouraged to bear the cult's philosophy in mind whatever they might be doing. At subsequent meetings they are invited to talk about how they have managed to apply what they have been learning. Those whose answers do not fit the SES doctrine are then corrected by their tutor. Initially the objective is 'self-realization', but later what is called 'the crystallization of the School' takes precedence.

8) **The dispensing of existence** In brainwashing environments, individuals who accept the ideology are granted the 'right' to live. Those who reject it have no such right. In a totalitarian state they are thrown into jail, exiled or executed. In the SES, those who accept the doctrine are on their way to eternal salvation. The rest of us are doomed to live in ignorance, evil and suffering.

These criteria are all apparent in the beliefs and modus operandi of the SES – just as they are exhibited by many other cults. But do they tell the whole story of why such movements in the Western world can precipitate personality changes which a totalitarian state might envy?

American R. K. Heller details how to break the influence of cults on the individual in his book *De-programming for Do-it-yourselfers: A Cure for the Common Cult* (The Gentle Press, Medina, Ohio). And in his treatise *An Opinion – The Relevance of Hypnosis to Acculteration*, he examines how cults, which seldom use physical coercion, nevertheless hold in their sway thousands of men and women, a substantial number of whom were apparently perfectly normal before joining up. He argues that Lifton's first criterion, environment or milieu control, may prove effective in a country where censorship and physical detention can be used. But how can it be enforced in a free society? The answer, he believes, is hypnosis, reinforced by self-hypnosis brought about by meditation techniques.

Heller points out that, contrary to what the more rugged individualists might believe, experts agree that everyone can be hypnotized. And it is not always apparent, even to the subject, that hypnosis is taking place. Heller contends:

> The cult is a sect of people wherein victims hypnotize each other, inadvertently and unconsciously, with disguised methods yielding the apparent belief . . . that no control is involved . . .

He argues that a hypnotic state can be discerned from, and caused by, two conditions of the mind – hyperaesthesia and anaesthesia. Hyperaesthesia involves:

> A heightened state of sensitivity or concentration. In this state a person's suggestibility is greatly enhanced. He is hyper-sensitive to stimuli from the operator. His tendency to adhere to the operator's theme is heightened or carried out. His ability to test suggestion is low. The focus of his concentration is so greatly increased that he can see, hear, taste etc. what the operator suggests . . . With his sensitivity to focussing on the theme increasing, his sensitivity to other input is decreasing. Concentrating on relaxing is a form of hyperaesthesia . . .

Anaesthesia is:

Also a form of hypnosis in itself. This form is more or less resultant from concentration. Unwanton or non-thematic input may be shut out – intentionally or inadvertently. The person may become insensitive to distraction . . . Inadvertently he may not react to suggestions from non-operators.

He states that five conditions are necessary for these mental conditions to arise, and hypnosis to take place:
1)   The arousal of emotions or anxieties, or promotion of relaxation;
2)   High-pressure or high-continuity attack by the operator;
3)   Suggestion;
4)   A non-distracting or thematically convincing environment;
5)   Repetition of themes.

He adds that 'these conditions by themselves are enough to bring about hyperaesthesia'. And then he makes a thought-provoking claim.

It does not take a formal use of hypnosis to produce these conditions. A high-pressure sales pitch is enough to produce this syndrome. If your attention can be diverted and your judgement caught unawares, wherein these five conditions exist, you may be brought to a state of hyperaesthesia and suggestibility by almost anyone.

He adds that by arousing guilt and fear a person can be made more suggestible, and the suggestibility will increase the more the emotions are played on. And he goes on to explain that relaxation results in hyperaesthesia setting in. The stage hypnotist often hastens this process by gently swinging a watch in front of the subject, or else using other methods of object fixation. Chanting a mantra, he claims, is no different.
   'Hypnotic relaxation and the relaxation of meditation are too nearly identical to ignore,' claims Heller, and he goes

on to compare step-by-step the process of self-hypnosis with the technique of meditation or deep relaxation. He finds little difference, adding that any good hypnotist could produce the sensation of journeying deep into Inner Consciousness which TM practitioners claim they experience.

If self-hypnosis instructions equal relaxation-response suggestions, and if relaxation-response equals self-hypnosis, and if relaxation-response equals TM, then TM is nothing more than self-hypnosis.

Regarding high-pressure or high-continuity attack by the operator, Heller explains:

The key word here is 'convincing'. The orator appears to know what he is talking about. He compels the person to try to understand. He doesn't allow enough opportunity for the person to test the conjectures. He may use known or general truths to generate his own inferences. He will use the individual's lack of knowledge to cultivate the inferences. The reinforced hallucination will reduce that person's capacity for reality-testing. Override information that is necessary to test a hallucination, and a reinforced hallucination will sustain. Numb the conscious mind and you've numbed the rational and you've numbed reality-testing.

Heller believes that his analysis explains why cult members feel such compulsion to continue with their membership. For in the context where the hypnosis takes place, be it a meeting, a meditation session or whatever, no provision is made for the hypnotic suggestion to be removed.

He states further:

A person who has the compulsion to carry out a post-hypnotic suggestion may state — with apparent sincerity — 'reasons' for carrying out that suggestion . . . Many, many subjects believe that they were not hypnotized, even when they achieved the deepest states. Truly, in the same fashion, a cultist does not believe he is being controlled.

167

The implications of all this for SES members are plain by now, in particular as a result of the movement's central use of Transcendental Meditation. The theory of self-hypnosis gives a very possible reason why the cultist's search for truth and inner consciousness becomes so all-consuming, and so self-perpetuating.

But are there implications as well for ordinary Christians in ordinary orthodox churches? After all, several of the criteria for cultishness and several features of a brainwashing or self-hypnotic environment apply to mainstream churches too. All Christian prayer contains an element of meditation; most Christians confess their sins sometimes; many Christians give a lot of time and money to church work; they believe strongly in a particular world-view; and they put their allegiance to Jesus Christ above all their other allegiances.

Does this mean the ordinary Christian is likely to be ultra-suggestible, externally controlled and obsessive?

The general answer is no, because cults meet all the criteria, whereas othodox churches meet only some of them. Yet there is an important lesson for the churches in these studies. Their ministry should always aim to set their members *more* free to think and act for themselves, not less. The normal cult-follower has surrendered his or her individuality to the movement; the authentic Christian is a free individual who has freely joined a fellowship.

CHAPTER SEVEN

A Private Education

The *Standard* story which produced perhaps greater anger from SES members and their sympathizers than the others was published on 9 June 1983. It linked the cult with four independent schools for children in London. Although the parents of many pupils were members of the SES, others knew nothing of the cult, or its connection with the education their children were receiving. No mention of the SES appeared in the schools' prospectus or advertising. It was a glaring omission, given the fact that all the governors and teachers were members of the cult, all the school-buildings were owned by the SES, the cult's philosophy was taught in the class-room – albeit in simplified form – and senior pupils were encouraged to join the SES. More worrying still, some parents had noticed behavioral changes in their children which made them uneasy, but for which there appeared to be no ready explanation.

Under the headline *The SES and its strange schools, The Standard* revealed that more than 600 pupils between the ages of four and a half and eighteen were being indoctrinated with the philosophies of the secret cult. The schools involved were St Vedast School for Boys in West Heath Road, Hampstead; St Vedast School for Girls in Queen's Gate, Kensington, next-door to the headquarters of the SES; St James School for Boys in Chepstow Villas, West London; and St James School for Girls, also at Queen's Gate.

Said one mother with a son at St Vedast School for Boys:

> They are indoctrinating the pupils. I feel my son is going away from me. He says I am wrong and the school is right when I try to talk to him about what they teach.

The father of two boys at the same school said:

> Before they went to school my sons were very happy boys. Now they stay by themselves in their room. They are definitely changed. I didn't know anything about the School of Economic Science when they started going there.

The Standard also highlighted the emphasis on corporal punishment at the boys' schools, and the use of cold showers at St Vedast School for Boys as an additional sanction.

A look at the exercise-books of pupils attending St Vedast School for boys shows just how far SES philosophy, much of it taken from the Hindu tradition, permeated the teaching. A twelve-year-old boy, who attended the school in the early 1980s, was instructed to write on Page One of his geometry exercise-book, under the heading 'Axioms':

1. The Absolute is Constant.
2. All and everything is Absolute. It begins in the Absolute, is sustained by the Absolute, and finally returns to the Absolute.
3. In order to create anything in time and space, the Absolute takes its stand in time and space.
4. Everything in creation is measured.
5. A point is a position in time and space. Where the forces of the Absolute are concentrated for creation, the point is a word.
6. Wherever there is multiplication there is division and vice versa. Wherever there is addition there is subtraction and vice versa.

The same child's history book provided further fascinating insights into the St Vedast view of a subject which for most schoolboys revolves around 1066 and all that.

On the first page of the exercise-book he has written:

> History is the story of man's return to his creator, his successes and his failures. We learn about great men so that by their example we too lead noble and upright and honest lives, suitable to the dignity of a human being. We learn about evil

men so that we may be aware of the dangers of selfish ideas and the evil they can cause.

On the next page appears a large table, entitled The levels of Man.

LEVEL	WORK	EXAMPLE
Humanity	Truth	Christ Krishna
Civilization	Law and Morality	Abraham Moses Socrates Plato
Culture	Education Music Science Literature	Shakespeare Mozart Newton Einstein
Nation	Government	Churchill Nelson Lincoln Alfred the Great Blackstone
City	Banking Finance Trade	Bank of England Shipping Companies
Town	Manufacture Selling Skilled Crafts	Major Firms Town Shops
Village	Production	Miners Farmers Labourers

The word HUMANITY appears vertically spanning the first four rows (Humanity, Civilization, Culture) on the left.

This is the table used by the School of Economic Science to illustrate their theories to their adult classes. We then go on to read about the four Ages — a concept which is pure Hindu cosmology. The child writes:

171

A Great Cycle of time in the life of a universe is called a Mahayuga which lasts for 4,320,000 years. It consists of four ages — yugas.

Golden Age: 1,728,000 years (Sat Yuga)
Silver Age: 1,296,000 years (Treta Yuga)
Bronze Age: 864,000 years (Dwaparyuga)
Iron Age: 432,000 years (Kaliyuga)
One Mahayuga =   4,320,000 years.

The child continues:

In the Golden Age man lives in a paradise under the direct grace of the Absolute. Everything works simply, naturally and beautifully. Man is so happy that relatively few seek to return to the Absolute. This is described as the Garden of Eden in the Bible. The Greek poet Hesiod described it like this: 'They lived like Gods. Misery was unknown to them. Hunger and thirst knew they not.'

It is a principle that everything in creation runs from fine to coarse (sic). It is said that the Golden Age ended when someone somewhere wanted some of this glory for himself. Others followed suit and ignorance entered the world.

Ten days later the child is writing of the Silver Age. The page reads:

In this age men no longer lived under the direct grace of the Absolute. Men are divided into four types of caste:

The Brahmins or wise men: These holy men devote their lives to God.

The Kshatryia: These are the warrior kings. They are noble courageous and just. They serve the wise men.

The Waiskya: These are the merchants. They are rich and love wealth. They are full of enterprise and skill in practical affairs. They serve the Brahmins and Kshatrya.

The Shudra: Full of devotion but without the abilities of other castes. They serve god by serving the other classes of men. The only surviving record of life in the Silver Age is the Ramayana of Valmiki, which was not written down until the end of the bronze age.

172

The legend of the Golden Age is one of the most persistent beliefs in the history of man's religions. Even some African tribes have their own versions of the story. But one can only wonder at its inclusion as concrete fact in the exercise-book of a twentieth-century schoolboy presumably laying down the foundations for O level history.

Another twelve-year-old pupil's Physics exercise-book shows an equally bizarre approach to the subject. Opposite a diagram of a circle with nine equidistant points drawn on the circumference the pupil wrote:

The whole universe and every creature in it is made up from elements.

There are in fact nine of these elements and the numbers on the diagram represent the elements. The first of these elements is pure consciousness which is often called the Absolute. This is the finest substance of all from which all other substances arise. It is so fine that it cannot be seen or touched. It is known only by itself, thus a person may only know it by becoming one with it, but not otherwise.

This consciousness is so fine and so full that nothing can penetrate it, but it can penetrate everything. Just as light penetrates air and water penetrates wood the fine substance of the Absolute penetrates everywhere.

After pure consciousness at one we have element 2. This is said to be the invisible nature of consciousness. Then at Number 3 is the element knowledge. The fourth element to arise in consciousness is very fine indeed but may be experienced by the mind. This element is experienced as the universal feeling of existence. Next in order is element No 5. This element is experienced as space, space is created by sound and we will be studying sound in detail. Then arises the element of air which has amongst its properties that of giving and sustaining life, for air blown onto a smouldering fire will cause it to spring into life. At No 7 we have the element fire and this element is studied in physics as heat and light. Next is Number 8, the element water which is responsible for bonding the whole universe together. Finally to the element earth. Earth is the glorious manifestation of all the elements. We remember that the very fine elements penetrate the coarser ones so that Earth is penetrated by all the elements that come before it.

The Ramayana is an ancient Hindu text.

Later in the book, in a section on Sound, the child has been taught:

> On the circle of nine points there stands at No 5 the element space. This element is exactly halfway between No 1, Pure Consciousness, and Number 9, the Glorious Earth. It is in this space that manifestation first appears. The very first thing to arise in space is Sound. Sound is a vibration which carries energy down from one point to another, sound can create forms and destroy them.
>   On the creation side, it says in the Bible, first verse St John, 'In the beginning was the word and the word was with God and the word was God' . . .

And in studying the element of Air the child states:

> The only real stillness (no measurement at all) is found in the Absolute from which all movement arises and to which all movement returns . . .

As explored in chapter 9, these concepts are essentially Hindu. Elsewhere in the exercise-books the subjects taught revert more or less to a traditional approach to the subjects – but by that time the foundation stones of the SES philosophy have already been laid.

The schools were set up in 1975 by SES members who were dissatisfied with the discipline, curriculum and principles which they saw in state and private schools in Britain. But enrolment was not restricted to the SES, for the schools advertised as normal private establishments.

Members' fears about declining standards had been fuelled at SES group meetings, as a set of 'tutors' notes' from the early 1970s illustrate. At one session in 1970 members were told:

Our concern is for the welfare of the world. Conditions are too urgent for concern about ourselves. No man can be happy on his own, however much he may delude himself to the contrary. The happiness of one is a reflection of the happiness of all; and if all are under a cloud, then no man is exempt.

You cannot be happy when you know that children of five and six are being launched on the road to drug addiction by daily doses 'to take the bounce out of them' and make them less troublesome to their parents. Or that countless young people are challenged every day at their school gates by dope peddlars offering free samples to those who look as if their pocket money would run to regular purchases. Or that educational authorities the world over are outlawing real learning and discipline . . .

Yet happiness is not far below the surface in every being; and to be aware of it, and so remind others of it, is perhaps our first responsibility.

Our second is to remind man of his dignity. How is this achieved? It is one of the fruits of real education . . . And because it affects many of us closely, let us start off with the education of a child . . .

It will be immediately apparent that most so-called education works to obliterate memory of who the child really is (this is called 'developing personality') and reinforces mental and physical habit (which is called 'self-expression' or 'creativity'). Instead of opening up great vistas of man's possibilities, his access to the treasures of universal mind, and the great dignity of his true role in creation, current education hedges the child about with limitations. For the younger one it is done by gearing learning to his environment; so fairy stories are being abandoned because they are not about mum and dad and fish and chips and television and the neighbourhood. For the older child, these limitations are imposed through subject specialization and the lack of demand made upon the real mind . . .

Towards the end of the same term women members were being told:

> We must accept the fact that children recently born may well receive no education at all of any value unless the mothers give it to them.

Some eighteen months later the situation had obviously worsened. Now the O groups were being told:

> Recently it has become clear that the assault on our culture perpetrated by forces within society dedicated to destroying it is growing. The spearhead of this attack is aimed primarily at the undermining of authority.
>
> Some ninety teachers in the school, meeting together just after Christmas, gave their evidence of these attempts to undermine authority in their field. They spoke of school television programmes which lionize criminals and praise anarchy; of a whole new body of nursery rhymes and jingles, urging the children not to accept the government of their teachers; of a highly organized movement to ruin the reputation of certain headmasters, as a prelude to having headmasters removed from their position in the state schools; and of syllabuses (linked to public examinations) designed to bring to an end the formal disciplines of study which carry knowledge of the Western culture.
>
> All this is the beginning of what must develop into a major conflict. It will be our children's war, not ours. But the least we can do is to equip them, so that those who survive may emerge capable of helping to restore a shattered society.

By this time Sunday schools had already been set up for children who attended SES philosophy classes, and attendance for the children was compulsory, unless there were special reasons – such as living too far away – which allowed exemption. With these schools the SES hoped to counter the influence of the education the children received during the week. But it was not enough. More drastic remedies had to be found, and so the Independent

Educational Association Ltd was formed to set up the St James' Schools.

The company, a registered charity, is limited by guarantee and has no share capital. The directors are all SES members of long standing. At the time of *The Standard* story they were Roger Pincham, Bernard White, Bernard Saunders, Emile Woolf (a city accountant), and James Armstrong. Pincham, Saunders and White were also the governors.

The plan was to take children between the ages of five and seven and keep them until their late teens, seeing them through O level, A level, and university entrance exams. MacLaren took an active role in dictating the principles upon which the schools would run, and he appointed the heads.

Nicholas Debenham, a former city businessman who had also taught at Westminster Under-School for a short time became headmaster of the boys' school, and Sheila Caldwell, a former deputy head of Downer Grammar School in North London, took charge of the girls.

The two St Vedast schools, catering for children aged ten and upwards, followed later that year. The accepted wisdom within the SES is that demand for schools for older children had become so great they were forced to expand. If so, they moved very fast indeed, with Debenham and Caldwell now taking charge of two schools each. Then, in 1980, with space at a premium, St Vedast School for Boys moved to Sarum Chase, and shortly afterwards Winchester-educated Julian Capper, a former advertising executive, took over as headmaster.

At first glance the schools appeared to be the answer to many a parent's dreams. The fees were appreciably lower than those of most other British private schools and, particularly appealing in London, there were no waiting lists for places. The school buildings, all lovingly decorated by SES members, created an aura of exclusivity which helped attract predominantly middle-class parents anxious to give their children a good start in life.

The apparent emphasis on academic rigour was underlined by the long school hours, from 8.30 a.m. to 3.30 p.m. for the youngest pupils and 8.00 a.m. to 4.30 p.m. for older children, who were also expected to attend on Saturday mornings from 8.00 a.m. to noon. Homework was given as a matter of course to all but the youngest boys.

The aim of the schools, according to a brochure issued by the Independent Educational Association Ltd, was 'fine and complete men and women'. It continued:

> Only such men and women may stem the current decline into confusion of spirit, thought and conduct and turn the energy, now running down towards violence, corruption and greed, into productive and creative endeavour.

The prospectus for each establishment stated that their aim was 'to provide a finely balanced education to encourage the unfolding and development of the whole person'. They claimed that each school 'seeks to inspire in the children the courage to defend what is simply true against what is plainly false, what is excellent against what is second rate, and what is virtuous against what is not'.

Their task, they claimed, was to render the boys 'effective, intelligent and responsible members of society'. Slightly different wording in the prospectus for the girls' schools gave the merest hint of the underlying SES philosophy towards women. For the girls' education was intended to make them 'useful, intelligent and responsible members of society,' who would be 'trained to serve and be helpful to others'.

But despite these grandiose sentiments, a number of pupils were removed on the strength of *The Standard* story. Other parents sought private meetings with us to find out more about what had prompted the article. *The Standard* stories had already been picked up by the national *Daily Telegraph* and now the BBC radio programme *The World at One* also ran an item based on *The Standard's* findings. That day the schools sent out a letter in a bid to reassure parents.

Sheila Caldwell, headmistress of St James and St Vedast girls' schools wrote:

> The articles in the newspapers are grossly misleading and we

178

are taking legal advice on how to proceed. Meanwhile, some of you may wish to ask questions of me or the Governors. I shall call a meeting of parents within a very short time when you will be able to ask anything you like. Thank you for your supportive attitude.

The meetings took place the following week. More than 500 parents from the two St James Schools and St Vedast girls' school attended a meeting in Baden Powell House, Queen's Gate, and the following night more than 150 parents from St Vedast School for Boys met at Sarum Chase.

A number of parents at both meetings, which were at times stormy affairs, raised the question of the secrecy over the links between the cult and the schools, and the excessive corporal punishment which they claimed took place in the boys' schools. Many who attended, however, were either members or sympathizers of the cult, who spoke out strongly in defence of the schools, and would not believe that others in the room knew nothing of the SES. One parent, the Rev. Stephen Terry, vicar of St John the Apostle, Whetstone in North London, revealed he had been a member of the SES for ten years. He had left two and a half years previously because of pressure of work. His father-in-law, however, is Mr James Armstrong, who at the time of *The Standard* story was treasurer of the SES. Mr Terry's two daughters, then aged eight and six, attended St Vedast School for Girls.

Despite the fact that he was a member of the governing body of St John's Church of England School, Whetstone, Mr Terry told the meeting:

I have seen quite remarkable educational progress – progress that I do not believe is genuinely available in the state system, and certainly isn't available in my own Church of England School. It is available in very few places. It is certainly not a common thing to find educational progress.

Mr Terry was later asked to explain these unusual sentiments by the head of his diocese, the Bishop of Edmonton.

Others who spoke in favour of the schools included David Boddy, the press officer of the SES, who is a former director of press and public relations at Conservative Central Office, and served as a press aide to Margaret Thatcher during the 1983 election. The *Observer* journalist and TV personality Sue Arnold, who is not an SES member, also spoke up. She had three daughters at one of the girls' schools. Father Kenneth Hewitt, vicar of St Augustine's Church, Queen's Gate, which was used for services by the two St James' Schools, also appeared to give the schools his blessing.

In an earlier interview with *The Standard* (see Chapter 8) he had admitted that he was worried by the secrecy of the SES, the anti-church attitude of some of its members, the emphasis on Eastern philosophy, and one of the teaching techniques he had heard used by a young member of staff at one of the schools.

He recalled the teacher, a man, tell a class of children aged about five: 'Don't forget, I am nearer to you than you are to yourselves.' Father Hewitt said the words had shaken him. He considered the teacher had been trying to inculcate absolute obedience into the children. But by the time of the parents' meetings his misgivings had apparently evaporated.

Despite such backing, some parents were not convinced. One mother at the Baden Powell House meeting said afterwards:

> There should have been an independent chairman and the chairman of the Board of Governors should have been there. I feel I haven't had the answer as to whether or not they are indoctrinating children.

Another mother said that the meeting had appeared 'packed' with members of the SES. She added:

> We knew we would be outnumbered. They were all very clever at twisting questions. The whole meeting seems to have been stage managed. They were selective in picking people to ask questions.

180

At both meetings, undertakings were given that the governors would consider forming a parent-teachers' association, and would consider allowing non-SES parents a place on the board of governors. These proposals did much to diffuse criticism, but so far neither development has taken place. In a letter to parents just a week after the meeting at Baden Powell House, the schools informed them that:

> The first thing to state is that we would not agree to the establishment of an association which had power to bring direct influence on the way the schools are run. We would consider that to be unjustifiable interference in the freedom of professional people to do their job. Besides, many parents have urged us not to allow our way of running the schools — which they like and trust — to be subject to pressures of this kind.

Instead, a series of small meetings between form teachers and groups of parents was suggested. If, after these, there was still a desire for such an association, the schools would be willing to meet parents and discuss how it should be set up. The schools added that one important prerequisite would be discussion of the relationship between such an association and the 'existing Friends of St James and St Vedast, a group of supporters from within and without the School of Economic Science who have given very generously of their time, energy and sense of humour over several years'. The Friends organization had not been mentioned to us by the schools at any time during our enquiries.

Late in 1983 the childrens' schools produced a newssheet called *Assembly* about their activities. In an article about the work of the Friends committee, it was revealed that since 1977 they had raised £40,000 for the schools, money which went on such items as laboratory and computer equipment, games equipment, library books, a minibus, cello, and rock climbing and sailing gear. The article stated:

> The function of the committee has been to organize events themselves, to co-ordinate the fund-raising activities of the members and well-wishers, and to liaise with the Governors and

teachers at the schools, so that funds raised may be administered usefully and effectively.

Fund-raising, however, did not appear to be top of the list of priorities of those worried parents who had called for a PTA.

The letter which followed the Baden Powell House meeting added that on the question of non-SES governors:

> After full discussion it was concluded by the Governors that at present, while the schools are still becoming fully established, no further members should be invited to join the board.

But parents were assured:

> We are reviewing our prospectus and other literature to ensure that our relationship with the School of Economic Science is fully acknowledged and all aspects of our education are explained.

At the Baden Powell House meeting Mr Debenham did not defend himself against *The Standard's* claim that not all parents were aware of the schools' links with the SES. Earlier, however, he had told the authors that he always explained to prospective parents the philosophy of the schools – and the connection with the School of Economic Science. But he added, 'It would depend somewhat on what the parent wants to know, obviously'.

At Sarum Chase, Mr Capper had a rougher ride. He told the parents' meeting:

> When parents come here I speak about the links the day school has with the School of Economic Science. The extent to which this link is heard and recognized will depend really on the extent to which I discuss it and it varies considerably. I do say that this building belongs to the School of Economic Science.

'No, never,' shouted a parent. 'It's a deception.'
Mr Capper demurred:

> It's not a deception. Whether it's touched upon, and it may
> seem to be in passing, or whether it's discussed more fully
> depends entirely on what sort of interest there appears to be
> at the interview. It may well be that at an hour-long interview
> several mentions of the School of Economic Science will not
> mean anything, but there's certainly nothing to hide about
> it.

The parent interrupted again: 'Many of these parents were
unaware of it, so it's hidden.'

Capper replied: 'The fact that one is not aware of it
doesn't mean that it's hidden.'

At both meetings pro-SES parents urged the schools to
issue writs for libel against *The Standard*. None have been
forthcoming. For what started as a mere suspicion that the
schools were being used to instill SES philosophies had
quickly hardened into fact, as the authors' research went
further. And the accounts from parents who contacted *The
Standard* in the days following the articles made that fact
unassailable.

In the words of one mother, the wife of a wealthy West End
property consultant whose eleven-year-old son was removed
from St Vedast the day after the story broke:

> The school is the strangest place I have ever seen, with the most
> weird practices. After your article last night he no longer attends.
> It was a combination of what you wrote coupled with my own
> feelings.
>
> When I first sent him there I asked who owned the buildings
> and was told it was the School of Economic Science. They didn't
> tell me that they were connected with it, and anyway, in my
> ignorance, I thought the SES had some connection with the
> London School of Economics.
>
> Where before he loved going to school, he grew to hate it.

He's the youngest of four boys and I could tell it was the school, not him being difficult.

Since the boy was removed, he has been attending a more traditional private establishment where he is said to be a 'changed person'. As will be seen later, this mother's account was by no means isolated.

The exercise-books aside, SES influences could be readily spotted in the curricula of the schools. But to parents who were ignorant of the cult, the influences merely appeared unorthodox – certainly not indicative of ulterior forces at work. Great emphasis, for example, was placed on the teaching of Sanskrit and Philosophy to children from the age of four and a half upwards. The Sanskrit was justified in the curricula with the words:

> Command of language is a key factor in every aspect of life, including the power to lead and undertake responsible positions in the world. The study of language is based on Sanskrit, which is acknowledged to have the finest grammatical system, besides possessing an incomparable literature. Most European and Asiatic languages are closely linked to Sanskrit which provides the student with a key to them all.

No mention was made of the philosophical importance which the SES attaches to this most ancient of languages. It becomes more apparent, however, when reading an article by chairman of the governors Roger Pincham, in the newssheet *Assembly*. He wrote:

> The children are taught the elements of Sanskrit for the purity and clarity of its vowels, as well as for the profundity of the philosophy which is directly expressed in its language. Learning another language gives access to concepts which are not immediately available in our own. This is especially true of the classical languages, and most of all so of Sanskrit.

Capper also explained its function in similar terms at the parents' meeting which took place at his school. He said it was taught in order to gain deeper understanding of the Eastern philosophies which helped the children develop and understand their own natures. He added:

> I must say there is no teacher in our midst who could get anywhere near O level and we don't intend to teach it for any examination. But some understanding of the language is useful to give us some understanding of the philosophy — and it is also clear that as a root-language Sanskrit does deepen broadly one's understanding of classics and indeed all languages.

It was not for purely academic reasons therefore that Sanskrit-chanting took place at morning assembly where the pupils prayed with their hands together in front of their foreheads, as they did at the beginning and end of every lesson. For the philosophical beliefs of the SES, passed to them from the Shankaracharya, were directly embodied in the sounds that were made. And while those philosophic concepts may be perfectly legitimate, they remain beliefs and nothing more. The SES may see them representing perfect truth, but that truth is relative to their own perception. Taught in schools which advertised in the local press as straightforward educational establishments, some may feel this approach to Sanskrit warranted a fuller explanation than the prospectus provided.

And even if one were to accept that the concepts embodied in Sanskrit were the real truth of mankind's place in the universe, it still needs asking who interprets those concepts. In four schools where every teacher was a member of the SES, the answer seemed fairly logical: the SES did.

Two hour-long philosophy lessons were held at the schools every week. Nicholas Debenham, in conversation at least, was rather more open about SES links with that particular subject. In an interview with *The Standard* he said:

> We do teach them philosophy and this is where what the schools do and what the SES does come directly together. I'm sure education needs a clear centre to it. If this were a Church

of England School it would be the religious teaching. If it were a Catholic school it would be that.

I went to a Church of England foundation and the education there was based on the church — the kind of moral training you got and everything. Now that isn't appropriate here and now. The church isn't strong. We have got a lot of different faiths represented here, Muslim, Jewish, Roman Catholic and Church of England. Quite a spread. We wanted to teach something which they would all understand, and which would we hope give them a simple basis for life based on the truths of all religions and all philosophies.

Now that is exactly what the SES in its lectures does; it is what it is trying to achieve. So that is where the two things come into line.

The interview then continued:

Q: You don't expect four to five-year-olds to go into the finer points of philosophy?

A: The philosophy starts at the beginning; it has to.

Q: Is the programme of teaching similar to the SES?

A: No, it is entirely devised by us here. Children need very simple teaching and what they want to know is that there is a God. That is the first lesson.

Q: There are many philosophers who would say you have to keep an open mind. Why teach them there is a God if you are being truly philosophical?

A: Because it's true; it depends what you mean by philosophy.

Q: Is it philosophy if you are teaching four-year-olds that there is a supernatural being?

A: We call it philosophy but in my view any philosophy that denies the existence of God is not much use. It is a universal religion. In my view religion and philosophy are the same thing.

Q: Where does Christ fit in?

A: He fits in as the incarnation of truth. He was the Son of God.

Q: The only Son of God?

A: No, I would hold that Krishna was also the Son of God.

186

Q: So that is where you part company with the Christian church?

A: Quite. That is why I say it is a universal approach.

Earlier in the interview Debenham had volunteered the information that:

So far as I am headmaster, I'm trying to bring up children within the traditions of this country – Christian, monarchist and all that.

Asked now how he could claim the education was Christian, he replied:

Because you have got to take a framework. It doesn't mean that other religions aren't true. In so far as your education is religious, you've got to adopt the culture and religion of the country you're in, and this is Christian, so it is right for us.

Mr Debenham's comments were borne out in the prospectus for his school. Under the heading 'Religious Education' it stated:

St James is open to pupils of all creeds and religious denominations. The teaching of Scripture draws on Christian and other traditions, and the study of Philosophy emphasizes their common features. The School has formed close links with St Augustine's Church, Queen's Gate and Church of England services are held there twice a term. All pupils are expected to attend.

But his concept of philosophy seems rather less than the all-embracing claim in the prospectus that 'From the outset spiritual nourishment is provided by introducing the boys to the great religious and philosophic teachings'.

The prospectus for St Vedast School for Boys included the same sentiments about philosophy and religious education, although in their case 'close links' had been formed with St Vedast alias Foster Church, Foster Lane, in the City of London.

Headmaster Julian Capper told *The Standard* that the approach of his school towards philosophy was the same as that of the SES in that:

> It draws from the same source, but it's not the same in that you are teaching ten-year-olds. When I say the same source, one can draw on our own religious traditions, or the Eastern tradition. There are many remarkable books which give one some guidance on the simple art of living, which is what philosophy is all about.

Asked how far the influence of the Shankaracharya penetrated the school Mr Capper replied:

> It's like everything else. One applies judgement and experience to what a man says whose wisdom one respects and whose guidance one respects. What one finds is that what he says about education is not at all different from what Plato says, or what one knows oneself. This must be the acid test: what one discovers in application.
>
> If you look at the great philosophers of any day, you will find if you really search deep that they are all saying the same thing. They may have branched out into different traditions, different expressions.
>
> As far as I am concerned the essence of philosophy — under which title you could have a discussion about practically everything under the sun — is to enable a human being to be more in touch with his surroundings, to have some understanding of his own essence and his own direction in life which he would find satisfying, with a certain permanence about it. Even though his job may come and go, even though his family may come and go, even if he lands on the dole queue, there's a certain permanence established in him, a certainty of knowledge. A knowledge about oneself which is not shaken whether an elephant or mouse walks through the door, or the world collapses. He has a certain anchor.

But Philosophy for five-year-olds was not the only surprise in the schools' curricula. Other curiosities included calligraphy, and a marked lack of emphasis on teaching modern foreign languages. All children learned Sanskrit, and from the age of ten also Greek and Latin. French, however, was not taught at all to junior pupils and remained optional for the over tens. One mother, who was an SES member for more than ten years and whose son and daughter attended the St Vedast schools said:

'There was the idea in the SES that Sanskrit was the only conscious language. All others were impure. I was told by my tutor that it was impossible to tell the truth in English. Of course the childrens' schools hardly bothered about modern foreign languages. Why should they? They are impure.'

Another parent cynically pointed out that by neglecting to teach pupils the rudiments of French, they were effectively closing the doors to other schools for the pupils should their parents wish to remove them.

In the curricula at the boys' schools one strange addition to the subjects taught was boxing. Boys had to take part from the age of four and a half to fifteen. The prospectus claimed that it was primarily intended 'as training in courage and chivalry'. In the Sports Report section of *Assembly* it was explained further:

It is the English art of self-defence. The method teaches courage, perseverance, skill under duress, coolness under attack, and a certain tough confidence when facing their peers. It's difficult to be a bully or a gangster in a school where every boy can stand up for himself. All boys fight at some time and it is essential that a man learns to fight in a disciplined and clean manner . . .

It has been very clear from the years during which we have practised this sport that many boys have conquered their early fears of pain or discomfort, and a sportsmanship has been engendered in the school where everybody who gives a reasonable account of himself is appreciated by the rest.'

While it all sounds vaguely convincing, it was perhaps a curious sport to make compulsory, especially for four-year-olds. Such an approach could foster as many feelings of inadequacy as of tough confidence. Sniffed one mother:

> Actually it's just two little boys hitting each other until one of them cries.

For senior boys, the emphasis on being able to look after themselves was taken even further, with membership of the Army Cadets compulsory from the age of thirteen upwards. Few opportunities were lost to show the boys off in their uniform. Open day at St Vedast School for Boys shortly before *The Standard* stories appeared featured two khaki-clad pupils rigidly at attention on either side of the front door. Those who attended an Independent Educational Association fund-raising evening at the City of London's ornate Barber-Surgeons' Hall were greeted with a similar, slightly incongruous, sight.

If this represented the traditional role for the boys, at the girls' schools modesty and decorum reigned, with senior pupils finding themselves obliged to go into ankle-length skirts at the age of sixteen. Headmistress Sheila Caldwell appeared reluctant to explain why she favoured long dresses when asked at the meeting which took place at St Vedast School for Boys. One non-SES mother asked:

> Could you tell me why the ladies connected with this school wear long skirts. I've asked because I think the truthful answer is that it is very important. I've been told that you all think it's very pretty and I don't believe that answer.

Caldwell replied:

> We do think that quite a lot of ladies prefer it. It gives them more dignity and stature. Most of us who wear them enjoy wearing them. Some ladies don't wear them all the time. I do. We think it is good to encourage young people to see people

well-dressed, and to take some trouble about it. I hope that satisfies you.

But the questioner pressed further:

Is it something in your philosophy that believes that women have to cover themselves. I would like to know.'

Caldwell admitted:

Yes, that is so.

Then why didn't you say that? Why did you just say that it looked smarter? I would like to know the truth. Why do you wear long skirts?

And at last the truth came out:

The truth is that ancient tradition has it that a lady does have her body completely covered. I do say to the girls, I said to some today, that it's only in this century as far as I know that this has changed.

One suspects that one must turn to the Shankaracharya's notes on 'The Education of Children and Young People' for a fuller explanation. In a copy of the notes distributed within the SES he says:

The age of sixteen is a dividing factor in the individual's life. It is up to this age the capital which has been provided to the individual is practically disposed of. After sixteen the life is more of a routine based on previous (before-sixteen) learning. The capital which is provided to the individual is the consciousness (brilliance and power) which he brings with him in this life. Thus it is up to the age of sixteen that most care is needed. It is at this stage that a discipline can take a firm root, and the life could become easy and happy. If the individual has spent his brilliance and power of consciousness in fruitless pursuits he really becomes destitute and leads a poor life. For such people a readjustment is difficult and hard, though not impossible . . .

Those who have no experience of the sexual realm usually have their character all right. When this takes place (at sixteen) all energies available to the individual are directed to this region, like a roaring stream. Usually the individual loses the concept of past and future, and all that remains is the present in this realm. The sensory, mental and intellectual levels are all affected by its force, and constant involvement with this realm comes into play. This limits progress in other fields because of the continuous bombardment of related impressions. Those engulfed with such impressions need some sort of instruction and discipline to ward off its effect.

The age of sixteen being the dividing factor, those before sixteen have their capital safe, fresh and unspoiled, because there hasn't been the chance to spoil. For them there isn't such a question to be considered. It arises for those over that age on whom such impressions are predominant. It is at this stage that the desire for worldly physical wants increases, and if the measures are upset then the question of character building arises. Then they need instruction for good character.

In relation to sexual laxity, too much association between boys and girls must be restricted. As far as the atmosphere in the society is concerned, which is the most impressive factor of all, through which they get these ideas and walk into the traps, hard discipline is necessary, either from parents or from those responsible to handle these people. Unless there is an authority to which, even through fear, they learn to respond, it is difficult to keep them from drowning in the deadly stream. Training and disciplining girls would be most fruitful. If one took care of the girls, the boys would behave themselves. So establishing a good appreciation of measure, related to every walk of life, in the minds of the girls, is most necessary. India, since ancient time, has held women in great respect. First of all the concept of goddesses like Shakti, Lakshami etc. associated with women. Shakti is incarnate sixteen-years-old, beautiful and fully developed forms of most pleasing measure. So when one looks at a young girl one sees divinity.

It seems that if a reverence and honour for womanhood is created in the minds of people, their attitude would change. For example, some young people have a young mother, young sister, or others have a young daughter, but they never have a carnal desire toward them. It is all because of an idea, although the form, the desires and the relation of male and female is just the same. Thus education of girls on measure and reverence towards womenfolk may well control this situation.

The ancient Indian tradition places women in three levels according to their age. From birth to the age of sixteen a girl is addressed as daughter, from sixteen to thirty or thirty-two they are addressed as sisters, and from thirty-two and upwards they are addressed as mothers. Most of the reasonable men still practise this. Once you bind yourself to these relationships, there arises a natural restraint.

In notes made by the SES about the Shankaracharya's view, members are told:

The age of sixteen should be taken quite literally. This is not a period of life which shifts with a shift in the average age of adolescence. There may well have been sexual exploration and experience before this age. But the opening of the sexual realm, as the Shankaracharya describes it, is of much wider import than sex as normally understood.

Whether these notes contain guidance given by the Shankaracharya, or simply the interpretation of his message by members of the school, is not clear. However, they continue that the two early references to 'discipline' by the Shankaracharya carry a much wider and deeper implication.

It should be understood as that which grounds a student in truth. When we speak of discipline in the classroom – for example whether the pupils are sitting in their places, listening to the teacher, paying attention, writing tidily etc. – we are speaking of basic conditions which the Shankaracharya takes for granted. Discipline – true teaching – begins when all this is in place.

The Shankaracharya's views presumably account for the SES belief, as explained by one former member, that 'a woman is not considered to have any powers of discretion until the age of thirty-two.' And it would also explain the fierce strictures at the boys' schools against pupils having girl-friends. Nicholas Debenham seems to have carried this zealous attitude even further at an 'urgent meeting' of parents called early in 1984 where the main topic under discussion was his concern about children listening to pop music. This music, he felt, would lead them straight to sexual activities.

The Shankaracharya also gives his blessing to another practice at the schools, that of meditation for children aged ten and upwards. It was not compulsory, and parents had to give written permission, but there is clear evidence that teachers actively encouraged pupils to take it up. Those that did underwent the full initiation at the School of Meditation. Says the Shankaracharya:

> The meditation can also be given for all cleansing processes for development of pure being.

Children who took it up started by doing five minutes at the beginning and end of each day. By the time they were sixteen, the sessions were twenty minutes long.

The pressure on non-meditators to take part included letters to parents from the schools extolling the merits of the technique. Teachers also sometimes encouraged pupils already initiated to give pep talks to those who were not, and some former pupils claimed that those who did not meditate had to do chores, such as cleaning classrooms and moving furniture.

Said Capper:

> Of course some boys will see it this way. The fact is that everybody tidies their classroom after the last lesson and this house has to be cleaned. It depends entirely on who is available. It's certainly not a question of either/or.

The mystique and secrecy which surrounds the initiation ceremony must be every bit as awesome to the youngster as a Roman Catholic's first communion. This also worried some parents.

One father, whose son had just started at St Vedast, expressed his feelings at the parents' meeting. He said:

> I would like to confirm that Mr Capper did tell us at the interview that the place was rented from the SES. I must admit that it just didn't mean a thing. I didn't know what the SES was and I failed to ask questions. Having listened to various comments and having read bits in the papers, I am very sorry I don't know more about the SES. I would like to know more to make up my mind whether the connection is good or bad. I am not in a position to at the moment and I feel uneasy for that reason.
>
> Confirming what was said earlier about meditation and the fact it was done with parental consent: we were asked to give our answer in writing. We took our son along to the initiation. He seemed very happy about it, and he still seems very happy about it. But one thing that bothered me was that after the initiation he told us that quite simply he couldn't tell us anything about it. We didn't press him but I would like to know why parents can't be told.

Mr Capper was understanding itself as he replied:

> I can speak from the point of view of one who meditates and whose initiation occurred many years ago. If anybody had told me what it was like to be initiated, I wouldn't have received it openly and wholeheartedly. I couldn't, because I would have had the experience of another individual standing in front of me as a sort of comparison.
>
> I went into it with quite an open mind. Meditation isn't available only for children. It's available for every human being. And it is a protection for the human being who does not yet meditate that he's not told in advance about it by anybody else. Because if he were, he might not go ahead. It's for his protection so that the door remains open. He comes to it from his own direction, his own desire and not from what another person says.

195

So at this level, the difference between parent and child disappears.

All children, whether or not they meditate, took part in the process known as 'pausing' at the start and end of each lesson. For two minutes they had to remain quiet and motionless in the SES manner, with knees together and hands resting palms down on their legs. The purpose, according to Mr Capper, was to ensure that they began any new activity 'from stability rather than emotion'.

The practice was not confined to the classroom. One twelve-year-old boy told us that while crossing Hampstead Heath with his class he met up with friends from his former school. As greetings were being exchanged, the teacher had called on the class to 'pause' where they were standing. The boys' resulting stance caused much merriment among his former contemporaries. The technique is, of course, used at the beginning and end of adult SES sessions.

Other SES influences at the schools included the diet, which was simply termed 'vegetarian'. In fact it was the same diet that SES members follow, culled from the Gospel of Peace, including wholemeal bread, cheese, butter, fruit, yoghurt, untreated milk, honey and nuts. For the children, however, there was also the addition of green vegetables.

No child was allowed to help himself, but had to be offered food by others at the table, and all the items had to be eaten in a certain order, the fruit first of all and the honey last. And while putting the butter on bread was allowed, the cheese had to be eaten separately. Hot meals, even in winter, were only provided as a special 'treat'.

The school uniform also accorded exactly with the dictates of the SES – only natural fibres allowed in the garments. This made them expensive items of clothing.

The emphasis on service for the girls was explained by Sheila Caldwell in an interview in 1979 with an education correspondent. She said of her pupils:

They need fully occupying, of course, and once they are over the age of eight or nine we give them quite a lot to do in the

196

way of service, looking after one another and looking after teachers. For instance, we say, 'You look after the school secretary this term'. The girl will go along after her lessons and ask the secretary if she's got any messages. They love it. Or she may fetch a tray for the secretary at lunch before her own . . .

But in fact in the past it has gone rather further than that, with senior girls being used as extra weekend help at Stanhill Court, cleaning and cooking for SES groups in residence there.

The persuasion to join the SES began when the pupils reached their mid-teens. The children of SES members would generally already have joined and non-SES youngsters were encouraged to follow suit. Said one girl:

The pressure put on them was fairly subtle. They were made to feel that it was the thing to do. All their friends were doing it.

Those that did join SES philosophy groups at the schools attended week-long residential courses at Waterperry or Stanhill Court, working in the gardens or kitchens, or cleaning the building. They were also expected to rise at dawn for meditation.

At one time senior pupils at the schools, whether or not they were SES-members, would be expected as a matter of course to attend several weekends a year at one or other of the mansions, where sleep would be restricted and the emphasis placed on philosophy rather than normal school pursuits.

SES influences aside, one of the greatest criticisms levelled against the boys' schools was the alleged use of excessive corporal punishment to maintain discipline. Canings were common from the two headmasters — they claimed only for serious offences — and other teachers were said to use the slipper or a ruler for lesser wrongs. A black-mark system meant that prefects were able to ensure pupils got caned.

And at St Vedast, cold showers were given, even in winter, for misdemeanours such as unpunctuality.

The emphasis on punishment could be seen as simply a reflection of the schools' approach to character building. But as one mother explained:

> The boys obeyed because they were beaten into submission. I would stress that they were submissive rather than obedient. I even heard of one child beaten for sniggering in philosophy, and another for not singing loudly enough.

The mother is one of several former-SES women who fought long battles to remove their children from the schools against the wishes of their former husbands, who are still staunch members of the cult. In all cases, the schools sided entirely with the husbands, making representations to the courts on their behalf. The woman added:

> My children were not getting on academically and were not happy. The children didn't want to learn because of the atmosphere. They were just sat on. You can't make a child learn. All you can do is put it in a situation where its natural desire to learn comes out. It was all clamping down; there was no encouragement.
>
> If you heard the boys talking about the schools, they were almost always talking about caning and punishment. It seemed that the positive side of any activities didn't make nearly as much impression as the harshness.

At the parents' meeting at Baden Powell House, one angry mother whose son went to St James said:

> I was shocked when my son, who is only five years old, told me he was struck on the hands with a ruler by his teacher. What's worse, older boys are now striking the little ones on the hands in the playground. Where do we go from here? Will my boy start hitting my two-year-old baby?

Mr Debenham's denial that any form of punishment

greater than a slap on the hands was ever imposed by his teachers on the juniors failed to placate the mother. And she was incensed when Mr Debenham added that nobody was ever harmed by the 'occasional judicial use of pain'.

She replied:

> Surely that goes against the fundamental principles of the schools to treat problems thoughtfully and spiritually?

Both Debenham and Capper had explained their attitude to corporal punishment in earlier interviews with *The Standard*. Said Debenham:

> The discipline is not savage. That is nonsense. I'm always very careful to explain the situation to parents. I don't want children whose parents don't want what I supply. I use the cane. It's reserved for serious offences like stealing, lying, cheating or gross insolence, which are very rare.

Debenham went on to deny that cold showers were used, saying the question sounded malicious. Capper, however, was happy to admit that the regime at his school included cold showers.

> There's nothing wrong with a cold shower, even in winter. It's used as a means of waking them up.

He added:

> I cane boys. I alone do it. I tell every prospective parent who comes to the school.

The offences which warranted it were said to be lying, cheating and stealing.

> They discover early on that for those offences the cane is supplied. For most it only happens once, but some need this sanction more than once. It's fairly rare though.

199

Asked whether teachers could give the slipper he replied:

> The only physical punishment is me applying the cane. There's no other. Someone may get a rap over the knuckles; I wouldn't exclude that.

The claims of the two headmasters do not accord with the many witnesses with whom we have spoken. And STOPP, the Society of Teachers Opposed to Physical Punishment, after interviewing a dozen cases, called in June 1984 for a government enquiry into beatings at the two boys' schools.

They wrote to the Secretary of State for Education, Sir Keith Joseph:

> These disturbing complaints about frequent and severe beatings and other physical punishments will cause great public concern. To safeguard the wellbeing of children attending these schools, we urge you to use your powers under Section 93 of the 1944 Education Act to establish an enquiry to investigate these serious complaints.

STOPP also called on the Archbishop of Canterbury to condemn corporal punishment at the schools, and asked him to warn Anglicans against sending their children there. And they urged *The Guardian* newspaper to cease carrying advertisements for the two establishments.

STOPP claimed that beatings were frequently administered at both schools. These were sometimes severe and left the victims badly bruised. The punishment was often given for trivial reasons, including the black-mark system by which prefects could effectively ensure that a boy was caned.

At St Vedast STOPP highlighted the case of two twelve-year-old boys caned for eating chocolate on a school trip to the university rugby match. They also claimed that one teacher frequently slippered boys in front of the class for 'trivial' offences. And they criticized the use of cold showers.

They also complained about a fourteen-year-old boy from

St James School who was caned so severely as to be badly bruised. His offence was of amassing too many black marks, one of which was given for having his hands on the table while meditating.

Despite the revelations of June 1983, followed by the STOPP investigation, the Department of Education and Science in Britain have consistently refused to order a full enquiry into the SES schools.

HM Inspectors visit all independent schools periodically to enable the Secretary of State to take action, under Section 71 of the Education Act 1944, against any which fall below the minimum acceptable standards.

Following *The Standard* stories, a DOE spokesman said:

> As far as St Vedast and St James schools are concerned, HMI have visited them in the past and not found anything seriously amiss.

In 1984 the Department rejected STOPP's demand for an enquiry saying:

> We have had no complaints from parents. In fact, our impression is that parents are in favour of the retention of corporal punishment. It is highly unlikely that we would start looking into complaints after a letter from an organization in this manner. We would have to be convinced that legally speaking the schools were objectionable before the Secretary of State would do anything about it.

The STOPP campaign came at a bad time for St Vedast School for Boys. Just two days earlier, Julian Capper had written to parents warning them of the dire financial position of the school. He said that funding covenants had expired and the Independent Educational Association had decided that they could no longer subsidize the school. The governors had therefore decided to close St Vedast from September 1984, the intention being that pupils should apply for transfers to St James.

But Capper had managed to do a deal with the governors.

Parents had *two weeks* in which to raise sufficient money to keep the school going. The amount needed was considerable. Some £30,000 would ensure the school's existence for a further year, and another £20,000 would give it two years' grace. By that time Capper anticipated that the school would be self-sufficient.

Among the reasons for the predicament were newspaper stories about the SES. Capper wrote:

> Many parents will recall the unwarranted attack which was made upon us in the Press last year, and will share my view that it would be especially deplorable if St Vedast Boys were to close as a result of the setback in numbers caused by that attack. We started this academic year with thirty pupils fewer than were registered before the articles in the Press appeared.

By the end of the first day he had received over £3,000 in pledged support, and with just three days to the deadline donations and pledged support stood at £23,500. Donations continued to pour in and the school was saved. £34,000 had been raised in two weeks.

St Vedast School for Girls was not so fortunate, and closed at the end of the 1984 summer term. The official reason given was that a boom in the primary school section of St James School for Girls at Queen's Gate meant there was no room for any new pupils at St Vedast, which was based in the same building. Some parents claim, however, that St Vedast had also been badly hit by the press articles. Whatever the reason for the closure, St Vedast pupils were merged with senior girls at St James, who by then had been moved into the SES building in Chepstow Villas.

The move to Chepstow Villas for St James senior girls was not an ideal solution, and before long the Independent Educational Association's Building Fund Appeal had sent out more than a thousand letters to 'all the people who have supported us previously, including parents'. Their aim was to raise between £700,000 and a million pounds for new premises. How successful they have been is not yet known.

The only real success story seemed to be St James School for Boys. In the winter of 1983 junior pupils were moved to Queen's Gate, while the secondary pupils moved to new premises in Ecclestone Square, Central London. The building there was the first to be purchased by the Independent Educational Association, and cost them £600,000, a good proportion of the money coming from the building-fund appeal.

The fund's patrons at the time of *The Standard's* initial investigations included the late actor Sir Ralph Richardson, who told the authors that he knew nothing of the School of Economic Science. Other patrons, Sir Lennox Berkeley, an eminent composer and President of the Performing Rights Society, and Sir Thomas Armstrong, a former Principal of the Royal Academy of Music, were in a similar position. Two other patrons, the judge Sir Kenneth Jupp, and the Recorder of London, James Miskin, refused to discuss their involvement. Jupp did not reply to either written or telephoned requests for information, and all Miskin would say was, 'I am afraid I cannot help'.

Today the schools do mention the School of Economic Science in their prospectus, and point out that secondary-school pupils can take up meditation (the word transcendental is omitted). The SES is, according to the prospectus, an absolutely worthwhile organization.

> The Fellowship of the School of Economic Science is an educational charity running a school for adult part-time students. It was established over forty years ago to study the natural laws governing relations between men in society, and it offers courses in economics and philosophy in London and a number of provincial towns and cities. It also acts as a sponsor of the arts, promoting new and worthwhile initiatives in art, music and education . . . The curriculum of St James and the philosophy that is central to it owe most of their original features to the studies carried out within the School of Economic Science. Present members of the staff are also students of the School . . .

Late in 1983 the schools all sought accreditation from the Independent Schools Association (not to be confused with the Independent Educational Association Ltd). The association is an umbrella body safeguarding the interests of most private schools in Britain. They carry out their own inspections before admitting schools to their ranks, and endeavour to uphold educational standards. Their backing is a marked asset to any school seeking new pupils.

Nicholas Debenham went so far as to describe it as 'the only objective seal of approval granted to independent schools'. He added:

> Accreditation would be a major step forward. It would end some of the crazier rumours about us. Parents would be reassured. It would make association with other schools — which is vital to our development — much easier. It would bring in many more pupils.

Whether they succeeded or not is unknown at the time of going to press.

Whatever the verdict, and whatever the problems the schools face in overcoming the suspicions they have raised by keeping their links with the SES secret, it is highly unlikely that the cult will relinquish their self-imposed task of moulding future generations into the SES version of model citizens.

As Peter Green, principal of the SES, said at the start of our enquiries:

> I hope that within two or three hundred years' time there will be a line of schools there which are something like the grammar schools have been over the generations.

The following case histories raise the question whether that is a prospect to look forward to — or to dread.

One eleven-year-old boy attended St Vedast for a year, but was then removed, in 1981, because of the 'excessive discipline'. His mother said:

> I was not particularly happy about the local school my son was attending and a married couple we knew who were SES

members suggested we sent him to St Vedast, which at that time was in Kensington.

When we went to see the headmaster, who was Mr Debenham, I asked if they were the same as the SES and he said it was just a school that had been set up to help people like ourselves who didn't have that much money. He added that they were looking for new premises in the same area.

The headmaster seemed quite nice, rather quiet and shy, and we were totally impressed by how polite and nicely mannered the pupils were. It seemed to be everything that we were looking for.

We went away for a summer holiday and came back to find that the school was to be moved to Hampstead. As we live in West London we would never have dreamed of sending him that far away, but there was no time to make alternative arrangements so we were stuck with it. We had been given no warning that such a move was imminent. It meant my son getting up at 6 a.m. every day, and when he came home at night he would bring so much homework he was often studying until midnight.

At first he seemed to be settling in quite well and enjoying himself. But I began to get worried about what was going on when a prefect kicked him while he was doing press-ups as a punishment, and injured his wrist. I complained to the school, but could get nowhere.

Then one day my son phoned home very frightened to say that Mr Capper, who was headmaster by then, had ordered him to have a cold shower because the top button of his shirt was undone. I told him I would phone the school secretary. I hadn't realized that the school had cold showers as a punishment, and I told her that on no account was he to have one. She said she would see what she could do, but doubted whether she could stop it.

Fifteen minutes later she phoned back to say the punishment had been carried out, so I told her to send the boy home. As I realized that he had no money for the fare, I requested that the school lent him enough for the underground and I would reimburse them.

When he got home it turned out that he had had to borrow

some money from another pupil. It wasn't enough, and so he had walked to Hampstead tube station and borrowed some more from the newspaper seller there.

It was a bitterly cold November day, and because he didn't have a towel with him at school, he had had to climb back into his clothes dripping wet. His hair was still soaking when he got home. The little chap was just eleven years old. I thought it was disgraceful, and he didn't go back.

I kept him at home until I could get him into a proper prep school the following January. After he had left, I was sent a letter from the headmaster saying that if I didn't do something with my son he would lead to bad things in future. I mean, he's just an ordinary child. He might talk a bit, but he's not that boisterous.

If you have too much discipline in a school without any family atmosphere, it's going to make a child hate school. That's exactly what happened to my son, he loathed the place by the time he left.

The second case was a well-known London broadcaster who removed her eleven-year-old son from St Vedast School in 1982. She told us:

My son was there for nearly a year and thank God I pulled him out. There is no way a child can leave that school after the age of about twelve and hope to get into public school. The standard is diabolical. He was getting the education that a nine-year-old would have been receiving elsewhere. The lack of French stops the boys doing the normal Common Entrance exam so they have to stay on there.

I saw the light after an incident which occurred in a Latin test. My son had been making his chair squeak and the teacher told him to get another one. When that also squeaked, he was punished in the most bizarre way.

He was told to remove his trousers in front of the whole class and he had to complete the lesson in his underpants, kneeling at his desk. The rest of the class of course were sniggering at him. When I found out I went to the teacher and asked what he had been trying to achieve by humiliating my son.

I said, 'Little boys of eleven are lavatorial enough without you making it worse'. And all the teacher could say was, 'That's hardly the point'.

There was always the threat of the cane hanging over the boys, and the threat of cold showers. I know my son was slippered at least twice by his form teacher. I am not one of those mothers who agrees with the abolition of corporal punishment. I think on odd occasions a boy might need a good whack. But there seemed to be such an emphasis on it. The boys were over-polite out of fear.

When I first visited the school I was impressed by the calmness of everybody. The children were all very polite and I thought it would be good for my son. I didn't want him to go to a comprehensive.

After about six weeks I started asking people why all the women wore long dresses and then I learnt that there was this strange group called the School of Economic Science. Before that I had no idea what the SES was.

Now I think that a boy going through the whole system from four and a half to eighteen would come out like a zombie, because they are trained to think in a certain way; he would lose his spontaneity. If anything, they teach children not to be able to cope with present-day living because they don't know what's going on in the outside world.

Their philosophy was brought into everything, whether it was history, geometry, scripture or science. And they taught that women were basically hysterical, inferior creatures. Once my son's teacher told the class that the man was head of the family, and oldest son next in line.

My son stuck his hand up and said his mother was divorced, so she was head of his family. 'Oh no', replied the teacher, 'you are'. I was furious. But it was indicative of their general attitude. As a divorced woman I felt that at various school meetings my opinion counted for nothing. There was a kind of 'dear, dear, pat her on the head' attitude.

Other aspects about the school which bothered this

particular mother were the power prefects seemed to have over younger boys, and the cleaning chores which pupils had to carry out in their expensive school uniforms. She also took exception to the vegetarian diet when she learned that the same food was provided day in, day out, with only slight variation.

The property consultant's wife already mentioned removed her son from St Vedast the day *The Standard* story broke. The boy, aged eleven, had been there just one-and-a-half terms. She told us:

My son had been attending a very progressive school where there had been discipline problems. I wanted something that would prepare him better for public school and I came across St Vedast quite by accident. A friend of mine, who has now also removed her son, told me about it.

I got the feeling that it was very weird from the moment that I sent him there. But when you go for the interview and are told what they do they skirt over things very quickly. They don't put a lot of emphasis on the unorthodox aspects of their approach.

They did tell me that they rented the building from the SES but they didn't tell me that they were connected. Anyway, I had no idea that the SES was some kind of sect.

The first thing that made me think something was funny was that all the women connected with the place wore long skirts. I asked the teacher why and I was told it was because they thought it looked prettier.

My suspicions were reinforced at the beginning of the second term when he got a black mark for not running fast enough, which I thought was ridiculous. He was also given cold showers for various trivial offences, and then I found out that for being inattentive in class he had been made to spend the rest of the lesson changing from his ordinary uniform into his sports kit in front of the rest of the form while they carried on working. Another time he was made to do squats with his hands on his head fifty times during a lesson. And on four occasions the prefects, who have a lot of power there, prevented him having his lunch for some offence or other and made him wash up and do other chores. The school day lasted from 8 a.m. until 4.30 p.m. and he was given nothing to eat!

When my son became very discouraged, I asked his teacher to have a talk with him. My son told me later that the talk had gone something like, 'I hear you're not very happy here and you feel very discouraged,' and I thought great, he's reassured him. But apparently all the teacher went on to say was, 'You must believe in the Absolute, the power of the Absolute'. I wanted him to help the child and all he did was go on about philosophy!

On another occasion I went with my husband to ask the teacher what all the meditation was about. We were shown up into a little room with a picture on the wall of someone I can only describe as an Indian guru. When I put my question the teacher said, 'Well, we go like this,' and putting both hands on his knees he sat up very straight and went into a trance which lasted nearly five minutes. We just couldn't keep straight faces. It was like a scene from a Mel Brooks film. We left and my husband said, 'Get the boy out, it's a loony bin'.

All this, coupled with the fact that the standard of work there seemed very, very low, made me think we should look for another school. The newspaper article confirmed it. I now feel I was very misled; they didn't tell us what was behind it all.

Case number four was related by the mother of two St James schoolboys, one aged six, the other fourteen. The six-year-old had been at the school for two years, the older boy for one year. She had known nothing about the School of Economic Science when she first sent her children to the school. Following the parents' meeting at Baden Powell House she decided to keep her children on in the hope that things would improve. She was disappointed, and a year later removed them. She said:

It didn't get better, it got worse. So many children left after the newspaper articles that I seldom saw any non-SES parents.

And those of us that were left were kept completely in the dark. There was a terrific gulf. As for the Friends organization, I don't think there was one non-SES representative on it.

I think the truth was not told to me at the beginning. For a school that places so much emphasis on truth they seem to tell an awful lot of lies; they lie by omission.

Several events which took place in the terms following the parents' meeting convinced me that my children would be better out of it. The first, which made me absolutely furious, was that my son was beaten for having his hands on the table when he was supposed to be meditating. They had a conduct book and if your name went into it four times you were beaten. Well, his name went in and as it was his fourth entry he was caned.

Then I got a letter saying that an urgent meeting of parents was being called. I thought it was something of world-shattering importance and I asked my oldest boy what it was all about. He said it was about the boys listening to pop music. I told him not to talk rubbish but he insisted it was to remind parents that their children shouldn't listen to pop music or see girls. Apparently they are terribly uptight about boys listening to such music because they think their minds are going to be brainwashed and the music will lead them straight to sex.

I went to the meeting and said I took my children to pop concerts, and that I also took them to classical concerts. I said there was a wonderful atmosphere at pop concerts and they said no, you come out on an unhealthy high. I said I've come out of operas on a high but they replied that was different.

Then a woman stood up and said she just didn't know what was wrong with her teenage boy as he kept going to his room to listen to pop music. She said that she talked about all the world affairs with her son and just couldn't understand it. I thought poor kid – he probably just wants to be a normal teenager sometimes.

Naturally, given a combined roll of some 600 pupils, there was a variety of opinion. There were many parents – not all of them SES members – who were well satisfied with the education their children were receiving. The following

210

excerpts were among the views expressed to the authors following the original newspaper stories.

An Essex man, whose parents and other relatives had been in the SES, wrote:

> I have a young cousin who attends one of the schools in Kensington. Like all her friends, she knows that *Vogue* is far, far more essential to daily life than the Vedic scriptures.

A mother who sent her children to the St Vedast schools wrote:

> In the mid-seventies, when many state schools were changing to comprehensive education, some members of the SES, at the urgent request of concerned parents, set up the four independent schools.
>
> Although not ever a member of the SES myself my trust was such that my children were among the first to attend the St Vedast Schools. To make this decision was easy — the schools set out to teach truthfulness, as well as the normal secondary education, with discipline, in peaceful surroundings. This I believe they still do to a large extent.
>
> There are some aspects which may be difficult to understand, but these are harmless. The teaching of Sanskrit, for example, is enjoyed, especially by the younger children. It is fun, and beautiful to write, as well as being the basis for all Indo-European language. The uniforms may be old-fashioned — but the girls who attend these schools do look like young ladies, and not the more usual denimed, unisex clones.
>
> Yes, there is corporal punishment for the boys. It is no secret. Nor is it harmful. I amongst many survived post-war Scottish education with the tawse very much in evidence. Once administered, a cane can be put aside; but it remains a deterrent.
>
> The children attending these schools come from many religious backgrounds. They are taught to appreciate the different beliefs, and that encompassing all beliefs there is one creator.

I cannot believe prospective parents of the school are unaware of the connections with the SES. I certainly was not. I agree there could be an air of secretiveness. I believe it is a quietness in an effort not to misinterpret the teachings of the school.

A non-SES mother with two sons at St James School said:

The standard of the educational system in England at the moment stinks — and there are very few schools that recognize this.

The children at St James are fantastic. They are not suppressed, repressed or worried about corporal punishment. And they don't go around with their heads in the clouds. They are very very self-aware, caring and loving, as are the teachers.

You can ring up the teachers or headmaster at any time of day or night. We are given their home telephone numbers from day one. They will spend ages with you; they're in no hurry to get you off the phone. I think it's a wonderful thing to have that. None of the state schools that I have sent my children to in the past have had that.

This mother also found it difficult to believe that some parents had no knowledge of the SES. She said:

One presumably goes into things pretty deeply before choosing a school for one's child.

But even among fellow-supporters of the schools there were some who had known nothing about the links with the SES. Said the mother of two girls at St Vedast, one aged twelve and the other fourteen:

The articles were the first time that I heard of the SES. I had no idea about it, but I don't think it would have made any difference to me. Let's say they do have some connection, as far as I'm concerned the teachers do not project this to the

212

children at all. So long as it doesn't affect my children in any way, it's not going to bother me.

I fully support the school. It's a very good, old-fashioned school and as far as I'm concerned my children have not been indoctrinated. Parents can normally figure out what's going on and I find my children absolutely normal.

I don't approve of fourteen-to-fifteen-year-olds going out dating, smoking and drinking. One of the differences between St Vedast and a lot of other schools is that the children are not that way inclined towards sex and alcohol. Miss Caldwell may be very old-fashioned. She may insist that teachers and students wear dresses down to their toes.

When I was young I went to a private Church of England school where the teachers were even stricter. That didn't turn me out too badly. I think there ought to be a lot more Miss Caldwells about.

My children have been there a year. They were at a comprehensive school which left me most unimpressed. And I was horrified at the so-called top schools where the end results were fourteen-year-olds who were pregnant, and drinking and smoking.

The emphasis on good behaviour also appeared to be a key factor in the views of a grandmother of four IEA pupils. She and her husband were not members of the SES, although the children's parents were.

She wrote describing her grandchildren – who were aged from seven to twelve – as 'particularly happy, polite and well-behaved' youngsters who showed no signs of brainwashing or indoctrination. The same comments, she added, applied to other IEA pupils that she had met. She went on:

We are very proud of our grandchildren and consider that their school education has contributed substantially to their good behaviour, happy outlook, sense of responsibility and consideration for others of whatever colour, social standing or creed.

213

The woman added that the vegetarian diet at the schools could hardly be said to be either undesirable or unique to the SES, and that while corporal punishment was administered where justified, it was subject to the same control as in many other British schools.

The woman also pointed out that it was not uncommon for some children to be unhappy at school, and IEA parents had the remedy immediately to hand — they could remove their children when they wished.

In the case of those parents who claimed to know nothing of the links between the schools and the cult, she felt it remarkable that they had not done adequate research before committing their children to the education the schools offered.

At least one parent thoroughly and vehemently agreed with that last sentiment. He was the father of an eleven-year-old boy who had attended St Vedast School for nearly a year.

> The article on the schools came out on the Wednesday, and I took my son away on the Thursday. I was going to remove him at the end of the term anyway as they were ramming down his throat a whole lot of religious nonsense. I learnt as well that he was expected to scrub floors and such like for things like forgetting his plimsolls, and I wasn't spending all that money for him to end up doing things like that.
>
> I was remiss. Having now looked at his homework, whether it's English, History or Scripture it's difficult to tell the difference between them because of all the philosophy in there.

And the mother of another eleven-year-old boy, removed from St Vedast two weeks after *The Standard* stories, told us:

> When I first went round the school it seemed too good to be true, but there was an uneasy current, a very strange feeling.

I mentioned it to my husband, but I thought I was just being a bit crazy. Perhaps I should have listened to my feelings a little more.

As far as I remember they never mentioned the School of Economic Science to me. Even if they had done, it would have meant nothing to me. I would have taken it as just a branch of education.

My son had been going to a prep school where they weren't being particularly helpful and we felt we really had to remove him. I didn't look too closely into what might be wrong with the next school.

In the beginning he seemed to quite like it but later it appeared that he wasn't happy there. He became very subdued. It wasn't natural, but we thought that quietening him down a little would do him some good. Now we're pleased we found out about what was going on as soon as we did. He's at a different school now and is very happy, much more outward-going.

We'd found things in his exercise-books which were a bit odd. The first term we thought it was just a different method of teaching, but by the end of the second term we thought this is not a normal school, and we weren't very happy. We took him out during his third term.

School is for learning, not indoctrination, which I'm sure is eventually what did happen to the children. Most of the parents seemed to belong to this SES anyway and for them the schools are fine. It's what they want for their children anyway. We moved ours out at soon as we could find somewhere suitable.

And the father of a thirteen-year-old boy who had spent nearly three terms at St Vedast, again leaving after *The Standard* story broke, said:

My son was going to a school in North London with a high academic reputation which we realized was ill-earned. We started looking for another school for him, but all those we liked were full, until we came across St Vedast advertised in the local paper. We went to see the headmaster and liked what we saw. All we were told was that the premises were rented. Even if he

215

did mention the School of Economic Science we would have been none the wiser.

After my son had been there for a while, however, he told us that some of the things he was being told were so way-out that he just couldn't believe them. I'm very pleased that we found out in time what was going on.

A teacher who was an SES member for many years had a deep insight into the movement's philosophy. Her children attended IEA schools until she became alarmed at the education they were receiving and disenchanted with the movement generally. She said:

> I became increasingly unhappy with SES methods and unwilling to attend the SES. I was also unhappy that my children should continue at the schools as they had neither wished to go in the first instance nor were they happy there.
>
> The teachers at the schools were in many cases unqualified to teach their subjects. Having taught myself, I was horrified at the unprofessional and rigid approach these schools made to understand and teach children. The attempted brainwashing through Sanskrit and Philosophy lessons was counter-productive in my children's case, but most of all they were deprived of being 'children'.
>
> Most of the children there looked and behaved like little old people. All their natural buoyancy was repressed, and they were expected to conform to excessively rigid codes of conduct.
>
> When I left the SES my husband was instructed to divorce me as I had 'turned away from truth'. Anyone believing that they have a monopoly of truth to this extent must be suffering from an enormous delusion. Our family was destroyed by SES and I have had a very difficult time since trying to restore my children to a normal view of life and the future.'

CHAPTER EIGHT

Illiberal Liberals

In May 1982 we met Roger Pincham, chairman of the Liberal Party, in the imposing foyer of the National Liberal Club in Whitehall Place, London.

We knew that Pincham, a wealthy stockbroker in his late forties, was a leading figure in the SES. He had given many years' service as its treasurer and was chairman of the board of governors of the SES independent schools. The purpose of the meeting was to find out whether the SES had been systematically infiltrating the Liberal Party with a view to gaining power and influence in the political as well as spiritual domain.

Pincham emphatically denied it. He took the precaution of bringing to the meeting Wyn Hugh-Jones, Liberal Party secretary general. Hugh-Jones professed no knowledge of Pincham's close link with the SES, indeed no knowledge of the SES itself. Throughout the interview he was supportive of his chairman and remained largely impassive except for the point where we asked Pincham if he believed that through meditation he could levitate himself. Hugh-Jones looked amazed when Pincham replied that though he did not believe he could do it, he nonetheless believed it was possible.

The rest of the interview was much more straightforward and dwelt mainly on Pincham's attempts to become an MP and his use of SES members to help with the hustings. Pincham had this to say about infiltration of the Liberal Party by the SES:

> Are you saying that a member of a church or a Jew shouldn't have anything to do with politics because they are living out what they have been taught in church.

217

There is a great difference between being inspired by what you have learned and going and doing something in public life, and being put into public life to do it.

All the (SES) philosophy can hope to do is alert and educate the kind of person asking fundamental questions. The School of Economic Science doesn't feel the Liberal Party should be supported. The SES doesn't have political views.

The interview lasted only forty minutes as Pincham had to get to another meeting, but that was not the end of his comments. He was, quite naturally, very worried about what we might publish about his links with the SES. Within a few days Louis Kirby, Editor of *The Standard*, received a long letter from Pincham amplifying what he had said at the interview. The letter appears as an appendix to this book. But equally remarkable was an article that appeared on 1 June 1982 in *Liberal News*.

The article was headed, *This school threatens nobody, neither do I*, and it puzzled many of the Liberal supporters who read it. Pincham wrote:

> The point which has aroused the suspicions of two investigative journalists is that I have also for many years been associated with the School of Economic Science.

However, at this stage we had not published anything about the matter and in the event it was another year before we did. In trying to anticipate what we might eventually publish, the Liberal Party chairman touched only obliquely on some of the SES's more controversial aspects. There was no mention of Hinduism, of allegations of brainwashing or of marriage break-ups.

Many *Liberal News* readers must have wondered why the Party chairman had commandeered such a large slice of their paper. The SES was described as an educational charity based in London with smaller centres elsewhere which gives courses in economics and philosophy.

This description is wholly inadequate as this book makes clear. It is not surprising that there was little apparent

218

response to the article. Only one Liberal activist followed up the personal statement by Pincham and asked us what we were looking into.

Inadequate though Pincham's statement was, it did provide some information about the SES's objectives and in a way indicated that the cult does indeed have political aims. As we have pointed out, the very origins of the SES stem from its founder's belief in a new system of taxation. Pincham explained:

> The founders of the School of Economic Science were Mr Leon MacLaren and his father, Andrew MacLaren, who was Labour MP for Burslem between 1922 and 1945. He was a great champion of the need for land reform, and became a great inspiration to me when I met him in the mid-1960s. He was then eighty-five.
>
> Leon MacLaren stood as a Liberal in 1950 and 1951, but since then has concentrated his energies on work in the school. Naturally its economic courses stirred up interest in politics but I would emphasise that the purpose of the school is not political. It does not seek to influence the way its members vote and includes active members of all the political parties.

The SES has tried to do more than stir up an interest in economics or politics. It has fervently tried to win acceptance for the taxation reforms it favours. It is not objective about it, and students are expected to follow the SES's economic dogma or leave.

MacLaren senior started the SES ostensibly as an economic study group. In reality its aim was simply to propagate reform. Economics courses were extended and refined but always based on the original ideas of the SES's two founders. Eventually Leon MacLaren committed the ideas to paper in a book impressively entitled, *Nature of Society*. It is said that while he was writing the book MacLaren began to think more deeply about the 'natural laws' that governed mankind, and turned towards the occult and mysticism. However, the book is a lucid exposition

219

of the SES's economic ideas and it is useful to quote from some of it.

The SES believes that most of our taxes are inhibiting growth and individual enterprise. Most are taxes on employment in one form or another. The SES would sweep most of them away and have one simple tax based on the theory of land value taxation.

This theory was most eloquently expounded by the American economist Henry George whose book *Progress and Poverty*, published in 1879, was once widely read. It has now been developed into the notion of site value taxation.

The tax would fall on sites and not on buildings, thus encouraging construction and development. Owners of land would have to pay a hefty tax to the government, but users of land would continue to pay an economic price for the right to exploit it.

In Britain the taxation system has the effect of penalizing human enterprise, the SES argues. We charge rates on building improvements but exempt from rates those who keep land idle.

The SES's plan is to levy a tax based on what a piece of land would let for if it had no buildings on it. The tax income would be greater for sites near to amenities provided by the state because such sites would be more valuable than those with a poor infrastructure. In the SES's eyes this system would penalize land speculators but protect and encourage those who wanted to bring land into productive use. More idealistically still, they see it as a solution to all our economic ills — industrial stagnation, low wages and unemployment.

Site or land value taxation has been introduced in some countries — South Africa, Canada, Australia and New Zealand, which are interestingly places where the SES is very active. But most economists believe the idea has one major drawback — it just would not, on its own, produce enough revenue. The notion that one single tax could be socially equitable is also difficult to accept, but the SES has no problems with this. It does not believe in social equality as we shall later see.

The SES believes in land value taxation because it accords with the natural laws that they claim govern mankind. Society has no power to change such natural laws.

Leon MacLaren wrote in *Nature of Society*:

> The people of this generation regard human affairs as naturally capricious, chaotic and cruel. On the other hand, they are so impressed with the feats of their own science and skill that they tend to believe there is nothing they cannot do. So, they set out to conquer nature, or organize life and to plan human relations. They might as well order the sea to retire or the earth to stand still . . .
>
> If land is enclosed and men cannot have access to it save by coming to terms with the owners, then rent and wages will be determined by the least which the labourer will accept in order to live. In these conditions this natural force, the operation of which has been called the law of rent and wages, will run counter to the fervent human desire to live, and to live more joyously. Men and women will be denied the opportunity to pursue those occupations which will give scope and expression to their native faculties and by neglect these faculties will wither.
>
> Moreover, they will be denied even the share they have earned of the wealth and services available in the community. Caught between these conflicting forces which they are powerless to control, between the law of rent and the desire to live, they will be frustrated and demoralized, and the resulting situation must lead to society being torn with dissension or paralysed by decay.

From this lofty viewpoint Leon MacLaren soon went on to explore the ideas of Gurdjieff, the Maharishi and others, and the SES turned from an economic pressure group into a religious cult.

The economic theory was not abandoned but accommodated in the SES's developing philosophy as MacLaren began to see more and more in the idea of 'natural laws'.

That a new religion should be preoccupied with changing the taxation system is a little difficult to swallow. It is largely an historical oddity. But remember, the School

221

started out as an economic pressure group and Leon MacLaren stood as a Liberal in furtherance of this cause. The aim was thus political, and though the economic wing of the SES is now much smaller than the philosophical wing, the political aim is still clearly evident. Roger Pincham's assertion that the SES is not political has never been true since the day the movement was founded.

Whether or not Leon MacLaren had other reasons for standing as a Liberal candidate there were strong SES economic policy reasons for him doing so.

The Liberal Party was keenly interested in Henry George's taxation ideas at the turn of the century and later. Though the party has turned away from such ideas in recent times there have always been a few members who kept the flame of land value taxation alive.

Perhaps this explains Roger Pincham's arrival in the Liberal Party with so many other devoted SES followers. Though they all deny they have been trying to infiltrate the Liberal Party — or in modern parlance are guilty of 'entryism' — there is no question that senior figures within the SES have been extraordinarily active and successful within the Party — and they have achieved this success without the vast majority of Liberals outside the SES knowing of the connection.

With one notable exception, it is the Liberal Party that has attracted the energies of most politically motivated SES members. The exception is David Boddy, former director of press and public relations at the Conservative Party. (Boddy's position within the SES is discussed in Chapter 10.)

Since the war, at least seven high-ranking members of the SES have stood for Parliament on behalf of the Liberals, and possibly several more. Many other SES members have been active behind the scenes but within the Party.

Robin Garton, a Mayfair art dealer, was a senior member of the SES until 1973 when he left and became a Christian. He remembers SES members being strongly encouraged to help with campaigning for the Liberal Party:

It was made clear that we should help if we could and it was

222

always the Liberal Party that was mentioned in this context. I can remember large numbers going off to help Roger Pincham in his campaign. If he had become an MP it would have been seen as a great coup for the SES.

Pincham has been by far the most successful SES member within the Liberal Party. He told some of his own story in an article in the 1980 Gladstone Essays, a booklet published by the Gladstone Club, a Liberal Party fringe organization:

> Such was the candidate shortage in May 1970 and such was the understandable lack of decision in the Executive of my local Putney constituency — rather dominated then by Peter Hain — that in the event I despatched myself to Leominster for the three most exhilarating weeks of my life . . .

Pincham got the candidature for Leominster because he was able to find the cash and the support to fight the seat. Surprisingly he had only joined the Liberal Party a few months before:

> At my candidate's interview I had to confess that I was not sure at what points I deviated from current Party policy for the simple reason that I was not entirely clear what current policy was, and I answered rather arrogantly that I had taken the precaution not to read the Party manifesto so that I should not be tempted to pretend an acceptance of policies with which I did not fully agree.

Over the next fourteen years he rose from this innocent position to the chairmanship of the party. He has fought the Leominster seat at every general election, building up Liberal support to the point where it was regarded as one of the best prospects for a Liberal gain from the Tories at the 1983 election.

Without question he was a diligent party worker and has been aided greatly by his SES friends. In 1973 Pincham founded the Gladstone Club and two years later the Centre for Industrial and Commercial Policy Studies. The

Gladstone Club meets monthly at the National Liberal Club, organizes dinners and lunches and publishes a Party newssheet, *The Liberal Clarion*. The Centre for Industrial and Commercial Policy Studies describes itself as a forum 'for promoting more detailed review and development of Liberal policies in a wider political context'.

The Gladstone Club has also published a useful directory of Liberal Party policy decisions and holds a fringe meeting at the annual Liberal Assembly. At the two most recent Assemblies – 1982 and 1983 – the speaker has been Emile Woolf, head of Emile Woolf and Associates, a big accountancy college in Old Gloucester Street, Holborn.

Woolf is a fervent SES follower and one of its experts on tax reform. His college premises are used as an SES London centre. But the SES connection goes much further than this, for the Gladstone Club is effectively an SES branch within the Liberal Party and the Centre of Industrial and Commercial Policy Studies is overwhelmingly made up of SES members.

The Gladstone Essays, mentioned earlier, are largely the work of SES members. Through the creation of the Club and the Centre, SES members had a convenient entry point into the Liberal Party, and a base for advancing the cause of land value taxation.

In his *Liberal News* article, Roger Pincham had this to say about the Gladstone Club:

> Some others who attend the School are currently active in the Liberal Party and tend to congregate in the Gladstone Club to which all Liberals are of course welcome. Had the Gladstone Club been a conspiracy – which it was not – to take over the Liberal Party it can only be judged an appalling failure!

He also supplied an explanation for SES members keeping quiet about their spiritual commitments:

> This reticence derives from the long-standing principle that one does not seek credit for work done there and that one does not chatter about whomever one meets there. These principles have

considerable advantages but they can also give rise to misunderstandings.

Another principle is that members of the School should not lead self-centred lives but try to make themselves useful in the community according to their talents and inclinations.

Thus through the seventies and into the eighties SES members modestly beavered away within the Liberal Party and kept quiet about their beliefs. Pincham and other Liberal activists have repeatedly said it is simply a coincidence that so many SES followers have become Parliamentary candidates.

In the general election of October 1974 Roger Pincham stood for Leominster and came within a whisker of unseating the Tory MP, Peter Temple-Morris. Temple-Morris won 15,741 votes and Pincham 15,162. His brother, John Pincham, stood for Uxbridge. He came third well behind the sitting Tory candidate. John, like his brother Roger, had been in the SES since his late teens.

At Maidstone the Liberal candidate was John Burnett, another leading figure in the School of Economic Science and a London accountant. He came second in the poll but well behind the sitting Tory candidate. Burnett is a long-serving local councillor, first winning a seat in 1973 and later becoming Liberal group leader.

Yet another SES follower was the candidate in Ealing North. Clive Phillips, a furnisher by profession, was a poor third.

It has not been an easy task finding out the names of candidates who are members of the SES because of what Pincham describes as the long-standing principle of reticence. No one in the SES was willing to supply a list.

However, it is believed that one or two other Liberal candidates were also SES followers.

This applies also to the 1979 general election campaign. But here at least five candidates can be identified as SES members. It was not such a good year for the Liberals as 1974 and Roger Pincham's Tory opponent had a 4,865 majority. However Pincham succeeded in increasing his vote. At this election brother John stood for Streatham, getting only 3,779 votes, and John Burnett was still well behind his Tory opponent in Maidstone.

Two new SES names appear in the list. Jeremy Nieboer, a solicitor, stood for the Liberals against Geoffrey Johnson Smith (Tory) in East Grinstead. Nieboer came second, with 11,102 votes but well behind Smith. Another lawyer and SES member, Alistair Brett, made a poor showing in Paddington, West London.

It appears that Roger Pincham's Leominster campaigns attracted most attention from his friends in the SES. Workers for other political parties told us of strange young faces suddenly appearing in the town not knowing where to deliver election material. One leading member of another party took a note of the strangers who were helping Pincham with his campaign. He gave us the list. There are sixteen names and every one is a leading member of the School. It includes Peter Green, the SES principal, Lesley Blake, one of three SES trustees and Margaret Bonstow the honorary General Secretary.

Green has the same view as Pincham of this phenomenon. In his *Liberal News* article Pincham wrote:

> My own decision to enter politics was fortunately greeted with enthusiasm by friends both within the school and outside, which was a great help especially in the early days of reviving a very rundown constituency. These friends no doubt share a certain similarity of thought but their help for me has always been a matter of personal support and not at the direction of the school.

The 1983 election saw a reduction in the number of SES members standing as Liberal candidates. The share-out of seats with the Social Democratic Party within the new Alliance meant that there were only half the opportunities for people on the Liberal Party's approved list of candidates to find a seat to fight. Roger Pincham and John Burnett were the only two left whom we could identify as being in the School.

Pincham held a packed adoption meeting at Leominster three weeks before the election. It was the first opportunity we had had of watching him and his supporters in action. Sure enough the audience was dotted with SES supporters, notably Richard Elias, a City insurance broker who acted as Pincham's agent in the 1979 election. He booked into the local hotel for the duration of the 1983 hustings. Also present for most of the campaign was James Dean, a Grays Inn barrister and like Elias a long-serving SES member. There were others too staying in Leominster but perhaps not as many as in previous campaigns. The locals by then had even coined a name for them - 'the London Mafia'.

The Liberals had great hopes of winning Leominster and many other seats in the 1983 election. As it turned out the Tories were able to gain an increased majority, and though the Liberal vote was respectable it did not produce the expected big increase in Liberal Members of Parliament. Pincham's vote was particularly bad. He blamed this on *The Standard*, for on the eve of the election and on election day itself we published our articles on the SES and the Liberal connection.

The story of Pincham's previously unreported links with the SES were splashed in the local Herefordshire papers. Pincham was to argue later that the final poll result — with a margin of 9,786 votes between himself and the Tory Peter Temple-Morris — was due to publication of the articles at a point where he had no opportunity to reply to the allegations.

There may indeed have been some last minute abstentions, but the seat had been politically altered by the boundary changes.

It is highly doubtful that we wrecked Pincham's prospects and that was most certainly not the intention. However, Pincham piled in with a more wide-ranging complaint. He wrote to the Press Council:

I am convinced that the articles had an adverse influence upon the results of Liberal candidates in the London area, none of

227

whom were in any way associated with the School.

The Press Council complaint had been spearheaded by a Mr Malcolm Hill who had written to the Council some weeks after publication of the articles in *The Standard* accusing the paper of deliberately timing their publication to do the maximum harm to Pincham and Burnett. Burnett later added his voice to the complaint, accusing us of deliberately trying to cause the maximum political damage. Of SES help in his campaign he had this to say:

> The number of people who helped with the election who were also members of the SES totalled six. Of those six people, four helped on one occasion only. The total number of people who helped was in the region of *100*. It is also the case that the few people of SES who helped, helped as friends of myself and not as SES members.

It is not surprising that Pincham and Burnett warmly endorsed Hill's complaint. Although neither Hill, nor Pincham, nor Burnett made any mention of it, Hill was for a long time a leading SES member himself. He left a few years ago but is still a sympathizer.

We had given Pincham ample opportunity to talk to us and on the day we published the articles we had phoned him to give him one last opportunity. James Dean answered the phone at Pincham's Leominster house and told us that Pincham had no comment to make.

The Press Council ruled:

> Newspapers are entitled to be partisan and *The Standard* was entitled to report critically on the activities of the School of Economic Science, which it described as a 'highly secretive religious cult'.
>
> The newspaper was entitled, too, to draw attention in the public interest to the involvement in the organization of some Liberal candidates and supporters, including in particular Mr Roger Pincham, a candidate for Leominster at the imminent General Election and a recent chairman of the Liberal Party.

The Press Council is satisfied, however, that *The Standard* made adequate attempts to interview Mr Pincham.

After bringing out into the open SES members' involvement in Liberal Party affairs, one would have expected some sort of response from the Party itself. That has not been forthcoming, but it may or may not be significant that Pincham failed to get as Liberal Party chairman permission to stand again at the beginning of 1983. Though he 'made himself available', he failed to get the backing of the national executive committee for constitutional rules to be bent. The meeting took place some months before we published our articles but well after we had first approached members of the executive about SES involvement.

The Party's candidates' committee has also discussed the SES links of some of the people selected for seats but seems to have taken no action. The presumption must be that the Party agrees with the SES that nothing sinister or underhand has been going on. Perhaps also the prospect of the adverse publicity that would inevitably follow any action has made the committee reticent.

Indeed why should anyone act? Is there any evidence that SES members of the Liberal Party are in any way unLiberal? Having met scores of SES members and studied the SES's viewpoint on many issues – women, discipline, authority and social change – it is difficult to see how any SES member can fit easily into the modern Liberal Party. Pincham perhaps recognized this when in 1982 he wrote in *Liberal News*:

> It is I think widely understood that my viewpoint tends to the traditional and certainly I believe that the problems of society can be put right by lawful and orderly reform.
>
> Some might mistake me for a Right-winger, but all who have read what I have written or listened to what I have said should realize that my position is deeply radical as well as traditional.

This is perhaps a good way of describing the SES: it is radically traditional. It harks back to an age when there was a widespread acceptance that someone's position in life was preordained. This makes many SES members extraordinarily unsympathetic to the plight of the out-of-work, disabled or sick. Beyond that, the SES view of Western civilization as it has developed this century is one of deep distaste. They believe old-fashioned standards have been destroyed by materialism and by the utterly misguided modern-day principle of equality. An end to all this is nigh. One woman told us at a social gathering:

> We haven't got long to put things right. We see ourselves as being ready to take over when the time comes.

This was not meant necessarily in the political sense. The view seems to be that there will be an apocalyptic ending to it all. The SES will survive this to nurture and lead a new Renaissance.

In the light of this, SES members' credentials for joining the Liberal Party seem a bit obscure. One wonders how many Liberals would agree with this statement by Pincham:

> I have never been able to equate the three battle-cries of the French Revolution with the principles of Liberalism because I see Liberty and Equality as incompatible. Replace Equality with Justice and I believe that one has introduced Liberty's natural partner — for justice as Justinian asserted 'is the constant will to render to every man his due'. That due depends both upon need and desert and upon every circumstance affecting his position . . .

CHAPTER NINE

The School and the Church

Roger Pincham wants to modify the catchword of the French Revolution. He wants to make it 'Liberty, Fraternity and Justice', rejecting the principle of equality. He was voicing a well-established SES idea that people are not equal and not necessarily deserving of equal treatment. This does not seem to fit well with the principles of Liberalism. It fits even less well with the principles of Christianity, with the notion that all men are created equal in the sight of God.

In this book we have taken some trouble to show that, while the SES may embrace some Christian ideas and show a selective respect for the Bible, it is a Hindu-based cult and not founded on Christian ideology. We need to make this point because the SES has involved itself with the church of England to a point where the church really should take notice. If the SES is not Christian, why has it been permitted to fund and help organize official church bodies? How can it hold meetings at Church House in London, the administrative nerve centre of the church? What are the clergy doing marrying SES couples as Christians and in some cases allowing its own clergy to remain members of the SES? SES followers have in the past been employed at Church House. SES members regularly worship at services at Westminster Abbey. The SES's children's schools have regular visits from two Church of England clergy who are fully aware of the SES's Hindu loyalties.

The church is noted for its tolerance, but if it is prepared to tolerate the SES helping to organize and fund church activities and play a part in its spiritual life, how can it logically be censorious of any of the other religious cults?

Attitudes within the Church of England are wildly conflicting. Some clergy are members of the SES. But others, notably Michael Marshall who was until recently the Bishop of Woolwich, describe it as an 'evil organization'.

We shall go on to show just how confusing this picture is. But first let us look at the SES's private attitude — an attitude they would never articulate in public.

A set of lecture notes for senior members of the SES's women's group has come into our hands. These were not meant for outsiders' eyes. They clearly illustrate how the SES manages to attach itself to institutions that follow a quite different set of principles.

One lecture given to the 'Ladies-at-Home O Group' in the spring of 1972 began with the chanting of the Te Deum, the church's principal song òf praise. The notes make it clear that the value of the chanting lies mainly in the sounds that are being uttered and not in the content. There is a bitter attack on the Roman Catholic Church for abandoning the plainsong Latin chants in favour of English versions:

> (Church Latin) relates very easily to the sound of the universal language . . . so long as the sound coming from the churches was of quite a different order from the sound coming from elsewhere, even the greatest miscreant held religion in some respect. Now it is becoming hard to distinguish the sound of some of the churches from the sound in the community at large.

This illustrates how the SES has become wedded to the idea that it is not the meaning of words and songs that matters but their sounds. This partly explains why SES members can attend Christian services — they will be absorbing the sounds and not the literal meaning of what is being said.

There is praise in the lecture notes for the way church liturgy had a civilizing effect on earlier times, and for the

Authorized 'King James' version of the Bible. But extraordinarily the SES takes credit for this, linking itself to other now extinct but similar schools of thought:

> England enjoyed the enormous blessing of the influence of School in the translation of the Bible.

The notes then become more difficult to grasp, but they illustrate another way in which the SES deviates from orthodox Christian thought. While the SES believes that man and God (or the Absolute) are one and the same, Christians believe that God and humanity are different in mind, however close the relationship between them. The following extract from the notes shows the degree of contempt the SES has for the churches, the Hindu terminology in which they analyse arguments, and the conflict of ideology between monism and Christianity:

> We started off with some general consideration of the function of the church − of religion, any real religion. Let us now be more precise. The function of the church is to uphold ignorance.
>
> It is ignorance which first separates a man from his Absolute Self and drives him from unity, finally into the Kali Juga, the age of ignorance. Thus duality, 'me and the rest', is fundamental to the condition of ignorance. The church's job is to make the best of this duality by substituting 'God' for 'the rest'; but it is still duality. Without the devotion which may arise from the idea of God, life in the Kali Juga would be intolerable; there would be nothing to save humanity from the descent into utter darkness. By teaching human beings some degree of unselfishness and service to others, the church holds society steady against the worst effects of ignorance. But it is still founded on ignorance and teaches ignorance, even though it may also hint to more wakeful members that there is a way out.
>
> To enable the church to fulfil this function, of upholding ignorance and also pointing to a way out of it, School has endowed her with great treasures, in particular the treasure of

the Scriptures. Therein lies the sound of the Self which may finally penetrate to the desire for truth in every man. Whether in its original form (where that is extant) or in classical translations or in the Authorized Version, the Bible still carries that sound – a sound to command, to bless, to civilize, to dissolve ignorance, to arouse emotion, to encourage devotion and service. As long as the church accepts guardianship of that sound and continues to let it be heard, its function will continue.

Thus in highly condescending prose the SES sums up the useful but limited role of the churches. The notes conclude with advice on the religious upbringing of SES members' children. Here in even more candid terms is the reason why these children should be allowed to go to church:

First comes the sound, then the meaning. That is why it is profitable to read to even the youngest children the words of the Scriptures. See that your children are acquainted with the Bible. Only after that turn to the rest of the treasure – the painting, sculpture, stained glass and church architecture. They are not truth, but they may be tokens of truth.

If your children are turning towards School, and attending classes, it is useful for them to know about the churches, as part of their general understanding of the society in which they live; and because one day, they may be called upon by School to assist the churches (as some of our members already are).

If your children are not yet interested in School, then let them become members of church. Many people have to tread the lesser Way of Devotion, before they can graduate, as it were, to the Way of Knowledge. Do not deny your child that possibility – provided he has not asked for the more embracing good of School.

Jesus said: 'Ye believe in God. Believe ye also in Me.'

'Ye believe in God' is for members of churches.

'Believe ye also in me' is for members of School, for what it is saying is *tatwa-maasi* – Thou art That.

234

As our chapter on the SES's philosophy has shown this simply follows the Hindu idea of other religions. Though SES members would deny they are Hindus it is difficult not to classify them thus. Imagine then the position of the Rev. Stephen Terry, Vicar of St John the Apostle, Whetstone in North London and a pillar of his local affluent, middle-of-the-road community. Terry is a fervent supporter of the SES, and was a member until 1981.

Could it be that his entry into the Church of England was because one day the School called on him 'to assist the church'?

After our articles were published in *The Standard* Terry was incensed at their content and vented his feelings publicly at a packed meeting of the parents of children at the SES independent schools. His speech from the floor was a wonderful piece of soap-box oratory, full of humour, irony and rhetoric. The SES could not have had a better cheerleader. His influence on the meeting is discussed in Chapter 7, but what is relevant here are Terry's view of the SES and the Church of England. He had this to say: 'It strikes me there is nothing that can be said of the SES that cannot also be said of the Church of England. The SES has its lunatic fringe, so does the church. The church has its devoted people so does the SES. It has its visionaries who perhaps are sometimes uncomfortable, so does the SES. Like all organizations it's imperfect. Like all organizations it's quite right that they should at times be taken to task for what they don't get right.'

Thus, with a slap on the wrist, he accorded the SES a clean bill of health. In doing so he had perhaps inadvertently made the SES out to be more of religion than the SES would itself like publicly to admit. But they loved Terry's speech and he was wildly applauded.

A similar ovation greeted another cleric, Father Kenneth Hewitt of St Augustine's, Queen's Gate. Father Hewitt's church is almost directly opposite the SES's headquarters and one of the children's schools. The SES rent buildings from Father Hewitt and attend some of his services.

He had granted us a long interview a few days before the public meeting and there was no doubt that he had great misgivings about the SES. He said that the way children were brought into SES group meetings was a great strain on them. He remembers one such child who was 'obviously at the end of its tether'. After spending all day at school the child had to attend a long evening SES meeting. At 9.30 p.m. the child burst into tears. Father Hewitt added:

> The child was totally ignored altogether until the class ended at 10 p.m.
> No one had the humanity to go and put their arms round that child — and I think that's what you mean by the lack of human feeling.

Father Hewitt also complained about the secrecy of the SES, its puritanism and the pressure put on people to stay in the SES. But he said the SES teachings were not incompatible with Christianity and that he had met many pleasant and polite SES members.

Father Hewitt gave this reason for not speaking out against the cult:

> I try to have a warm relationship with every member of the school, teachers and some ex-members and the children. They know that I'm not in any official way related to the School so that they can feel that there is somebody they can turn to with warmth, compassion and understanding when they come to that point where they feel they cannot stand that lack of humanity any longer. Anything which would harm that relationship . . . would be disastrous for those individuals . . .

But Hewitt's comments at the Parents' meeting gave the impression that he was utterly besotted with the work of the SES, and provided sparse comfort to worried parents. Gone was the criticism expressed in our interview. He poked fun at *The Standard* for levelling criticism at the SES and gave not one hint of having any reservations about the cult.

Not surprisingly the SES still quotes Father Hewitt when anyone asks what the SES's relationship is like with the church.

Andrew Mottram, a curate at Old Hatfield parish church in Hertfordshire, had rejoined the SES when we met him in June 1982. His wife was also a member, but Mottram's connection with the cult goes back to his sixth-form days when he first began attending. His mother was a member and his brother is a teacher at one of the SES's independent schools.

He joined the SES youth group under its leader, former army sergeant major Michael Nash. Mottram says that 'amazing changes' took place in the group:

> It was a motley crew. There was a cleaning up. I suppose you'd call it a grooming effect. I'd dropped out and didn't know what to do. It helped people to grow – the sheer physical work.
>
> I wouldn't say it was quite a question of teaching people to conform. You reach a point where you are ready to co-operate with other members of your group and your tutor.

Mottram left the SES when he was at university but returned in 1981. By then he had joined the church and saw no contradiction in serving both organizations:

> Both the church and the SES are seeking to help individuals find union with God. I can't be a party to the view, which is a supreme arrogance, that claims a monopoly of access to God. The crucifixion and resurrection are events which are unique. I believe the Creator enables himself to be seen incarnate in Jesus Christ. But I don't believe that God made himself incarnate only once.

Here Mottram departs from orthodox Christian thought as he does in other respects. He described his initiation into the SES – 'the giving of meditation' – as a kind of baptism ceremony. Of the SES's leader he had this to say:

> Leon MacLaren is a fairly amazing man. He has an amazing

237

insight and sensibility to what is needed in individuals — the ability to reflect what an individual is seeking. He is a great teacher. I regard the Shankaracharya as the representative of God on Earth like the Pope. The Shankaracharya is one of the great holy men of India. Through that person the teaching of truth is presented.

Mottram was honest enough to admit that he had misgivings about some aspects of the SES:

I wouldn't doubt that there are people who have been very hurt while they were associated with the School. I know the church has dealt with a great number. . . Some get very involved and contact with friends outside the SES becomes very limited. This is something that concerns me. I wouldn't deny it's true that many people are too involved. It becomes a race to progress as fast as possible.

He acknowledged that some are in it for power:

There is a darker side of us and it appears also in the Church of England. There is a desire to control others. There is arrogance, a subtle self-righteousness.

The School is about enabling people to find union with God, enabling them to live in a harmonious way. Standing for the Liberal Party is thus compatible with SES aims. I believe the people I know — Roger Pincham — don't have a desire for their own power. I believe the School must be brought into the life of the nation when the nation is in darkness.

Mottram's membership and commitment to the SES was later to end abruptly, but not because he fell out of sympathy with its ideals. When his bishop found out about his SES loyalties an interview was arranged. Mottram was instructed to quit the SES. He did so and his wife left as well. Since then he has continued to meditate, though not regularly, and has remained of the same mind about the School. Clearly he would rather have remained both a member of the SES and a Church of England curate.

238

Where the established church and the SES come even closer together is through the work of Tom Chapman, former industrial adviser to the Archbishop of Canterbury and Secretary General of the European Christian Industrial Movement. Chapman denies being a member of the SES, but in most respects he could be described as an honorary member. His SES links are so close as to make the distinction almost irrelevant.

He is a former trades union leader whose rise to prominence in the lay work of the church is largely due to the financial and organizational help of the SES. It is an extraordinary story which we have only limited space to describe.

While working for the church and the ECIM, Chapman was also regularly assisting the SES in holding public-speaking classes and courses on civics. He would travel abroad with MacLaren and help teach the SES meditation technique. Once he gave a lecture to SES members in Malta. Chapman was set up in a comfortable house in Chelsea by the SES. The secretary he employed at Church House while advising the Archbishop was the SES's Honorary General Secretary, Margaret Bonstow.

The European Christian Industrial Movement, popularly known as the 'Bridgebuilders', is an official Church of England body. It encourages groups of Christians in industry and commerce to get together. It is Chapman's brainchild. He told us:

> If only management and workers would tell the truth to one another there would be no disputes.

Thus another aim of the Bridgebuilders is to break down barriers between management and workers. Chapman writes lengthy bulletins which are circulated nationwide. The theme is frequently virulently anti-communist and anti-strike.

The President of ECIM is the Right Rev. Ross Hook, formerly the Bishop of Bradford but more recently in the highly influential post of chief of staff to the Archbishop of Canterbury. ECIM was set up in 1975 with a great deal of help from SES members as we shall show. But Chapman had been hatching the idea for much longer. For him it was a means of continuing the work he had already begun to perform on the payroll of the church.

Now nearing seventy, Chapman is a jovial, energetic man who now has only one interest — ECIM. In the late sixties, however, he was enmeshed in a public row within the Amalgamated Engineering Union of which he was an organizer for North London. In a battle with left-wingers he lost — and lost his job.

It was a low point in his life, but the post of industrial adviser at Church House was found for him. Around this time he was befriended by Leon MacLaren:

> SES members were a very great help to me when I needed help. It wasn't a question of money; they gave me moral support and I'm thankful for it.

Today, as Secretary General of ECIM, he is its only full-time employee. He denies any links with the School of Economic Science. But the links are there, hidden.

The ECIM has been set up as a charity and has three official trustees; Mr Chapman says they were approved by the Archbishop of Canterbury in 1975. They include Peter Green, and James Armstrong, SES treasurer and a leading member.

Then there are the people involved in the work of the ECIM. Mr Chapman last year sold his £120,000 house in Pimlico and moved to the English Lake District, but the man he left in charge in London is James Dean, Liberal activist, SES member, barrister and son of Sir Patrick Dean, a former US Ambassador. One of the guest speakers at meetings which Mr Dean conducts at St Vedast Church in the City is Mr John Jessop, a City metal broker and long-serving SES member. The ECIM's current London address is Flat 2, 1 Montague Place, W1 — Dean's home.

The SES also helped with Mr Chapman's former home and ECIM's London headquarters in Westmoreland Terrace, Pimlico, the one recently sold for about £120,000.

240

After being pressed, Mr Chapman agreed that SES members originally found the house for him and extensively converted in at considerable expense. But Mr Chapman says that he then bought it from them with the help of loans from friends who were not SES members.

He later needed the roof repaired. Roger Pincham, Peter Green and Leslie Blake, all leading SES members, arranged for a loan and personally took a legal charge on Mr Chapman's property. Mr Chapman said he was told the money was found from a trust administered by the trio:

> I was a little surprised when they lent me nearly twice as much as the roof was costing, but I believed them when they said it was for the good of ECIM.

Mr Green, a recent speaker at ECIM's London conference, agreed that many SES members had become involved in the ECIM and have attended classes run by Mr Chapman in public speaking and committee procedures:

> People who are interested, as many in the School are, in general welfare and good citizenry are also interested in Tom Chapman's good work and there is no other connection than that. I think what he is doing is absolutely splendid. I've known him for many, many years and when he left Church House we, with the (then) Bishop of Leicester and one or two of his friends, worked together to establish his movement around his work. It is as simple as that.

Mr Green said he and other SES members had given Mr Chapman a loan because of their friendship with him:

> It may be that SES members have been Tom Chapman's main source of moral and financial support, but when you get to know someone these things do happen. Many of our people are anxious to encourage anything which they think is a worthwhile fight against what they view as being a menace in this country.

241

The SES's encouragement even runs to providing Mr Chapman with music for his ECIM conferences. The ECIM Brass Ensemble is really an SES music group led by one of the cult's most fervent followers, Loulla Efthimiou.

ECIM's influence within the church cannot be considered great and it is difficult to see why so much assistance has been provided by SES members. However, ECIM is also active in Belgium and there are regular conferences held in Antwerp organized by Chapman. Some leading church figures there have been involved in conferences, but attendances have not been large. One wonders whether the involvement of the SES stretches to the Antwerp venues.

When we met him in 1982 Bishop Ross Hook said he had not realized the connections between ECIM and the School of Economic Science:

> I have never heard of the School and did not realize there was any connection. I shall certainly take a look at any evidence that there might be. I've always looked on the ECIM as a little dull and rather right-wing. I took on the job as President because I was asked to do so by another churchman. I haven't been able to attend many meetings.

But Bishop Hook has recently declined to take too close a look at the SES's influence on the movement of which he is President. He told an inquirer:

> The impression I have been given is that, although they appear to be a syncretistic body very much based on Platonism, their chief offence is the same as the Masons, namely their secretiveness.

He said that as he was getting near retirement he could only pass on information to others.

Peter Green's remarks, quoted earlier, about SES members being willing to help ECIM were put in another context by an ex-SES member who was told to attend a meeting at Church House one evening some years ago. When she arrived Tom Chapman was making a speech and the

242

audience was full of SES members. She had not come across ECIM before and her only reason for being at the meeting was the SES instruction.

On the other side to these sympathizers within the church are some who are ranged aggressively against the SES — prominent churchmen who are gently trying to persuade the Church of England to investigate the movement. But perhaps the most robust and comprehensive denouncement of the SES has come from Malta.

The SES has been active on that island for many years and is known there as 'The Study Group'. More of its history is given in Chapter 3, but what is relevant here is a pamphlet published ten years ago by a Roman Catholic priest, Father Salvino Galea. The pamphlet entitled *The Ganges Flows into the Grand Harbour*, is a direct attack on the Study Group. It begins by quoting Matthew's Gospel, 'Be on your guard against false prophets, men who come to you in sheep's clothing, but are ravenous wolves within. You will know them by the fruits they yield'.

Galea introduces his attack in these terms:

> The purpose of these notes is to put you on your guard against attempts to steal Christ Jesus away from you by a movement of Eastern origin that is seeking to spread Hinduism in the West, taking advantage of 'the thirst for the divine' which Western decadence and atheism are causing among many . . . At a moment of crisis for our Christian civilization (discernible in Malta as elsewhere in immodest dress, lewd entertainment, idleness and crime) the Study Group aims at ecumenical alliance with all movements which truthfully seek to stem this tide of destruction.

Father Galea spent many years in India and was able to learn a lot about Hinduism. He is in no doubt that the SES is fundamentally a Hindu movement and being a fiery Christian he saw it as his duty to warn that people were being drawn into Hinduism without realizing it. Clearly he must have taken some trouble to learn the SES's modus operandi and the subtleties of the cult's recruitment techniques:

> Since there is play on the term 'philosophy', which now stands for a truth about some natural principle and now for natural religion, expect these teachers of Hinduism to tell you that your objection to their teaching is 'Religion' while they are dealing *only* with 'Philosophy'.

In Malta the courses were very much the same as today at any of the centres:

> Since the approach to you is gradual and surreptitious, expect them to tell you, in their courses or school, they do not 'give labels'. That means they do not call things by their name. They give you the substance and leave the names to you. Thus, if you were to remark that universal awareness is an attribute of God, expect neither a denial nor a confirmation, but the enigmatic: 'We do not label things in this school.' This non-labelling goes as far as concealing the true nature of the school.
>
> When the approach in these schools is not a straightforward one, expect to be told at the very beginning of the lectures that you listen and take what you think is right and leave what you think is not for you. It is one way of disarming you and brainwashing you into the sin of presumption and pride.
>
> When the approach is not an open one, expect to be told not to discuss with others outside the school what you hear in the school. The reasons given for this complete contradiction of the words of Jesus: 'Preach from the rooftops what I tell you in private', may be many and specious. The fact that the injunction is made is the central and damaging and dangerous fact. Thus, if somebody tries to explain to you that when you are being taught in the school to invoke in your 'meditations' the name of Ram this is nothing else than invoking the name of a false Hindu God, you will be able to reply, 'I do not discuss these things outside the school'. Very convenient! But is it very helpful? Is it very truthful?

Father Galea went to some lengths to explain the differences between Hinduism and Christianity. In summary he picks on the following points:

Whereas Christianity is a revealed religion, whose followers believe it is the only true one, Hinduism is a natural religion thought up by the human mind and not claiming a monopoly of truth.

Christians believe God created the world from nothing; Hindus that the world emanates from God. In Hinduism life and nature and existence are bad as they keep us from God.

In Christianity God created man in his own image but not in his own divine identity (the duality idea). In Hinduism we are already divine but we do not know it.

To Christians life is a gift, whereas Hindus believe life is a chain to be broken as it represents a failure in a previous existence. Souls pre-exist and get reborn until freed.

Christians believe Jesus is the Eternal Son of God but Hindus see Jesus, like Buddha and Muhammad, as an exceptional religious leader who has acquired a form of divinity. Christ is not the only way to the Absolute.

In Hinduism gods may be reincarnated, either of their own free will or by order, to fulfil a mission such as bringing aid to humanity in distress.

Father Galea's list was longer and in more detail. Its importance is not that it distinguishes Hinduism from Christianity but that it distinguishes the SES from Christianity. To the Christians of Malta he gave this stern warning:

It is one thing to know what Hindus, or Muhammadans, or Buddhists think, but quite another thing to be drawn gradually to think like them and to enter with them into 'a community'.

This 'community' may be built through the 'sacrament' of Music or of that of Handwriting, or through the close circle of those that 'see'. The fact remains that you would be allowing others to steal away Christ from you and to steal you away from the Body of Christ which is his Church.

245

r Galea's pamphlet had the desired effect of weaken-
e SES movement in Malta. In Britain there has not
such overt opposition from the churches except for
the comments of churchmen published in *The Standard*
articles.

Michael Marshall, then Bishop of Woolwich, a London
diocese, has had the most contact with former SES members
seeking the church's help. He accused the SES of ruining
people's lives.

> When religion goes wrong it doesn't just go a bit wrong, it goes
> very, very wrong. This is an insidious organization. They are
> power maniacs and really do want to manipulate people's lives.
> They are a society with spiritual aims that have gone wrong.

The bishop first came across the SES in the early seventies
when he was vicar of a Central London church — All Saints
near Regent Street. He began to get more and more people
coming to him in various states of mental distress. Some
were sent to religious retreats in Kent to recover:

> Every person I saw who had come out, and I am talking of about
> twenty to thirty people, all say there is a lot of good in it. That's
> the disarming thing about it. There is a lot of good in evil. It's
> good corrupted. The worst evil is the corruption of the best.

The bishop had to deal with mental breakdown cases and
a number of broken marriages. He believed the type of
meditation practised by the School helped to seal off a
person's mind from the sexual, emotional and fantasy
worlds:

> All images are suppressed. They are very articulate and begin
> to speak slowly and precisely while fixing you with an incredible
> stare.
> They are fastidious about cleanliness and they are legalists.
> Life becomes a lot of rules. You get the feeling almost of
> fascism.

In my experience it flatters a certain type of snob, a Hampstead semi-intellectual. They feel they've found the answer others are searching for.

The bishop had an enormous reponse from the publication of these remarks, mainly from people who had suffered just like the people he had helped.

Another involved in this counselling work was Dr Martin Israel, a lecturer in pathology at the Royal College of Surgeons and an ordained clergyman. He was based at Holy Trinity Church, in Kensington not far from the SES's headquarters buildings. He characterized the SES in this way:

> I always knew the School was evil. There is a tremendous lust for power there — I felt that right at the beginning. It was made clear to people joining that they had to give up a great deal of time to it. It completely intruded into their private lives and often made family relationships extremely difficult. Furthermore it was obvious they were given a certain way of thinking. They couldn't think spontaneously — and that is what worries me.

From the people he helped Dr Israel got the impression that their sense of inner identity and individuality had been taken away:

> They became somewhat like automata. They thought according to a pre-conditioned pattern. Obviously it couldn't have been completely gone otherwise they couldn't have left the School.
> The type of people involved would be fairly intelligent, middle-class people of the professional type — lawyers, that sort of thing. It they did leave the School every effort was made to bring them back. They visited and phoned, and then they were ostracized completely — treated as pariahs.

More recently the pressure put on people to remain members of the SES seems to have been reduced. A number of ex-SES members have said they were not contacted after leaving their groups — but the process of ostracization still continues. SES members were not encouraged to stay friends.

In some cases people are still warned of dire consequences if they leave the cult, as Canon Colin Slee discovered when trying to help a London University student. Canon Slee is Sub Dean at St Albans Cathedral, but he was chaplain at the University's Kings College until early 1983. He found the SES was very active in the college particularly in the classics department. A girl student came to see him who was living in a flat belonging to a number of SES members; she was a member of the SES herself:

> When she wanted to leave she was told she would become a prostitute if she lived apart from the SES. Eventually she managed to make the break, but she had a terrible row with the SES about it.

Parents of another girl student came to Slee and pleaded for help in getting their daughter out of the cult. He told us:

> I'm very worried they are brainwashing people. Members seem to give up their critical faculties, which is completely contradictory to the aims of being a student.

While at Kings he discovered SES members in his choir.

> I married two of them but I wouldn't do it again. The church needs to make a statement against the SES and explain how it is theologically full of holes.

The same view is held by the vicar of Hampstead in North London, the Rev. Graham Dowell. Within his parish is the SES's palatial mansion Sarum Chase on the edge of Hampstead Heath. Graham Dowell has helped a number of SES members and their families and has become concerned at the SES's growth in his area. He prepared a statement for us after talking to people who had been in the SES.

He says the training provided in prayer and meditation

certainly makes a lasting impression on SES followers and fills deep needs. The discipline of having to give time, talents and money to the cult makes enormous demands on members 'who respond to the point of heroic, sacrificial dedication'. He adds:

> The strengths of the SES are very much the weaknesses of my own church. This tends to disarm criticism and lend credence to those of its supporters who view it as a complement to specifically Christian loyalties and not as a rival or alternative 'church'.

But Mr Dowell gave these four warnings:

> Like most other 'heresies' in our history it seizes on particular 'Truths' and facets of Truth to the exclusion of others.
>
> There is an element of Masonic secrecy: an elitism that fastens on potentially successful, middle-class executives. An SES gathering gives an irresistible impression of 'cloning'.
>
> As with the Moonies, marriage partners are selected. Where partners are not members of the School the pressures on the marriage are severe and often lead to break-up of families.
>
> Children are indoctrinated from an early age. Some parents are unaware that St Vedast is geared to a particular philosophy. Sleep deprivation, severe discipline (including corporal punishment), dietary and other techniques are used that seem very like brainwashing.

Graham Dowell said that as Sarum Chase was in his parish he was naturally concerned at reports of activities there:

> These reports come mainly from non-members who are married to members of the School and who feel it is a threat and not a support to their marriage.
>
> Members themselves are asked not to speak about the School to 'outsiders', so impressions and criticisms are inevitably second-hand. Ex-members, some of whom spent many years with the School, speak more freely. Though the aims of the School don't appear to be overtly political, the stress on the

inevitability of cataclysm and training in survival techniques suggest that members are or will be expected to 'take over' when the need arises. I find the analogies with Mosley's private armies frightening enough to warrant special investigation.

Mr Dowell said he was not speaking of paramilitary-type survival training but training in leadership aimed at being equipped to take charge when the cataclysm arrives.

The church's response to the SES can thus be divided into three camps. There are those — though only a few churchmen — who are tolerant of the cult or even members of it. There is a much more powerful group who see the SES as a danger, not just to the work of Christian ministry but to social harmony. By far the biggest group of all have no views either way, despite the fact that the SES is active in most of Britain's major cities.

The church as an institution has been putting off taking up a position, not merely on the issue of the SES but on all new religious movements. The argument has been that 'knocking copy' might be counterproductive — lay people might think the church was getting peeved at all the competition. There is also the principle of tolerance which the church holds as one of its great virtues.

It is the same sort of debate that surrounded the emergence of the National Front fifteen years ago. Most people at first thought it best to keep quiet, but as the NF grew in strength opinion switched. Opposition became public and campaigns were launched which brought people out onto the streets.

In Britain it is the newspapers that have been largely fighting a battle against cults. Corporately the churches have stood aside, with the exception of the shortlived Nationwide Initiative in Evangelism, which produced study kits and videos on the cults. But now there are signs that this reluctance might change. Arising from the articles in *The Standard* about the SES, the issue was ventilated at the

General Synod of the Church of England in November 1983.

The Dean of St Albans, the Very Rev Peter Moore, put a question to the Archbishop of Canterbury, Dr Robert Runcie, in the following terms:

Will the House of Bishops put in hand a consideration of the influence of so-called 'new religious movements' in this country and invite the Board for Mission and Unity, and the Board for Social Responsibility, in consultation with other appropriate bodies (e.g. the BCC, the Centre for the Study of New Religions at Kings College London, FAIR etc.) to examine the teachings propounded and report to Synod advising the clergy and people of the Church of England how to respond to help those who are damaged, and to teach the faith more clearly in order to remedy the influence of such movements, particularly with regard to (1) those who claim membership is not in conflict with holding Christian faith, and (2) those which do not specifically claim compatibility with Christian faith but use holy scripture and church property in their activities?

The Archbishop said he was prepared to raise the matter with the House of Bishops. In a supplementary question posed by Canon Alan Freeman from St Albans the Archbishop was asked if it would be useful to have more information about the School of Economic Science and two other cults — the Emin Foundation and the Children of God. He added:

It has been suggested that a majority of the trustees of one of the organizations listed in the Church of England Yearbook are members of one of the bodies I have mentioned.

Canon Freeman was referring to the European Christian Industrial Movement.

Dr Runcie said he would seek the advice of the church's Board of Mission and Unity — a Synod advisory body — about the matter.

Since the General Synod there has been a slow response to the raising of the issue. The matter may be gradually dropped but there could be the beginnings of a stirring of interest in cults and their more worrying aspects.

What many would like to see is a statement from Dr Runcie from the British Council of Churches or from General Synod on the church's attitude to the spiritual challenge presented by cults. There needs to be a strong condemnation of practices that break up families. At the very least the church should have something to say about secrecy and infiltration into its own ranks.

CHAPTER TEN

Power — For What Purpose?

Many old soldiers never stop talking of war. Many ex-SES members never stop talking about the SES. It has a compulsive fascination — not least because they are still puzzled how it had such a profound effect on their lives. Some are angry, some are ashamed and sadly some are psychologically disturbed. Others have left the SES with no ill-effect or ill-feelings. They see it just as a phase they went through. But they recall the experience vividly. Everyone finds it unforgettable.

Those who feel bitter about the SES are liable to exaggerate its power and influence. Many within the SES have similar misconceptions. When there was a delay in *The Standard*'s publication of its investigations it was widely rumoured that some occult force had prevented it. Some people warned us we would be in physical danger, but we have seen only one example of the SES resorting to violence. That was outside Chelsea Town Hall where Leon MacLaren had convened a meeting of the faithful soon after *The Standard's* initial articles. Photographer Paul Massey was pushed and jostled as he attempted to photograph MacLaren leaving the meeting, and when Andrew Hogg intervened, a small fracas ensued. Mr MacLaren is apparently very camera-shy, and some half a dozen young SES men were determined to preserve his 'privacy'. The fact that the incident took place on the public highway made their actions illegal. That incident aside, most members of the cult are far too intelligent to indulge in tactics that would provoke an outcry. They are trained not to act spontaneously, emotionally or without authorization. The SES is a disciplined force in which the lower ranks are not encouraged to ask questions or query decisions.

It is therefore difficult to accept the argument that if any long-serving member of the SES gets involved in extra-curricula activities such as the Church of England or the Liberal Party then this is entirely an act of individual choice. But first a word of caution.

It is tempting but irresponsible to see in every SES member a potential 'sleeper' bent on infiltration. Any organization that is highly secretive will be viewed with suspicion, even if its objects are entirely innocuous. One must beware conspiracy theories.

But the SES is certainly not an innocuous organization. As we have reported, it has been branded 'evil' by some churchmen, alarmed at the cult's psychological hold on its members. Others have called it sinister and seditious, with motives that are kept hidden from a large bulk of followers as well as people outside the movement. A substantial body of ex-members have accused the cult of brainwashing them and we have drawn parallels between SES practices and characteristic brainwashing techniques.

But what is the aim of this cult? What drives MacLaren and his senior associates to want a bigger and bigger movement? Is it power? Is it money? Or is it simply what the SES fervently states it is – a desire to lead people towards greater enlightenment and 'realization'?

Many SES members are sincere, guileless and baffled that we see anything untoward in their beloved ideology. They sometimes admit that there are others who show a fanaticism and dedication that goes beyond healthy enthusiasm.

There is another category of followers, many high in the SES hierarchy, who do not adhere to 'The Measure' and in whom it is difficult to detect a genuine desire for spiritual enlightenment. It is said there are such people in any movement. But that does not explain why in the SES a blind eye is apparently turned towards those who act with questionable motives. And why are so many members left to cope alone when their fallibility is shown up? Why is cruelty condoned when it could so easily be stamped on?

If the cause is to lead as many to enlightenment as possible, then compassion for each individual suffering distress would surely be a must. But many we have interviewed have found the SES totally unhelpful in such situations. This surely suggests that there is another cause uppermost in the minds of those who control the cult. The consensus of opinion from ex-members is that the cause is not individual enlightenment, but individual subjection. They are not after money except as a means to an end. They are after power.

This assertion must be speculative, because the person most able to refute it — Leon MacLaren — has refused to be interviewed. Other leading members who have talked to us adhere to the view that the SES is simply helping people to become more aware and useful citizens. Speculative though it may be, here is a theory: The cult's leaders — or at least some of them — are seeking power over others to further an aim that they all admit to, to create a more perfect society. It is difficult to see how any movement bent on creating a new Renaissance would not need some means of influencing events.

At its most benign, such influence could take the form of encouraging people to enter politics, organized religion or any other area through which society can be 'rehabilitated'. There is nothing wrong in that; indeed, it is a laudable aim. But surely people with such an all-embracing ideology should declare an interest when they enter public or church affairs? It is the secrecy of the SES that is most worrying; it is this which casts doubts on what its members are up to.

Such suspicions led us to take a closer look at the 'extra-curricula' activities of Timothy Glazier, a hat designer turned public relations man and TV producer, but above all one of the SES's top people.

Glazier's reputation as an activist begins in the late 1970s in the bitter dispute between the British print union SLADE (The Society of Lithographic Artists, Designers, Engravers and Process Workers) and graphic designers and artists working largely in the advertising industry. SLADE was attempting to recruit members through the crude means of blacking their work if they tried to resist. A special section was set up — the SLADE Art Union — to look after the interests of this group. Unfortunately they proved to be a rebellious and articulate lot. Glazier and another member took their new union to court in a bid to allow the SAU to formulate its own rules and in particular allow freelancers equal rights within the union.

The battle became a major issue in Britain and SLADE was branded by Tory politicians as exhibiting the worst traits of trade unionism. Glazier and his colleague won the day, aided by a professional firm of political lobbyists — Lloyd-Hughes Associates, and a government inquiry was set up into SLADE's practices. Its findings were damning. Published in September 1979, it concluded that when conventional recruitment methods failed SLADE 'embarked on a deliberate plan to 'organize' the industry and it was conducted without any regard whatever to the feelings, interests or welfare of the prospective recruits'. Glazier could take pride in having forced SLADE's practices out into the open, but his activities did not end there. He and some colleagues also saw potential for 'organizing the industry', but not under the control of SLADE. The Graphic and Creative Arts Association was formed with moderate, unmilitant objectives. To that end a link was sought with the only union to fit that description active in the printing world — the EETPU (Electrical, Electronic, Telecommunications and Plumbing Union). Perhaps this union was tempted by the prospect of another 25,000 members.

To begin with Glazier was the only SES follower active in the Association, but that was to change in November 1981 when GAACA held its first annual general meeting. Many of the old committee or trustees were persuaded to take a back seat.

Whatever their reasons for resigning, it meant that new blood had to be brought into GAACA. Here is the official account of the committee elections:

The main business of the evening was to elect a Governing Committee to take over the running of the Association from the trustees. Since there was only one candidate for each of the principal posts on the Committee there was, strictly speaking, no need for an election but the candidates were called upon to give a brief account of themselves and they were duly accepted on a show of hands.

Jill Havergal (Chairman) has experience in illustration and theatre design and has taught at Maidstone and Hornsey art colleges. She now works in a small publishing company with responsibility for the origination and commissioning of artwork. Trevor Bounford (Secretary) has worked his way through the studio business and is now a director of an information graphics company. Rosanne Knox (Treasurer) has worked in regional TV and is now the advertising manager for the international section of a large manufacturing group.

What none mentioned — neither Jill Havergall now Jill Dean, wife of James Dean, nor Bounford nor Knox — was their membership for many years of the School of Economic Science. Glazier still remained a driving force in the background but the SES connection did not end there. A stranger to all but the SES members at the AGM was introduced and proposed as the association's first President. It was Tom Chapman, the SES's favourite non-member and a man with no previous background in the world of commercial art.

It was suggested that, although the constitution stipulated a governing committee, an additional honorary post of President should be specially created. The official report says Chapman was introduced as 'a man whose wide experience in trade union affairs would be very valuable to the committee'. He was voted in on a show of hands with no other candidate in view.

In February 1983, Chapman's photograph and signed letter to GAACA members covered the glossy front page of the association's newsletter. In a stirring call for support, heralding what he sees as 'the beginning of the twenty-first

257

century of Trade Unionism', Chapman concluded with this stirring message:

> We must have the strength to protect any single individual from any form of intimidation. We have that potential strength, there are at least 25,000 people in the creative arts industry, you are one of them. As a united group, imagine the possibilities of such co-operation in the many fields of ideas, unimpaired by the sordid political manipulations of industrial trade unions or any others who would interfere with creative ideas. Our chairman in the last letter adequately spelt out the other privileges; I would add one line only, it is the duty of artists to portray the new era to the world that is waiting for their ideas. Nothing less than that is the intention of this Association.

Rosanne Knox has now left the SES after twelve years' membership, but she remains treasurer and membership secretary of GAACA. It has failed to get more than a few hundred members so far, she says, and she maintains that the only reason the top committee posts and Presidency are in the hands of SES members and associates is that no one else was prepared to volunteer. She admits, however, that it looks to outsiders as though there is more to it than that. One such outsider was amazed at what he saw as an SES takeover. David Thomas, a well-established painter who does a limited amount of commercial work, wrote to us of his impressions of the 1983 annual general meeting. He said he was dismayed at the involvement of SES members.

Thomas had been in the thick of the SLADE battles and was present at GAACA's inaugural meeting. He describes how he was unknowingly roped in to the SES's own art world by Glazier:

> At the inaugural meeting Tim Glazier had proposed that Tom Chapman should be President. I thought that Tom Chapman was simply an old-fashioned moderate trade unionist, the like of which I have always admired.

In the summer of 1982 Tim Glazier persuaded me to go to Waterperry near Oxford for something called 'Art in Action' to demonstrate painting at their annual show. Art in Action is the Art Department of the School of Economic Science. I had never heard of it and was given to understand it was an organization to promote art. I was horrified to find what it really was.

David Thomas added that he had not been active in union affairs for two years and had only attended the AGM of GAACA to meet old friends. But his discovery of the SES at Art in Action aroused his suspicions at the meeting and he ended his letter with this comment:

> If GAACA is an association to protect artists from the excesses of the NGA that is all right with me, but if it is a far-right-wing anti-union group I would deplore it. I have no concrete evidence that the School of Economic Science is actively connected with GAACA but if they are playing politics I think their status as a charity registered with the Department of Education should be reviewed.

Timothy Glazier's activities have not been confined to trade unionism. In the late seventies he also became keenly interested in the politics of Namibia and a fervent supporter of the South African-backed regime there. His interest began as a professional public relations man, but more recently he has given many seminars on the subject in Britain. His audiences have included senior members of the SES.

Glazier first started working as a press officer of the Namibian Information Service, a propaganda agency in London run by Lloyd-Hughes Associates – the same firm of political lobbyists that helped with Glazier's SLADE battle. The firm is run by Sir Trevor Lloyd-Hughes, a former press officer of British Prime Minister Harold Wilson.

There have been many allegations that the Namibian Information Service is funded by the South African Government. Sir Trevor stridently denies this, but he openly admits that the Information Service is funded by the government in Windhoek, the Namibian capital, and that its job is to take a pro-government line. One of the Service's main objects is to attack the paramilitary organization SWAPO and weaken sympathy for SWAPO in Britain.

To that end, Glazier has arranged meetings between politicians from Windhoek and a variety of influential groups in Britain.

In December 1980 he set up a meeting between a member of the ruling National Assembly and the British Council of Churches, with the clear object of getting the Council to change its view of the political picture in Namibia. The Council has been a leading opponent of South Africa's attempts to impose its own puppet government, and has recognized that SWAPO has widespread support within Namibia. A report of the meeting, produced for internal use by the Council, concluded that funds would be made available by the Namibian regime if a delegation wanted to visit Namibia and see how the situation was developing.

Presumably funds might have been channelled through the Namibian Information Service. Certainly Glazier has made two all-expenses-paid visits to Namibia and remains a bitter opponent of SWAPO's cause. More recently his work with Lloyd-Hughes Associates has taken a different turn. Glazier is now in partnership with another long-serving SES member, Neville Wortman, a television director. Their company, Venture Communications, has made two films for Lloyd-Hughes on Namibia. They have a clear message promoting the current political development of the country.

Sir Trevor Lloyd-Hughes said he knew nothing of the School of Economic Science and had not talked to Glazier about it. He said that Glazier and Wortman were paid for their film work and other design services. However, Glazier gave frequent lectures on Namibia — to Eton College and Westminster School, for example — and this had been done 'for love rather than money'.

When we talked to Glazier about his political activities he was careful to explain that his involvement was his own personal interest and not at the behest of Leon MacLaren. He admitted, however, that he had given talks on Namibia at SES gatherings. In the light of what others in the SES have told us, this could well have been interpreted by those present as being an SES line.

We were surprised to discover that Glazier had also taken the opportunity to promote the Namibian cause at other functions where the SES was involved. Bishop Ross Hook recalled being 'bombarded' with pro-Namibia propaganda following a chat with Glazier at a meeting of the European Christian Industrial Movement. Again Glazier denied there was any significance in such anecdotes. But he agreed that the SES sometimes lays itself open to suspicion of covert infiltration:

Yes. I would acknowledge that very probably the way the SES is run, it lays itself open to all kinds of conjecture for being an extreme right-wing, pro-racist organization, for being an infiltrator of the Liberal party, for being a brainwashing organization and an organization which leads astray. I don't know what other conjectures you might put on it. Maybe it does lay itself open to that, but the fact is that it is none of these things. It is a totally dedicated and sincere organization striving in whatever way it sees available to itself, in this present day and age, 1983, to discover the truth, to achieve fulfilment of the human spirit and to enable others to be the same and to be a positive instrument of good and an alleviator of suffering in society. Now there, if you want it, is my formulation of what I see; now if it at any place falls short of these things, if there are individuals in the organization who have in any way gone outside those terms of reference, this is because it's only a human organization. But I see that it's entirely compatible with objects of the Fellowship of the School of Economic Science to discover and teach the truth in society.

The best-known SES member active in politics other than Roger Pincham carved out a successful career for himself in the British Tory Party. David Boddy was Director of Press and Public Relations at Conservative Central Office and one of Margaret Thatcher's closest advisers on press matters. As a devout SES member there has been speculation that he may have secretly infiltrated the inner sanctums of Toryism for some sinister purpose. There is not a shred of evidence or basis for such a view. Boddy simply worked his way up the career ladder as a protégé of former Party chairman Cecil Parkinson. His membership of the SES never seemed to have the slightest bearing on the way he carried out his duties for Mrs Thatcher. He never talked about the SES with her, he says, and saw no reason why he should.

Boddy, who is also the SES's press spokesman, in many ways typifies the new breed of young, disciplined and devout SES follower. At the MacLaren meeting at Chelsea Town Hall where *The Standard's* photographer was attacked, Boddy was at 'The Master's' side easing him gently into the waiting limousine in just the way he assisted Mrs Thatcher during election tours.

David Boddy's full-time career at Conservative Central Office ended in early 1983 when he resigned to launch a new British weekly magazine. It was a puzzling move for someone evidently well thought of and set for even higher things in the Party. The magazine, called *Out of Town*, was a bland but expensively produced journal on countryside matters. Boddy's major coup in setting up the new publication was to persuade the National Trust to endorse the venture and advertise it widely in National Trust publications in return for two pages of free editorial matter in every issue and a down payment of £30,000.

The deal caused some puzzlement in the Trust. There were questions asking why a new magazine, untried and untested, should receive such gushing praise. The answer appears to be that the Trust saw the £30,000 deal as a sound business proposition. It seems to have worked out that way and there is no evidence that the magazine is developing into an SES propaganda medium. Nevertheless, the SES connection with *Out of Town* extended beyond Boddy's editorship. The publisher, Christopher Shepheard-Walwyn, is also an SES member of long-standing, and one of the founder directors is Roger Pincham, although other directors were not SES members.

This grouping of SES directors seems rather more clannish than clandestine. We asked Mr Shepheard-Walwyn if *Out of Town* was effectively an SES publication. He bluntly denied the suggestion. The venture went bust in October 1984 owing £300,000, and the title was sold. Nevertheless it illustrates again how the SES has members in influential positions in many walks of life. In this way it differs markedly from other religious cults, many of which do not seem to appeal to what marketing experts would denote as A-B category customers.

The signs are, then, that the SES is after power for a purpose – that of promoting a new Renaissance. Not all their members' involvements are part of any secret plan, but wherever they have opportunity they pursue objectives which accord with the teachings and attitudes of the School. They are SES people above everything else.

The SES is rather different from other cults because it is a British institution that has spread itself around the world. But that does not make it unique. In many ways it is a typical cult, however much people such as Glazier, Boddy and Peter Green would deny it.

Philosophically and organizationally it is just as complex as the Moonies, the Rajneesh or the Children of God. The psychological commitment to the movement is similar. The reports of casualties tell the same sad story.

It is not easy to analyse the strong appeal of new religions. Certainly Gurdjieff seems to have hit on one fundamental principle – the more demands that are made of followers, the more they will become committed. There is the appeal of a strong social structure where everyone has clearly defined roles. There is the prospect of escape from the rat-race.

But anyone seeking such a change in lifestyle could equally well opt for a commune or kibbutz. The 'magic' of most cults seems to be the prospect of achieving what the SES would term spiritual enlightenment or realization. Within many people is an urge to have answers to questions science has failed to solve. This urge seems to be greater among the educated. Perhaps they grow to believe that there are ready answers to all questions. Perhaps they are trying to answer the wrong questions.

This search for enlightenment can be obsessive in any movement. After all you can find highly spiritually motivated people in every parish church, let alone cult. But where the SES and other cults must accept criticism is in their very intolerance of criticism. There appears to be no place for the rebel, the person who will not accept every tenet of the faith. There is therefore a weeding process whereby only the most devout and obedient remain. In this milieu competition for one member to become holier than another is enhanced.

The inevitable result for some people is that the pressure becomes too great. They become a typical example of a cult casualty, full of guilt at failing to progress, and perhaps suicidally depressed. This aspect of cults is all too often ignored by commentators. Many press articles dwell on the wacky practices of a cult and perhaps make it sound quite an amusing organization to join.

Our researches into the SES show that people join and remain attached to cults for much deeper reasons than that. If they enter into such a commitment knowingly, then who can blame the cult if they end up in a bad way? But if they join in ignorance, and are drawn in further and further without realizing how they are becoming subjugated, then it is the cult's practices that are to blame.

The SES has a motto which is often quoted by the more starry-eyed followers. It is, 'To Thine Own Self Be True'. Can we suggest that anyone interested in a cult should adopt another motto? 'To Thine Own Self — Be Careful!'

Postscript

It has been a difficult task to portray an organization that wished for no publicity and afforded minimal co-operation. Right through the process of writing, stories have continued to flow in from around the world. Ex-members of the cult had passed on the news that the first detailed account of the School of Economic Science was in preparation. Three long, vivid letters simply couldn't be ignored. They contain some new information and much to corroborate what has already been written. We include them here as a postscript because they also provide a sad final warning of how people with intense spiritual ambitions can become corrupted. The Bishop of Woolwich said the SES was ruining people's lives. Here are accounts from Canada and Australia that show just that.

Carol Peters; Toronto, Canada

All the names in this account have been changed. Carol is now a successful journalist in Canada but was born in London and married there before emigrating to Toronto in 1967. Carol's husband, Ian, had joined the SES in London but left after two years. Ian, she says, was the strong figure in their marriage. In 1969 they had a son, Jeremy, and after a stormy marriage, in which Carol frequently felt lonely and depressed, the pair began to take an interest in mystical schools.

Ian saw an advertisement for the Toronto School of Philosophy and in 1976 was back in the cult. Carol began to find that she must act the role of the dutiful wife. She is certain that her husband was strongly influenced by the

School's leader, Geoffrey Ramsey. Together, she believes, they planned how she should be cured of her temperamental and wilful behaviour:

Ian seemed to come very much under Ramsey's spell. He spent a great deal of time, not only on school activities, but at Ramsay's house. For example, every Sunday morning he would get up early, meditate, do calligraphy, then visit Ramsey who 'checked his meditation'.

I began to feel rejected and unimportant. I was loved, Ian assured me. I was needed to run him to work in the morning, make his tea, mend his clothes, put food on the table, look after Jeremy. When I told him I felt I was wasting my life even though I seemed to be stabilizing after several years and wouldn't hear of me taking any kind of job beyond the two evenings a week I spent teaching breathing and relaxation techniques to pregnant Mums and Dads.

Carol began to stand up to Ian but it led to more and more figh' ,. She is now sure that Ian's lack of sympathy was a direct consequence of his increasing commitment to the School of Philosophy. By 1980 the marriage was on the rocks:

There were several occasions during those final months of breaking up when Ian hit Jeremy, something which I found intolerable and which often triggered another fight. It was also at around this time that I noticed Ian was changing. He seemed to have become very distant, cold, unfeeling, cruel often in word or deed, and reminded me of a wall. He told me he was achieving objectivity. He said he certainly had feelings and loved me. I kept thinking he seemed rather like a robot. He was by now starting to eat the school diet so I had to put up with strange plates of cheese on the kitchen counter, going bad, because the use of a refrigerator killed the life force of the food. I was expected to cook, or provide, two meals. Mine and his. I complained and said it was too expensive.

'Eat my diet,' he told me. 'No, no more housekeeping money.'

Carol does not try to hide her own failures within the marriage and admits to having an affair during this period. She often felt it was her fault that her husband seemed to have changed so radically. But she also knew she couldn't stand being treated as a chattel. She left Ian in 1981 and struggled without financial support to create a new home for her son. Ian would ring to say she could come back but only on his terms. Slowly she began to build a career for herself in TV. While researching a story in 1983 she came across *The Standard* articles:

What I read shocked me more than I can tell you. For the first time I began to realize that it was not I who was a bad wife to Ian, because of my 'past'. I ceased to believe that I was 'lucky' to have been rescued and taken in by him. And I knew that it really was quite OK to have left him. All the insults he had hurled at me for years and years which had brainwashed me into thinking I was no good didn't mean I was no good. I was angered. I went in to work the next day and I was sort of numb and 'out of it'. I went home early. By that night I began to experience incredible grief. My dear friend who lives next door called me and when he heard my voice asked me what was wrong. I told him I felt like Ian had died – years ago – but that I was only now feeling sad. I still feel sad today when I think about it. I feel sad writing this to you who I don't know. It's a very deep, very personal grief. It's crying for someone I once loved long, long ago. Someone who, if they had never found that goddam school, would probably still be an intimate part of my life today.

Carol has now also come into contact with other former members of the School of Philosophy. She relates some of their experiences, one of which is particularly heartbreaking:

John was diagnosed ill with terminal cancer. But because he had cancer he was being punished, apparently, for his miserable sins. The School decreed he should not be taken too much notice of. Thus John wasn't cared for properly – not fed properly, not washed or given a shave, not cleaned or bathed. And if he fell out of bed there he was to stay. John was also not allowed to receive pain medication because any medicine that isn't 'natural' (herbal or homeopathic) is disallowed by the School. It also insisted that John be brought to class for the good of his soul and to hear 'the truth'. So he was dragged out of bed, put into a suit (as per school instructions for dress) and brought to school. At first he was propped up in a chair. Later it was suggested a mattress be brought in so he could lie comfortably to hear the truth. The School also decreed that John was to die consciously.

Carol says that the School was thwarted in this endeavour because he fell into a coma for three days before dying. The School was dismissive about this, saying he was not worth knowing. John's wife turned her back on the School and returned to England with her children.

John's treatment may have been the cause of a large number leaving the cult including one of its most prominent members. Kenneth, a former Benedictine monk, joined the School and was soon made a tutor. He had organizational talent and became the 'front man'. Some saw him as a rival to Geoffrey Ramsey. The break came after Kenneth and Ian went to Walkhill in New York for a School retreat:

Also present was the spiritual leader of them all – Leonardo da Vinci MacLaren, with five young maidens, as they are called, all in their early twenties, and one young man, waiting on him hand and foot. There was one to discreetly pour wine into MacLaren's glass standing at his shoulder, another at his elbow to light his cigarette, and so on.

It was that week, plus the shoddy way in which John was treated, that turned Kenneth against the school. The atmosphere at Walkhill was one of insanity. People had hysterical fits; they became psychosomatically ill; people were like robots literally moving from one task or place to another. He said it was dreadful. During one question period with MacLaren, a Toronto woman asked why men should treat women in the School the way they do. MacLaren poured forth a diatribe and yelled at her at one point that 'all women do is lie around dreaming of how to seduce a man'.

More than twenty members of the Toronto branch left the School of Philosophy with Kenneth and he now is an active campaigner against the cult.

Celia Ravesia; Sydney, Australia

Long after Anthony Ravesi wrote to us (see chapter 3), we received an extraordinary letter from his wife Celia. She outlines graphically some of her experiences and some of her views of the cult. She has intense feelings about the way the School in Sydney is operated by Michael Mavro and his wife Nina, aided and abetted by Leon MacLaren. MacLaren gave a lecture on one occasion that included the assertion, 'The Australian Aboriginals and the native animals must be allowed to die out. They are the last of an ancient civilization.'

On another occasion Celia was dining with MacLaren. She asked if there were any Maoris in the New Zealand School. He replied: 'No. They are not sufficiently intelligent.'

There were equally strong views expressed about people with physical disabilities:

Mr Mavro's habit was to stand at the end of the room and indicate by a facial gesture whether he approved of the student enrolling or not, just on appearance. Those who received the 'thumbs down' were either caught in time and refused, or given their money back with some excuse that the course might be too difficult or too practical for them, or a suggestion they try the WEA instead. Mr M. (as he was known) arrived while a student was in the process of enrolling a man with a hare-lip. He spoke in the distinct manner people with this impediment often have. Mr M. called over the senior man and said, 'See that he gets his money back. We don't want deformed people here'.

Once on the way up through the School, followers were subjected to tests of endurance that would indeed have been

269

difficult for anyone disabled. Celia describes what happened at the exclusive township of Mount Wilson, a pretty area in the mountains where School men were creating a property out of raw bush:

At Mount Wilson one got a taste of what the early convicts went through. Weekend after weekend my husband would come home black, red-eyed from lack of sleep, filthy and barely able to walk from breaking through the bush. They had to work alongside snakes, and funnel-web spiders which they killed by the score.

The time came for us ladies to go there. The married men were not allowed to go up that time; I feel even their hardened hearts would have felt for us. The bachelors were put in charge. And humiliating it was after a day of hard labour to hear them all together with Mrs Mavro in her well-appointed tent, complete with carpets, laughing about our miserable performance.

For three hours I was put onto a fifteen-pound sledgehammer (I was started on fourteen pounds) swinging it continuously over the head; one was not allowed to stop. There was a fifteen-minute break in the middle during which there was no time to get to the earth toilets at the bottom of the hill. After lunch we continued with gardening, moving earth etc. For about an hour I was put on a two-man chain-saw – my back was really hurting but I was told to keep going. One lady slipped a disc. We were put to rolling tree trunks, woodchopping, moving boulders.

On a previous occasion in the country I had seen a lady lose a fingernail when two men dropped a rock on it. She was not allowed to speak of the pain, nor were we allowed to discuss the incident when we returned home. Men have lost parts of fingers on the woodwork team – always these things are not to be talked about.

Mr Mavro called us together after he inspected our tent. 'You women,' he roared. (Sorry, the word Ladies was more often used.) 'You love your comforts – I can see from the way you have set up your tent that you indulge your bodies'. Some of the women had brought camp stretchers and quilts – it was very cold in the night there. We had to wash in public in a tin bowl in the dark. We had to rise in the pitch dark and be dressed and out in a few minutes. I found myself helping a lady next to me with severe arthritis with her boots. As a result we were the last out — too late for a cup of tea — and told to go to groups at once. We never had breakfast and it was tiring having to do that work on nothing.

I went for two of these weekends. On the second one we cleared the bush in the afternoon with brushooks, swinging these as we stood in rows. Our bachelor overseers would urge us faster and faster — 'double your speed'. I became angry and I swear he was very close to losing a leg. We always worried about the spiders which are deadly — but it was not quite warm enough for them — the men had to cope with that.

Coping became all that mattered. Celia remembers how life became an endless train of tasks. Towards the end she was crying a lot, interested in nothing, having to organize the family to attend yet another evening of duties. The questions had all stopped: 'You do not question, you obey.'

It all stretched away into old age, death, one's children marrying other School children, keeping it all going and the most terrible thought — being born again. As Mr MacLaren had said, we would be into another School family, going through the 'whole circus again and again until we had done the 'work' we were supposed to do. Incidentally, Mr MacLaren told the Senior Group after we had left that these people who had left the School would all be in School again in another embodiment. He told them that he himself had already chosen his future parents and his embodiment. We were told by Mrs Mavro: 'Mr MacLaren is very powerful, he knows all about every one of you; even if you are not in the room he knows what you are doing. One would not dare to think an impure thought in his presence.'

The break with the School was difficult because all the Ravesis' friends who were still members turned their backs. They had been taught that those who leave never improve, so not to communicate: 'They will feed on your energy if

271

you talk to them.' But Celia realized a whole new world was opening up. She was surprised to find she could chat with people in shops. She missed the ordered life and security of School, but she was free.

It was four months before she had the nerve to buy a skirt that came just below the knee but she only wore it if she was unlikely to meet anyone from the School. Finally she had her hair cut, defying the edict from School.

She had a whole wardrobe of unfashionable long dresses:

> We had been told that ideally every woman should have 300 dresses, silver and gold were appropriate. The men had to have a collection of expensive suits which they wore even for woodwork.

Celia regrets the way her children were treated when she was a member. They were permitted a reading list of only a dozen scriptures but no children's favourites. These were labelled 'untruth'. They were discouraged from playing imaginative games. Other comforts were prohibited.

In one instance an eight year old who was very attached to a baby doll had it taken away.

> My little girl loved dolls and I turned a blind eye when I knew she was playing with her sister's dolls, but I didn't buy her any or encourage it. The little boys were not allowed to play with guns. However they were taught to box at Sunday school, 'to make men of them'. Personally I do not approve of little boys hitting each other about the head, but I said nothing. The mothers were invited to watch one day and had to maintain emotionless faces while their boys as young as seven and eight boxed, some of them with tears in their eyes. Punishing the boys with a thrashing was encouraged. My daughter remembers sitting through the girls' group at 7 Wilmot Street, hearing the boys being punished upstairs by their male tutor with thrashings all round.

> I ran a small group of children from two and a half to five years old. They too were not allowed to cry, especially when their mothers left them. They were ordered to stop and if they

persisted we had to smack them. When I asked Mrs Mavro if they could not be given a hug and distracted by being taken off to do something I was told for their own good they had to break the attachment to their mothers and must not cry when they left.

The instructions to wean the children early followed the same theme. The boys had to start weaning at four weeks and be weaned by six weeks. The girls about a fortnight later. The reasons given were that boys become more attached to their mothers and it is unhealthy. When my baby girl was about eight weeks old Mr Mavro called me into his room and said that Mrs XYZ had said that I was not weaning the child. (Mrs XYZ had a baby the same age and did a 'Duty' with me.) 'Why not?' I was asked. I replied that I had given her a bottle of cow's milk and she had cried with pain for about an hour and I was reluctant to do it again. (Other mothers reported that with the sudden weaning to cow's milk — formulas were not allowed — the babies became very constipated and uncomfortable.) Mr Mavro said that women get sensual pleasure from breastfeeding and it was not to be encouraged beyond the first weeks.

The women went to great lengths to show that they were not attached to their children. Ill with measles, a child would be carried to a babysitter when duty called. The children too had to play their part:

As soon as my daughter reached eight she was put to cleaning the flats of the bachelors, usually with another little girl and other ladies. She was out four nights a week until she was eleven, attending one compulsory duty after the other. At Mr Mavro's house she was given the job of picking up the German Shepherd dog's faeces with her bare hands. She was told that women should not be too proud to do this. (She had had extensive surgery on her hands as the result of an accident.) She was also made to clean the toilets with her bare hands (this was a favourite one to get us to put our hands into the toilet without reacting). On the residential weekend when she was ten, she was made to carry buckets of earth on her head for three hours, starting before six in the morning when the frost was on the ground, no breakfast; the rain poured down and the ladies and the little girls were made to keep working — there were one or two grandmothers there. They were made to run up and down a hill with the buckets on their heads.

Celia says that in the weeks after leaving the School she was filled alternately with loathing and compassion for Mavro:

I do not want to be an instrument in his destruction, but if anything could be done to show him and his superior the harm they have done and may do to others so that he could at least stop before too many more lives are broken . . . There are some very tender souls still under his so-called care — people who have been given a place so that they feel part of something, so that they feel they are working towards some sort of ideal for a better world. But in losing their own personalities and surrendering their wills to such a person they have allowed this sort of power to gain hold. To quote Mr Mavro: 'You cannot decide anything for yourselves. You cannot even think for yourselves.'

It is not pleasant to write these things down. After three years one is endeavouring to make the experience a thing of the past. The fact remains that one will never be the same as when one walked into Part 1 — and enthusiastic, fairly conservative English girl in Australia on a working holiday, with a good job and young friends, a social life, but curious always on the meaning of it all and our purpose in it.

Kathleen Ellinger; Queensland, Australia

Kathleen Ellinger joined the Sydney School of Philosophy in 1969 when she was twenty-four years old. For years she struggled to become a model follower, but by 1980 her disillusionment with the movement was so strong she left. She is now profoundly critical of the School's beliefs and practices, and feels a particular resentment towards Leon MacLaren, who was a frequent visitor to the Sydney establishment, and the Mavros. MacLaren she believes to be a fraud, while the Mavros are said to have relished the power they held over members — a power which Ms Ellinger considers was often used in a tyrannical and destructive manner. In October 1984 Ms Ellinger wrote for us a twenty-three-page statement about her experiences with the SOP. The document is a searing indictment of a movement which exerts a draconian power over its followers. Ms Ellinger, now forty years old, attended university after leaving the SOP and is training to be a teacher.

She told us:

Since leaving SOP I have read much on the psychology of totalitarianism and fascism, and I count myself lucky to have gotten out when I did. For the following reasons I hold that the SOP is a fascist organization.

1 There is an official ideology which is 'revealed', not set down for inspection and analysis. Everyone must adhere to this dogma by which there will arise a perfect society, an enlightened state of mankind.

2 The organization is not open to inspection and criticism, it is led by one single, powerful leader who heads an elite hierarchy.

3 Followers are conditioned to believe that salvation can only be gained through SOP. People who leave SOP are in 'outer darkness', never spoken to by those still in SOP, and shunned like the devil.

4 They have an exaggerated sense of SOP's importance in society and hence an unwarranted sense of self-importance.

5 Michael and Nina Mavro, and Leon MacLaren, are idolized. They give their lectures on platforms covered in costly Persian carpets. Very throne-like. At first I thought the platform was so that everyone could be seen, but it is also pyschological: we have to 'look up' from our lowly position, and respect everything they say, no matter how stupid.

6 Students are unable to act as individuals — all decisions and actions must be referred to the leader. Mavro was called 'The Leader' while Nina Mavro often called him 'Father'.

7 Following meditation initiation there was a systematic routine called 'checking', where the mind was brought under even more

275

control and we became dependent on whatever the Mavros said. If we were told that we were bad, people believed them. Group nights, under the Mavros, were little more than systematic psychological attacks on ourselves.

8 SOP centres are opening up all round the world, and this brought both a sense of pride and also a sense of respectability and authority. There is a feeling of spreading the good word, spreading truth which gives the student a sense of unity, of belonging to something real, powerful and authentic.

9 *Fear* is the dominant factor in SOP and each student is kept 'on the boil' for years, always on edge, never able to relax or let go. There was no freedom in our lives and we spied on one another, so no one lapsed into bad habits. There was always the constant need for mass effort to counteract the evil in the world.

10 There is total disrespect and disregard for the individual, except as a means to an end. If anyone complained about being ill-used, Mavro made it clear that there were always others just waiting for the 'opportunity to serve'.

11 The illusion of saving the world is fostered through a simplistic, rigid system of regulations, laid down by a select few and patrolled and controlled by the manipulation of peoples' weaknesses. Mavro is a master of emotional, not rational, persuasion. Our so-called progress in SOP depended on gaining favour with Mavro, not effort, virtue or self-sacrifice.

12 The leader is kept in power by a doctrine which enforces compliance on its followers and excludes all rival systems of thought: 'School is the expression of the Truth; only a fool looks elsewhere.' Although Mavro called himself 'just another student', he encouraged the attitude that he was special. He claimed his authority directly from the Shankaracharya, who told him to go to Sydney and form a 'good company'.

13 Ironically, many of us dissenters, before leaving SOP, called the school the Greek Gestapo because we were afraid to put a foot wrong, say the wrong thing, or be seen daydreaming by another student. The pressure was never-ending.

14 A disregard for the legal system of this country was obvious. Mavro said: 'Do you really think your vote makes any difference to what happens in Canberra?' And yet he encouraged us to

all vote for the Liberal Party.

15 There was a suspicion of rival ideologies. Mao's *Little Red Book* was called the work of Ignorance, and yet any member of the SOP led a life circumscribed by mental disciplines, the holding in mind of certain quotations and loyalty to the School. People were frightened into submission and the individual was isolated, leaving him or her very lonely and shut off from ordinary family and friends. Free association with people not in the School, such as workmates, was forbidden.

16 Although there was an unwarranted belief in the School's invulnerability, we were told to be on constant look-out for those 'who are trying to destroy the School'. The School was supposedly 'inviolate' because, of course, it was straight from God.

17 The SOP believed they were producing 'special and superior' people who would be the 'leaders of tomorrow'. Children raised in the School were said to have an advantage over those outside. This was nonsense, of course. Our children were cut off from normal society and had trouble adjusting to normal children. They were special, in that they were especially lonely and unhappy.

18 The School was always right, there was never any deficiency. If I saw something amiss it was because of my wilfulness, or disillusion. All personal defence mechanisms were exposed and destroyed, leaving only Mavro and the SOP in their place.

19 The School was said to be absolutely necessary to the universe. Mavro told us it was the bridge between the inner and outer circles of mankind, and without it mankind's energy would run down. SOP was said to be the Absolute's instrument for the salvation of humanity.

20 We had to wear a uniform. The men almost invariably wore dark suits and ties. The female students were told to wear long dresses all the time, including long nightgowns in bed. Women and even little girls had to drag themselves around in ridiculous long dresses while scrubbing floors, gardening, clearing dense bush or cleaning the car. This, of course, cut out all sport, and horse riding was taboo because we couldn't wear trousers. One of the first things an ex-SOP woman does to proclaim her liberty is get back into trousers. We were told women wore pants to

277

'take over the world'. Long dresses were said to 'bring out the lady' in us, but really they were to imprison us, and weaken us psychologically. Even our hair length and styles were dictated to us. Mavro wanted us to wear our hair long 'so you can do lots of different things' to it. They seemed to want to turn us into composites of Hindu goddesses and Victorian aristocrats. Mavro told us that 'School people are the aristocrats of the universe'.

Ms Ellinger, who has one son, is particularly resentful of the way children and women are treated by the cult. She said:

Our children were subjected to inhumane, cold and cruel treatment. There is no doubt that SOP adults and parents love their children. We were all what could be labelled 'good' parents. But we made the mistake of abdicating our rightful responsibilities to our children in letting Mavro dictate how they should be raised. Mind you, the Mavros had no children of their own and to my knowledge had no training in the care and education of the young.

A totally deaf little boy, about two years old, was forbidden the use of hearing aids because his deafness was the result of his 'ignorance in a past life', and hearing aids would only increase his ignorance. (Many students did not take recourse to medicine because we were told that it only played with the symptoms. Get to the cause and you change the disease. We were required to 'work' against physical ailments, thus erasing that problem for next time.)

The children were taken from the breast as early as possible because the mothers had such heavy responsibilities in SOP. My son, aged one month, went to SOP babysitters or child-minders whenever I had evening duties. These were often young adults who had little knowledge of the care of the young. We were told that parents were frequently the worst people to raise their own children. We did not 'see' the needs of our children because our claims on them blinded us to their real needs. Hence we were not allowed to say 'my' children, but always 'the' children. The emphasis was always on discipline, never, never love, warmth or affection. That would have been considered

278

to be 'wrapping them up in cotton wool', or the expression of claims on them, and unnecessary. In eleven years in SOP I have never heard one word about loving our children, only about discipline, keeping them under observation, being strict because the outside world was so loose and evil, and being perfect models for them. The children were never allowed any unstructured time for natural play and interrelating with other, non-SOP children. Their friends could only come from SOP because everyone else was 'bad company'. Therefore they were isolated and cut off from normal society from their earliest years. They were being turned into little nuns and monks who were pushed into young adulthood, against their will.

Like the children, women were always to be under authority and allowed no liberty to make up their own minds. MacLaren said that the education of women should always be for pleasing and being useful to men. Girls and women must always be restrained and kept under strict control, made to obey immediately and without question. A woman's salvation was solely through service to a man. We were supposed to be treated as 'goddesses' (a Hindu idea) in our own home, but in fact we were treated like dirt and blamed for all the ills of the world. If a senior student left SOP, it was the woman's fault because we had not provided enough 'space' for him.

SOP students seem to have a chattel/slave personality, an abnormal, maladjusted need to be told what to do, to give over personal responsibility to another, to deny control over one's own life. This was called freedom — because we would not then be under the rule of our own ideas and desires. We had absolutely no voice in our lives. We were not free to choose our own jobs, houses and cars, or to have children when we wanted, wear clothes of our own choice, or eat food to our own liking.

I deeply resent the utter waste of eleven years of my life. I am a very different person now; university has re-awakened my inquiring mind and my critical faculties. I have, with a vengeance, regained my self-confidence and self-esteem. I have become an active feminist, strong and independent. My motto is now: 'Trust no one, believe nothing.'

A Letter to 'The Standard'

Louis Kirby, Esq.,   26th May 1982
New Standard,
Fleet Street,
London E.C.4.

Dear Mr Kirby

At the suggestion of my lawyer I am writing to clarify, emphasise and expand upon some of the principal points which arose in my interview with your staff reporters, Mr. Hownan and Mr. Hogg on Monday.

The subject of the School of Economic Science and the activities of its members both within the ambit of the School and quite outside it, is a fascinating story which deserves telling properly. I would not expect either the correspondent or many readers to agree with or understand every aspect of the School's work or thinking, but there is much that any fair-minded person would applaud. I would therefore hope that any account would resist the temptation to dwell principally on the least familiar aspects and in so doing, fail to give a broad and balanced view of the direction and motive of the School as a whole.

An account based upon the views of a few disaffected ex or current students, or on reporters' attendance at the School on two or three occasions could not achieve that balanced objective.

Over the past forty years or so many thousands of students have taken the School's economics and philosophy courses, some staying for a term, some for a year, some five years and some twenty. I have no doubt that the great majority have gathered much of value during their time in the School. Unfortunately, there are a few who have not found their work in the School helpful, and who may be moved afterwards to be resentful or depressed. I trust that these cases are very rare and my simple advice to those who are not finding happiness and fulfilment in the School would be to leave it and turn to something else of positive interest. There are other cases where one partner in a marriage resents the other's interest in the School as might be the case with golf, politics or religion. Everything possible is done to alleviate and accommodate these problems but when one is dealing with adults, one partner may not expect to be sent home to the other! There are many, many happy marriages where one partner is in the organisation and another outside it, and there is not the least reason why this should not be so.

Much has been made of the School's recommendation of a simple, wholefood diet and a measured life, rising early in the morning. Such advice is to be interpreted with intelligence, but I can only say that if I myself succeeded more often in following this lead I should be the the fitter for it.

It must be underlined that all students attending the School do so by enrolling at very modest fees three times a year and are of course, free to abandon the course at any time they wish. Non-attenders may be reminded once or twice but there is certainly no pressure upon those who wish to leave not to do so. Unfortunately, some find it difficult to decide whether they wish to go or stay which is never a comfortable position in any circumstance.

However, it is not my intention to give a full account of the philosophy and economics courses. I know that Mr Green has already spoken at length on these matters, and I am sure that he is willing to give further information at your request. Since my entry into politics I have had less and less time to be of use in the School. I resigned from the Executive and the Treasurership on becoming Chairman of the Liberal Party, and my contact now consists of leading a small senior group in discussion once a week.

My concern here is with the St James and St Vedast Independent Schools and with the link you suppose to exist between the School of Economic Science and the Liberal Party.

The day schools were founded in 1975 by a group of parents and potential teachers who were unhappy about some aspects of educational standards, and also wanted to give their own and other children the opportunity to receive the simple truths upon which teaching in the School is founded at an early age. They sought to establish schools which would give balanced care for mental, physical and inner development. Since those small beginnings we have expanded to over six hundred pupils, all of whom are accommodated at present in the buildings of the School of Economic Science. These are now overcrowded, and one of my immediate objectives is to raise sufficient funds to acquire a well-equipped school and thus ease the accommodation pressure throughout. Much has been made during the interviews of our use of Sanskrit, and naturally, many prospective parents are puzzled and perhaps a little sceptical about this. The young children begin with writing and sounding the characters which have the advantage of being wholly phonetic. They move on to simple words expressing concepts which have no precise English equivalent. But let me emphasise that the point in no way is to turn the children into Hindus. The point of the exercise is to help them discover more about themselves and the natural working of all their faculties. In any case, this elementary study of Sanskrit is a great help when other languages are introduced later on. The philosophical teaching they receive derives principally from conversations between Mr MacLaren, who is really the founder of the School itself, and the Shankaracharya whom he meets every couple of years in India. These conversations are characterised by their great simplicity and relevance to the questions and problems of the modern world. By tradition the Shankaracharyas have been ready to answer the questions of all who have come to seek their guidance, whether of their own tradition or of another.

The essence of this philosophy is the essential unity which pervades everything and is itself a characteristic of the omniscient and omnipotent Creator from whom everything flows. None of this is in conflict with the principal tenets of the great religions, and it is certainly our wish that a child coming from a religious home, be it Christian, Jewish, Muslim or Hindu, should gain a deeper penetration of the essential truths of their own religion and their own tradition.

For example, the Christian child might be helped to understand more fully the meaning of the phrase that 'The Kingdom of Heaven is within you' or the famous reply of Jesus that 'Before Abraham was I am'.

In addition to the philosophy classes scripture is taught as an exam subject, there is Assembly each morning and Church Services several times a term, attended by all.

Perhaps I might add at this stage that my own years in the School have in no way diminished my devotion to the Christian tradition — very much the opposite.

I can assure you that our children are not turning into religious fanatics but I hope that the approach is away from the old idea that the Creator is remote or contained within any religion. The children will be invited to consider the essential nature of the number one in arithmetic, of the centre of a circle in geometry, and the still spaces between the notes in music.

After the children are ten, they are invited to receive a very simple method of meditation from the Vedic tradition. Parents in the School are likely to be familiar with the meditation and in all cases, the proper permission of parents is of course, obtained before the practice is given. The children meditate for short periods which make a useful interval in an otherwise very active day. I would emphasise that whether or not the children receive the meditation is up to them personally. Some do and some do not.

I have laid emphasis upon the philosophical and religious aspects of the schools for obvious reasons but you should also know that ample time is given to all the other usual subjects in schools' curricula with the addition of English Law, and every effort is made to give all the children a period of physical exercise each day. In short, the provision of a rounded and successful education is our overall objective, and anyone who meets the children will soon discover that their minds are by no means dominated by religious or philosophic considerations.

I am not pretending that these schools are yet perfect in any respect. We are still learning many things but the Inspections we have had have generally been complimentary although the lack of space is a manifest problem. The Inspectors have commented in particular upon the excellent relationship between teachers and pupils.

We are only now coming to the point where pupils are passing out of the schools and every effort is made to set them on course for a satisfying and hopefully, gainful occupation. Several from our small Sixth Forms have achieved university entrance and overall the examination standards are by no means unreasonable, although we hope to do better in future.

A specific criticism is that we have failed to stress the link between the day schools and the School of Economic Science. The Head Teachers assure me that the great majority, and probably all, the parents are aware of the link and that there is no endeavour to disguise this at any stage. However, to make too much of this would be confusing because the schools are an independent Charity with their own constitution, their own Board of Governors and Board of Management. They really do not need the School of Economic Science to explain themselves. The vital common link is that both organisations have looked to Mr MacLaren and his conversations for philosophic guidance.

In short, we have every cause to be proud of what has been achieved and what we now need are good friends to help us forward because it is impossible from termly fees to accumulate sufficient to acquire vitally needed accommodation.

I am sure that the work of the schools is greatly valued by the parents whether or not they also attend the School of Economic Science, and I would suggest that it is the duty of the responsible media to help rather than in any way to hinder further development. We have had many visitors to the schools on both Open Days and ordinary days, and all have been impressed and interested in what they have seen. For example I myself took Mr Edward Heath for an inspection of the schools last spring.

It is a great mistake to distrust something just because it is new and rather unusual. While I can be useful to the St James and St Vedast Day Schools I shall continue as Chairman of the Governors bearing in mind that all the day-to-day organisation is, as usual, the responsibility of the Head Teachers.

Let me now come to the simpler matter of the School's alleged interest in politics. As is known, both Mr. Leon MacLaren and his father, Mr Andrew MacLaren had political interests. Mr Andrew MacLaren started as a Liberal in Glasgow in the early years of this century, and subsequently sat as a Labour M.P. from about 1922 to the end of the second World War. Mr Leon MacLaren stood as a Liberal candidate in 1950 but has taken no active part in politics since about that time.

On the economics side of the School, there is a great interest in the land question and the extent to which other forms of taxation could be reduced if only revenue available from communally-created land values were collected.* This was seen as one of the vital keys to achieving a more just society whilst still retaining all the benefits of a free market economy. This is by no means all that is taught in the nine term economics course, but the essential approach is in each case to try to discover the underlying economic law and to see it at work.

Until 1967 I personally had been concerned with the philosophy course, but then switched to the economics course which undoubtedly fired my interest in the subject. Mr Andrew MacLaren was still alive in those days, and was personally another great source of inspiration. In subsequent years, I have frequently referred to him and his influence on public platforms. Unfortunately, his name is not now generally remembered. Several of the day schools' patrons, including Sir Ralph Richardson, were willing to help us because they remembered Andrew MacLaren with affection and respect.

However, it should be emphasised that neither then nor at any time since has the economics course been conducted in support of any political party or for any political purpose. Not only did the Charitable Rules forbid it but everyone concerned respected the objective of trying to discover the truth about the subject which would then be available to everyone of whatever Party. That may be an unusual view but it is a valid one.

My own move towards the political world arose from an unsatisfactory correspondence with my local Conservative candidate at Putney, Mr John Wakeham, which concluded with his writing that 'he respected my high ideals but in the end, I should have to make up my mind either to vote for him or to vote for the left-wing Labour M.P.' I determined to vote for neither and called upon Mr Adrian Slade, the then Liberal P.P.C. at Putney who in due course enrolled me into the Party. When later, Mr Slade retired from the candidacy, I was resolved that the seat should not go unfought by a Liberal and volunteered to stand if no more experienced candidate came forward.

I would emphasise that my decision to enter politics was entirely at my own initiative and in no way at the behest of the School of Economic Science or anyone else in it.

Fortunately for me, my move into politics and subsequent candidacy in Leominster aroused a lot of enthusiasm amongst friends both inside the School and elsewhere but again, I would emphasise that those who came to Leominster did so of their own accord and by no means at the direction of the School. We all had a whale of a time and in the outcome, I just held second place, eleven thousand votes behind the sitting Conservative M.P. There is of course, an underlying Liberal tradition in the Welsh Marches which has been strongly revived over the past decade.

I have remained the Liberal P.P.C. for Leominster from that day to this, and at each of the subsequent General Elections have enjoyed the help of a lot of friends and supporters, members or not of the School, coming to augment the growing army of constituency workers. Ideally, any candidate would prefer to fight entirely with local resources but I know few who would turn outside help away.

By the generosity of my local Association I now have a full-time Agent and although friends from elsewhere will be as welcome as ever when the next Election comes, I am confident that local members will do 95% of the work. There is a strong constituency Executive and over one thousand enrolled members.

As your staff know, there is one other Liberal P.P.C. who is also a member of the School, and there are various others working in their own constituency parties.

Some of us meet monthly at the Gladstone Club — which is open to all Liberals — and some of us help with producing the occasional Liberal Clarion, but otherwise there is no co-ordination or central direction of members of the School who happen also to be members of the Liberal Party.

Let me emphasise again that the School does not seek to influence the way in which its members vote, and I know of senior members of the school who are currently members of other political parties. In short, the suggestion that the School has mounted some concerted effort to take control of the Liberal Party is absolute nonsense. If we had, it could only be judged an appalling failure!

As you may imagine, my own life is extremely full, and more and more other interests, including career and family, have been neglected in favour of my work in the Liberal Party. This process is set to continue and naturally, I have to spend an increasing amount of time in Herefordshire, looking after a multitude of constituency affairs.

I am in the Party for the simple reason that I am a Liberal and I believe that everyone in the party recognises that fact even though they may also be aware of the independence of my views. When I speak, I speak from myself and from the views I hold myself, and I trust that that is also apparent. I have sat upon numerous national committees over the past eight years, following upon election within the Party. There is also the suggestion that I have been somewhat secretive about my part in the School.

For one thing, there is the old rule that we do not publicise or claim credit for work done in the School. Those who have known me for some years are undoubtedly aware of the connection. With newer acquaintances I am much more likely to talk about the Liberal Party, and of course, the day schools for whom I have written many hundreds of letters.

Your colleagues commented particularly that Mr Hugh Jones, the Secretary-General knew nothing of my attending the School, or of the day schools, but in fact, he receives a schedule from me week by week setting out all my appointments, including frequent Appeal Meetings for the day schools. When one's life is full one tends to deal with relevant matters to get the business done.

It is a pity there is not more time to talk of deeper things. When there is the chance I find myself speaking more of what I have come to understand myself, partly through half a lifetime spent in the School than of the organisation of the School itself. Perhaps hereafter I shall have to be more forthcoming.

I hope I have said enough to convince you that if you decide to publish anything about the School, the day schools, my part or anyone else's part in them, you will do so in a serious and constructively critical way. Your people have not stumbled across a collection of battered and brainwashed lunatics but a body of generally respectable and respected people who have learned the value of sensible discipline, and choose to find time to study and work and think and converse together in common cause. They do not imagine that the majority of people would wish to make the same effort, and they certainly do not wish to push the School down other people's necks. They are quite content that its benefits should flow into the community untrumpeted and if you want an example of that, then I would suggest you attend 'Art in Action' at Waterperry in early July. Of course, newcomers are welcome and are received regardless of where they come from, but it has never been our tradition to do much more than make public announcements and leave existing members to recommend friends who they think might be interested.

As a Liberal I value every positive aspect of freedom which includes freedom to assemble, freedom to worship, freedom of reasonable privacy, the freedom to teach and the freedom to learn, the freedom to seek excellence and the freedom to aspire to virtue. I have every reason to believe that the Standard shares these objectives.

Yours sincerely
Roger Pincham

Roger Pincham,
CHAIRMAN OF THE LIBERAL PARTY

P.S. * This principle has long been respected in the Liberal Party but is from time to time brought into ridicule by those who insist that no other form of taxation should be necessary. I would emphasise that I do not adhere to that extreme view.

Copies to: The Rt Hon. David Steel, M.P.
Secretary-General
Party President.